Help Him Make You Smile

Psychological Issues

Psychological Issues is a monograph series that was begun by G.S. Klein in the 1950's. The first manuscript was published in 1959. The editors since Klein's death have been Herbert Schlesinger, Stuart Hauser, and currently, Morris Eagle.

The mission of Psychological Issues is to publish intellectually challenging and significant manuscripts that are of interest to the psychoanalytic community as well as psychologists, psychiatrists, social workers, students, and interested lay people. Since its inception, a large number of distinguished authors have published their work under the imprimatur of Psychological issues. These authors include, among many others, Erik Erikson, Merton Gill, Robert Holt, Phillip Holzman, David Rapaport, and Benjamin Rubinstein. Psychological Issues is fortunate in having an equally distinguished Editorial Board consisting of leaders in their field.

Help Him Make You Smile

*The Development of Intersubjectivity in
the Atypical Child*

Rita S. Eagle

JASON ARONSON
Lanham • Boulder • New York • Toronto • Plymouth, UK

Published in the United States of America
by Jason Aronson
An imprint of Rowman & Littlefield Publishers, Inc.

A wholly owned subsidiary of
The Rowman & Littlefield Publishing Group, Inc.
4501 Forbes Boulevard, Suite 200, Lanham, Maryland 20706
www.rowmanlittlefield.com

Estover Road
Plymouth PL6 7PY
United Kingdom

British Library Cataloguing in Publication Information Available

Library of Congress Cataloging-in-Publication Data

Eagle, Rita S., 1938-
   Help him make you smile : the development of intersubjectivity in the atypical child /
Rita S. Eagle.
     p. cm.
   Includes bibliographical references and index.
   ISBN-13: 978-0-7657-0496-2 (cloth : alk. paper)
   ISBN-10: 0-7657-0496-X (cloth : alk. paper)
   ISBN-13: 978-0-7657-0497-9 (pbk. : alk. paper)
   ISBN-10: 0-7657-0497-8 (pbk. : alk. paper)
   1. Developmentally disabled children—Care. 2. Self in infants. 3. Social interaction.
 4. Intersubjectivity. 5. Infant psychology. 6. Child psychopathology. I. Title.

RJ135.E244 2007
618.92'8527—dc22   2006030833

Printed in the United States of America

⊗™ The paper used in this publication meets the minimum requirements of
American National Standard for Information Sciences—Permanence of Paper
for Printed Library Materials, ANSI/NISO Z39.48-1992.

For Anny and Lydia

My other special children

With all my love.

Step-dad: "Benjamin, you know, I really love you."
Benjamin: "I know . . . *who wouldn't!*"

Contents

~

Acknowledgments

This book owes its conception to the marriage of two major themes in my life. The first is my dedication to the study and treatment of developmental disabilities, and to autism in particular, in my professional work as a psychologist. The second is my dedication as a parent to a son with developmental disabilities. Once the book was conceived, many people helped me nurture it through repeated revisions, over the past fifteen years.

The idea of writing this book came to me over thirty years ago, after about two years of putting down my thoughts, almost daily, about my infant son's development. Rather compulsively jotting down progress and setbacks, and my thoughts about them, might have been my way of coping with the challenges of raising a child who was atypical from birth. However, it felt much more like a necessary part of my role as his parent, to create a written "photograph" of his development, one that helped to capture and contain my interest and enthusiasm in watching him develop. I embraced and enjoyed the intellectual challenge of trying to make sense of what I was seeing, using all that I knew, or *thought* I knew, about child development. When I finally began to write the book, some twenty years after the diary was begun, the chronicle was there, ready to be looked at again, at a time when there was growing interest and scientific study in the very areas I had been writing about during my son's early years.

So—first of all, of course, I owe and dedicate this book to Benjamin. It would not have been written without him. Then, I owe it to all of the many people who loved him, and had faith and pride in him, for they helped him to become the baby, child, and young man that inspired the writing of this book. They are, first and foremost, his sisters, Anny and Lydia, who felt proud of him from the start. They shared the belief that he was their *special* kind of baby, and that he really *was* special. Their love and admiration of him helped me to see and accept him just the way he was, so that who he was could emerge and develop, proud and confident.

Part I of this book covers the first four years of the diary. During those four years, the people (after his sisters) who most helped me to be there for Benjamin were: Lenore Greenberg, who amongst my friends was the only one who "had the nerve" to come and see me and my (initially) disfigured baby, once he was home from the hospital; Ray P., who thirty-four years ago chastised me for worrying and complaining so much about my new infant, and for missing in the process what a sweet soul he had; and Dr. Hilda Knobloch, whose careful evaluation of Benjamin and sensitive, truthful, and accurate communication of his diagnosis started Benjamin and me on the road to working together, bolstering each other's self-esteem. I also owe much to Jean, the quiet, gentle, but very competent young woman who cared for Benjamin, as if he were her own, on the days I was away from home at work. The loving nuns and teachers at Kennedy Child Development Center in New York City introduced Benjamin to a world outside of his family; they supported him in learning how to be one among many. Benjamin's father, Leonard Simon, was there when he was born and expressed unconditional faith in him, from the start, when I was still too scared to do so.

Part II of the book includes review of theory, research pertaining to social interaction in infancy, and interventions to foster it, in both normal and atypical children. I must acknowledge all those who helped me to stay abreast of the rapid expansion of interest and study in these areas. John Heng, librarian at Surrey Place Center and doctoral student in medical philosophy, was so helpful in always finding the books and journal articles I needed. I must thank, too, my original Macintosh computer, for being user-friendly to this technologically challenged author, when I started writing this book almost fifteen years ago. A special thank you to Dr. Peter Hobson, whose appreciation of the excerpts I sent him six years ago gave me the confidence I needed to try to get this book published. As well, his supportive comments in reviewing a recent draft buoyed me through yet another revision. Some six years ago, Clara Claiborne Park's interest in the book also kept me going. Her superb books, *The Siege* and *Exiting Nirvana*, have been an inspiration to me in proving that a parent can write a book for professionals and parents alike. I know of no other books that give so much insight into autism. Finally, I acknowledge all that I have learned from the many, many children I have met, and their families, in over forty years of clinical practice in developmental disabilities.

Many people over the years have helped care for and educate Benjamin with love, humor, commitment, and devotion. All of his friends have become mine, and all of mine, his. I could not have maintained my enthusiasm in raising him were it not for being able to share the experience with them. I cannot list them all. Thank you, Ramzi, Julian, Lynn, Nicole, Margie, Bernard,

Maria, Aly, Deirdre, Ms. Forbes, Ms. Draper, and Peter (of Peter's Garage), to name a few.

My husband, Morris Eagle, has known Benjamin since he was born. He has lived with him, and shared in his upbringing for half of Benjamin's life so far. He appreciates Benjamin, is proud of him, and, like everyone who meets Benjamin, enjoys him and finds him loveable—while putting up with some of his not so loveable traits. Morris is a professor, clinician, researcher, prolific writer, and prodigious reader in the field of psychology. I trust his judgment about the value of anything I write more than anyone else's. He has always encouraged me to keep going through multiple revisions and given extremely valuable suggestions.

Most of all, though, my thanks are to Benjamin, for teaching me so much, and to Anny and Lydia, for sharing me and allowing me the time and devotion I needed to learn from him.

~

Introduction 1: Intersubjectivity

"Intersubjectivity" refers to the mutual communication of ideas, feelings, and intentions between two individuals that takes place even without the use of words. It is the intangible connection between two minds, the effortless bridging of the space between two people. Over and above the capacity to recognize and understand another's inner experiences, intersubjectivity also involves the desire to share and communicate those experiences. As such, it is at the heart of every social interaction between two individuals.

The first indications of intersubjectivity emerge during the first year of life; the capacity then remains with us all of our lives. Babies smile with eye contact when the caregiver smiles at them. A bit later, they will check with mom through eye contact before trying something new; they will make gleeful eye contact to share their pleasure with a new toy and point and vocalize while making eye contact to bring mom's attention to something of interest or to request something they want or need. In these behaviors, the baby demonstrates an interest in and capacity for "connecting" with another person, not physically but across space, to share his inner world with that of another. He also is demonstrating a capacity to comprehend the gestures and affects of the individuals who are engaged in communicating about their inner world to him.

The "intersubjectivity" behaviors that take place in infancy instantly identify the baby as a social being, like us, to whom we can relate. We enjoy these encounters—there are few things as enchanting and endearing as connecting in this way with a baby—but we also tend to take them for granted. We expect babies to do this; this is what makes them so "cute" and loveable. It is only when these phenomena do not emerge, when the baby's behavior does not suggest a sense of contact or shared meaning with another person, that we become aware of how critical this behavior is to our sense of what a baby is—a little human being who is "one of us."

1

This book addresses the question: How does an interest in, and capacity for, the mutual sharing of experiences between two individuals develop, beginning in infancy? How is it possible? What makes it happen? And what can or should be done, when it does not? It approaches these questions in two ways: first, by presenting a unique set of data describing the step-by-step emergence of intersubjectivity in one particular child, and second, by reviewing theories and research findings relevant to this topic. On the one hand, the specific developments in the infancy and early years of that child are examined in the light of the existing theories and findings about intersubjectivity; on the other, the existing theories are challenged to account for some of the specific developments that were observed in the early years of the one child. In the attempt to reconcile observation and theory, certain themes emerge, with implications for a theory of how intersubjectivity develops and for how to intervene when it does not. In the end, however, neither source provides conclusive answers to these important questions. Rather, the book acknowledges the inroads that have been made and raises some new issues and new questions to inspire and guide future research.

This book is intended for a wide audience—clinicians, researchers, theorists, academics, students, and parents—in short, anyone with an interest in how intersubjectivity develops and in what to do when it does not. These are questions that have attracted a great deal of attention in recent years in connection with the developmental disability of autism, since individuals with autism appear to lack affective connectedness with others. They appear to have no interest, investment, or joy in sharing and communicating with others about their experiences, nor do they seem to have the ability to do so. They appear to be unable to engage in give-and-take interactions with others. Many people view early developmental phenomena related to intersubjectivity as the key to understanding the etiology and nature of autism and related ("autistic spectrum") disorders. Therefore, research about early developments in intersubjectivity has received considerable attention of late in connection with the diagnosis of autism.[1]

There is a subplot in this book, however. It is to challenge the notion that atypical development in intersubjectivity is the sole province of autism, or that atypical development of intersubjectivity is always associated with the other characteristics of the autistic syndrome. Atypical development of intersubjectivity may appear in other conditions and developmental disabilities. Moreover, on the so-called autistic spectrum, there may be many variations with respect to the capacity for "intersubjectivity." It is the thesis of this book that little is gained in our understanding of autism and how to treat it if every child with any type of problem in intersubjectivity is considered autistic, just as it is a disservice to efforts to understand intersubjectivity to ignore the existence of variations in intersubjectivity in other conditions, as well.[2]

Finally, intersubjectivity is a phenomenon that takes place between two *persons*. The baby communicates to and with another person, not with inanimate objects; the parent communicates with the baby as if the baby were a little person. Intersubjectivity, then, is inextricably bound up with the "personhood" of each of the parties. This book, then, will also need to address how the baby comes to perceive a "self" in the other person and, as a necessary corollary, how a sense of personhood develops in the baby.

Help Him Make You Smile is in three parts. Part I comprises entries from the first four years of a diary about the development of my son, Benjamin. Benjamin was born in 1970 with multiple birth defects and cognitive/developmental disabilities. In his first months and early years, he appeared to lack the irresistible, communicative "little person" quality that normal babies develop early in the first year of life.[3] As I had done with my other two children, I kept a diary of his development. In Benjamin's case, it was focused on any hints of the emergence of that missing interpersonal spark, and on my struggle to find ways to foster mutuality in our relationship. Over time—slowly, in not one, or even two, but perhaps three or four years—Benjamin did become a "little person," initiating social interaction and apparently comprehending something about his shared humanity with others. In normal infants, the steps in this development are rapid-fire; the transitions seem imperceptible. Within the first years of Benjamin's life, however, they appeared to be in slow motion. The diary account of his first four years thus promised a unique opportunity to observe the step-by-step emergence of selfhood and intersubjectivity.[4]

In part II, these observations are discussed in relation to existing theories and research about selfhood, intersubjectivity, and the relationship between them, in normal development and in children with different kinds of developmental disorders. Part II also examines the strategies that seemed to help Benjamin develop selfhood and intersubjectivity and compares them to various interventions currently in vogue to foster development in atypical children. Chapter 52 explains why, in such endeavors with an infant, one must "help him make you smile."[5]

Part III describes Benjamin's sense of himself, and capacity for intersubjectivity, *as an adult*. The outcome of the particular challenges Benjamin had presented as an infant should be of interest to parents, clinicians, and researchers alike. Part III includes a series of "Benjaminisms"—remarks by Benjamin and verbal interactions with him that reflect his special way of understanding and relating to others, two and three decades after the period covered in part I. They are, I believe, fascinating and often unexpected. They illustrate how difficult it is to pin down exactly what may be wrong about or missing in the capacity for intersubjectivity in individuals with developmental disorders.

A Single Case?

Some words are in order in defense of the "single-case" biographical basis of the book. Infant observers and researchers have identified several discrete milestones or components in the development of intersubjectivity. Each of these, however, appears to be a qualitatively different and new phenomenon—Newson (1978) refers to them as "Copernical" leaps. Butterworth (1990) notes that the *why and how* of these qualitative changes in development remain to be explained. It appears that Siegler and Crowley (1991) have this in mind when they champion the "microgenetic approach" (i.e., frequent and continuous observation over the long term) to understand developmental phenomena.

Although there is now much research on early infant development, observations in the laboratory tend to be scheduled weeks or months apart. Subjects may be studied at different ages (e.g., at two, four, or six months) and the phenomena then identified that are characteristic of the infant at each point in time. But this method cannot capture what goes on between the lab sessions and between the emergence of each milestone. They cannot capture the minute-by-minute events that may constitute the transitions from one phase of development to the next. Caregivers, in contrast, are uniquely positioned to engage in the kind of observation described by Siegler and Crowley and, thereby, to witness and document the continuity of development.

There is, of course, a long tradition of using parent observations to assist in describing and documenting developments in infancy (e.g., first and foremost, Piaget 1952, but also Church 1968; Bloom 1973; Carter 1978; Gray 1978; Wolf 1982; Nelson 1992). Since intersubjectivity is a two-person phenomenon that first appears in the infant–caregiver interaction, it may seem especially fitting and desirable that it be observed and studied in the day-to-day context of that interaction. However, there are problems in this scenario. Data about the infant's development is perforce confounded by the effects of the child's behavior on the caregiver and by the caregivers' responses to it. The parent is likely to try to reverse or stem development that appears to be going awry. This is true even in laboratory studies about social interaction in infancy, such as those currently being performed with the infant siblings of autistic children. It is inevitable, for humanitarian reasons, that interventions be introduced when "atypical" development is suspected.

The diary entries therefore reveal much about the relationship between Benjamin and myself. The question then is inevitable: How can one draw general conclusions about development and interventions from the observations on only one child, in one particular parent–child interaction? Might not Benjamin's development have been different if he were raised in a different family, with different caregiver responses? Conversely, might he have developed in the same way, regardless of the way I had responded? And what if, in the context of the family and parenting that he did have, he had been a different kind of child to begin with?

Certainly, caution is necessary in generalizing from the particulars of Benjamin's development. Still, the emergence of intersubjectivity, or something like it, in Benjamin's style of relating was so long in coming, and the stepping stones to its eventual appearance so dramatic, that the story seems worthy of being told. If existing theories are correct, Benjamin's story should provide evidence to support them, and in this book we will be checking to see if they do. On the other hand, if new explanations with general applicability are yet to be discovered, then it should be possible to catch a glimmer of them in this chronicle of his development. Hopefully, too, the questions and hypotheses raised by observations of this one child will stimulate more controlled explorations that will result in findings that pertain to many. At the same time, Benjamin's story does illustrate one thing very well, and it is clearly my bias that this one thing has wider applicability. No two children, typical or atypical, are alike. In a time when there are many interventions for sale to help a child, often provided by professional interventionists at considerable cost, a great deal of good can come from getting to know one's child very well and learning from him how best to help him out.

In Part III, "Benjamin Today" (chapter 54) begins: "I would never have predicted the young man Benjamin is today from the infant and toddler described in the diary." I doubt many readers would.[6] In writing this book, I marveled at how far he had come. I laughed a lot in revisiting his infancy and in following through the years his unique way of making sense of the world. Re-reading the diary brought back the joy of watching him develop a sense of self and self-worth, the capacity to share emotions and ideas with others, and the ability to enjoy life and to spread joy, immeasurably. For Benjamin has never stopped making people smile. I hope this book will remind parents, professionals, and service providers who work with children with developmental handicaps that it is possible to appreciate and enjoy the *differences*. For parents of normal children, I hope it reminds them to wonder at and celebrate their children's desire and capacity, beginning in infancy, to share experience and to reach out to connect their lives with others.

Notes

1. I first came in contact with severely autistic children in 1956, during an undergraduate psychology practicum at the League School for Emotionally Disturbed Children in Brooklyn These were joyless children, without the capacity to play and to share emotions with others. I continued to work with autistic children throughout graduate school and thereafter, as a professional psychologist, first during six years of both clinical work and research (at Master's Children's Center in New York City with the psychoanalyst Margaret Mahler and clinical research psychologist Fred Pine) then, in a variety of clinical, research, and educational settings in New York, Toronto, and Los Angeles.

2. Several researchers and clinicians now view autism as a continuously distributed dimension, rather than a "qualitatively discrete" condition (see Rutter 2005 for a recent discussion). They point to mild forms of autistic characteristics in the "normal" relatives

of individuals with autism. It seems to me, however, that describing autism as a single dimension, with variations in *degree*, leaves less room both for *qualitatively* different variations within a particular characteristic (e.g., the focus of this book, intersubjectivity) and for the appearance of these variations in the context of other characteristics that are less likely to appear in full-syndrome autism—that is, in the context of other conditions. Considering autism as a single, continuously distributed dimension also raises questions about which of the several characteristics conventionally considered to be part of the syndrome is the core deficit that defines the dimension. The jury, I suppose, is still out with respect to whether research into etiology and genetic factors will be helped versus hindered by a lumping of conditions, rather than continued efforts to identify qualitative differences and refine diagnostic categories.

3. Additional description of Benjamin's "personality" as an infant may be found in the letter written to Dr. Hilda Knobloch, when Benjamin was about twelve months old, several months before she examined him. This letter appears in the appendix.

4. The diary spans twenty years of Benjamin's life. However, only the first four years contribute to this book.

5. I generally refer to a child as "he" and occasionally as "she." For the sake of readability, however, and also since virtually all study of infant–parent relationships has referred to the *mother*–child dyad, I always refer to the caregiver as a female.

6. At his birth, one doctor actually had remarked that Benjamin might be "a totally defective organism." I am confident that the reader will find it difficult to reconcile that insensitive prophecy with the young man who steps out of the pages of part III.

~

Introduction 2:
Intersubjectivity and the
Atypical Child

An "atypical child" has what is often referred to as a "developmental disability," which may be "mental retardation" and/or what is now referred to as an autistic spectrum disorder (ASD) or pervasive developmental disorder (PDD). All of these terms refer to conditions which are present at birth or assumed to be genetically programmed to become manifest within the first few years of life. Mental retardation appears in a number of different syndromes, with many different etiologies. The autistic spectrum or pervasive developmental disorders also cover several syndromes, which may have different etiologies (Bauman 1994; Gillberg 1992), with autism or autistic disorder considered the most severe. Mental retardation always involves both cognitive and adaptive limitations. The pervasive developmental disorders may or may not involve cognitive limitation. In current usage, according to the widely used *Diagnostic and Statistical Manual of Mental Disorders* (DSM) published by the American Psychiatric Association, the diagnosis includes children with autism and children presenting with either less severe manifestations of autism or certain features of autism but not others (see American Psychiatric Association 1994). The PDD-NOS (pervasive developmental disorder, not otherwise specified) diagnosis may also include (amongst others) children who in the past may have been diagnosed as "borderline" or "borderline psychotic," "psychotic," atypical ego development, or schizoid. Children who have been diagnosed in the past with a semantic-pragmatic disorder or nonverbal learning disability may also now be diagnosed with an "autistic spectrum disorder."

The diagnosis of "autism" (or "autistic disorder") requires that the individual have significant *qualitative* impairments in three areas: reciprocal social interaction, communication, and the flexibility, range, and spontaneity of interests and play. (The third group includes the presence of diverse behaviors including, but not limited to, motor stereotypies, perseverative behavior, rituals, unusual preoccupations, and/or resistance to change and transition.) This is the "triad" of impairments as described by Wing in 1988. By current DSM criteria, children diagnosed with an autistic spectrum or pervasive developmental disorder may or may not have significant impairment in *all* three areas. However, there must be a severe and qualitative impairment in the area of social relatedness. Thus, severe and qualitative social impairment is considered to be the sine qua non of autism and autistic spectrum disorders, their signature symptom (Wing 1998; Mundy and Crowson 1997; Grossman, Carter, and Volkmar 1997). An individual who is able to comprehend and engage in age-appropriate give-and-take social interaction could not be diagnosed autistic, no matter how many other "symptoms" he may have that are suggestive of autism in areas other than interpersonal interaction (e.g., a language disorder, motor stereotypies, or limitations in interests and imagination).

In contrast, atypical development in interpersonal relating is not considered a necessary characteristic of mental retardation. Although children with autistic spectrum disorders may be "mentally retarded" or appear to be so, their problems in interpersonal relating are presumed to relate to their autistic spectrum diagnosis, not to their mental retardation. In fact, not too long ago, according to the DSM, the differential diagnosis between autism and mental retardation could be made on the basis of the individual's capacity for social relatedness (see American Psychiatric Association 1980). The mentally retarded child was socially interactive, the autistic child was not.[1]

Intersubjectivity is at the heart of the reciprocal social interaction that is so impaired in autism. The diary in this book documents my son's delayed and atypical development of intersubjectivity. Benjamin, however, was diagnosed (in 1971) as "mentally retarded," *not* as autistic. Does this mean that Benjamin was (is) in fact, autistic? Do his difficulties in achieving intersubjectivity suggest a pervasive developmental disorder? If not, should we expect similar atypical development of intersubjectivity in other children who have been diagnosed "mentally retarded" but not "autistic" or PDD?

These questions are not easily answered because, within the general area of developmental disabilities, diagnosis is quite complicated. There are myriad variations and tremendous individual differences amongst persons diagnosed with "developmental disability," "mental retardation," autism, and/or a pervasive developmental disorder (see Pomeroy 1998, and Volkmar and Klin 1998, for recent discussion and review of these issues). The diagnostic criteria for and boundaries of the autistic spectrum disorders are still very much in flux (see, e.g., Wing 2005) and, it appears, ever widening. Some writers suspect there may be different subtypes of ASD, characterized by different types and degrees of interpersonal skill (Volkmar and Klin 1998; see Beglinger and Smith 2001 for a review of subtypes; see also Wing 2005). As well, autism and mental retardation can coexist; yet the more severely the individual is affected by either or both conditions, the more difficult it is to differentiate the two. Thus, for example, apparent symptoms of autism can be artifacts of low developmental level (see, e.g., deBildt et al. 2004), while more severe forms of autism may be associated with lower intellectual functioning (Wing 1981, 2005) or will bar access to the individual's cognitive functioning (Eagle 2002). It is true that many mentally retarded children do not appear to have a *qualitative* impairment in selfhood and interpersonal relating, although they may show somewhat delayed or dulled development in these realms (Cicchetti et al. 1989; Field 1987). On the other hand, some individuals who have been viewed primarily as "retarded" or "developmentally delayed" *do* share characteristics which border on or overlap with problems in intersubjectivity and communication. These characteristics include limited pragmatic skills and limitations in the quality of social interaction and "theory of mind" (see, e.g., Begeer et al. 2003; Njardvik, Matson, and Cherry 1999; Yirmiya et al. 1999; and Yirmiya et al. 1998).

Thus, where the mentally retarded or developmentally delayed spectrum ends and the spectrum of autistic disorders begins is not at all clear. Nevertheless, since mental retardation is typically diagnosed on the basis of an IQ score and adaptive functioning, alone, it seems likely that diagnosis of a pervasive developmental disorder will be added to a diagnosis of mental retardation (or mental retardation added to diagnosis of a pervasive developmental disorder), when the individual with mental retardation also displays deficits in social relatedness. On the other hand, the most current DSM definition of mental retardation (see American Psychiatric Association 2000) requires significant limitations in adaptive functioning in at least two skill areas, one of which on the list is now "social/interpersonal skills." I would add that most forms of autism also appear to involve some kind of cognitive irregularity (e.g., concrete thinking), including some that involve very severe cognitive impairment. Autism and cognitive irregularity or limitation may not be independent (Wing 1981; Rutter 2005).

Finally, the autistic spectrum seems to shade into other diagnostic categories (e.g., schizoid, childhood degenerative disorder, semantic-pragmatic disorder, nonverbal learning disabilities, etc.), and there is much controversy over whether these disorders are within the spectrum and about what qualifies a disorder for inclusion in the spectrum (see Schopler, Mesibov, and Kunce 1998). As already mentioned, it is likely that disorders with very different neurobiological substrates have been included within the pervasive developmental disorders category currently defined by the DSM-IV-TR. Limitations in the DSM method of diagnosis (in which a certain *number* of characteristics selected from a list is required to meet criterion, rather than specific symptoms) also contribute to this problem (see Beglinger and Smith 2001).

The range of individual differences within existing diagnoses of atypical early development has led some clinicians to propose a diagnostic approach that cuts across different diagnoses, by focusing on different psychological functions rather than syndromes. The "regulatory disorders" or "multi-system developmental delay" proposed by Greenspan (1992) is an example. In this diagnostic system, regulatory difficulties (which may be biologically based) will be identified in auditory/verbal, visual/spatial, and/or perceptual/motor processing. These difficulties interfere with relating and communication on the part of the child, often resulting in negative interactions with caregivers that intensify the difficulties. The disturbances in relating and communicating are considered more secondary than primary (i.e., biological, as presumed in autism/PDD) and amenable to therapeutic intervention.

There are, of course, some cases about which there would be little doubt that the child is "autistic"—that is, he or she seems quite neatly to match the cases originally described by Kanner in 1943. Yet by virtue of much earlier diagnosis, early intervention, and therapeutic preschools and home-based programs, it has become increasingly difficult to say what a "classic" autistic child looks like. Such children may behave differently in different environments, at different ages and at different stages in their life, and/or as a function of the amount of early intervention they received (Mundy and Crowson 1997; Camaioni et al. 1997). Although diagnosed as autistic in early childhood, their presentation (in some cases) will have changed considerably by adolescence or adulthood, and this too, in any case, may vary, as a function of their environment (i.e., whether it accommodates their needs and provides necessary supports) and the extent and nature of interventions throughout the life cycle (see, e.g., Seltzer et al. 2003).

To complicate matters further, differences of opinion exist regarding whether absence or limitation in the capacity for social-emotional contact is, in fact, the primary deficit of autism. Some theorists and researchers (e.g., Baron-Cohen 1988, 1995; Baron-Cohen, Leslie, and Frith 1985) believe the primary deficit is in metacognition, leading to a failure to understand mental states in others (described as a deficit in "theory of mind"). Others view the primary deficit as a failure in the "executive function" (e.g., Ozonoff 1995), referring to a variety of cognitive functions such as planning, attending, and initiating, or in "central coherence" (Frith and Happe 1994), referring to the ability to focus on the context rather than specific features of stimuli. Proponents of facilitative communication argue that the autistic individual's problem is primarily a problem in motor planning (Biklen 1990). He is viewed as, in fact, willing and desirous of making contact with others, even as capable of understanding another person's mind and motives, but simply not able to demonstrate these capabilities and propensities, due to a motor disorder (apraxia) affecting communication. In the past, and still nowadays, especially "on the continent," some psychoanalysts view autism as a failure of "psychological birth," a defensive "encapsulation" created to protect against awareness of a precocious separation from the maternal figure (e.g., Tustin 1981). Or the autistic individuals may be viewed as desirous of human contact but withdrawing from it defensively because (as a result of primary processing difficulties) the interaction is too difficult and painful to endure (e.g., Bemporad, Ratey, and O'Driscoll 1987).

When Benjamin was born, the diagnosis of pervasive developmental disorder did not yet exist. The diagnosis of autism did, although much more circumscribed than it is today. The term conjured up images of somber, unrelated, unresponsive children, rocking their bodies and flapping their hands, screaming or banging their heads, mute or echolalic. No one, including myself, ever considered that Benjamin was or would become like that. Although he seemed delayed in all areas from the start, he smiled on time, and seemed relatively *responsive*, socially. Doctors were reluctant to diagnose him anything, anyway, for most of his first year. They attributed his initial delays to the fact that he had undergone surgery at age two months; they thought he might catch up during the first year. When finally diagnosed (with mental retardation) at age fourteen months, there was no mention of autism. In any case, autism, at that time, would generally not have been identified that early.

Dr. Knobloch, the renowned developmental specialist who evaluated Benjamin in 1971, described him as developing at about two-thirds the normal rate, with the implication that he was "retarded." She also commented that he appeared to have "give and take" (not, however, observed by his family at the time—see the appendix), perhaps in this way reassuring herself and confirming in her own mind that he did not appear to be autistic. At the time, I thought I knew a lot about autism but I did not know anything about retardation. I therefore spent much of Benjamin's infancy and early childhood trying to figure out what *retarded* really meant—that is, exactly *what* is slower, and why do various skills and characteristics develop too late and/or differently, or not at all.

The DSM criteria for autism and autistic spectrum disorders have changed over the years, so that these terms now cast a much wider net and include milder and/or less atypical symptoms. How does Benjamin fare now against current DSM-IV criteria for a pervasive developmental disorder? Depending upon the assessor's personal understanding of each of the criteria and how well he or she knew him, Benjamin might well be checked (or have been checked, *at some point in his development*) as positive on each of the following:

Alb: failure to develop peer relationships appropriate to developmental level;
A2d: lack of varied, spontaneous make-believe play or social initiative play appropriate to developmental level; and
A3c: stereotyped and repetitive motor mannerisms.

Moreover, with the exception of the designation of degree (e.g., *lack* versus *limitation*; *encompassing* versus merely *frequent*), he would appear to fit, if not now, then at one time or another in the past, virtually *all the other criteria* in the areas of social development, communication, and range of interests.

Nevertheless, based on my clinical experience with individuals diagnosed with or suspected of having an autistic spectrum disorder, my reading of the literature, and my tremendous familiarity with Benjamin, I am inclined to say that he is *not* now "autistic," and that he never was. And indeed, most people meeting him, enchanted by his outgoing nature, would argue that, most definitely, Benjamin is not "autistic." But does he have a pervasive developmental/autistic spectrum disorder? Is he PDD-NOS? Should he be diagnosed as mentally retarded with PDD features, or even as a mentally retarded child with Asperger's syndrome (an apparent contradiction, or "oxymoron" [no pun intended!], but one which at times seems best to describe him)?[2]

Benjamin has always had several of the characteristics found in children diagnosed with autism or other pervasive developmental disorders.[3] These characteristics of Benjamin include the following: a restricted range of interests (but with passionate and obsessive attachments to them!); problems with change; motor stereotypies; perseveration, and compulsive rituals; atypical prosody; limited or atypical natural gestures; disordered pragmatics; an apparently atypical course of development of intersubjectivity and "theory of mind"; and subtle differences in the end product of these cognitive-social developments.

With such a list of symptoms, why do I *not* think Benjamin is autistic? I would probably refer to his interest in people—his friendly, outgoing nature, and, albeit late in developing, his social reciprocity. He has all these qualities, but all in what I will refer to throughout this book as a "same but different" form. But so, too, do certain types of children and adults who are now being diagnosed with autism or other pervasive developmental disorders. As mentioned earlier, these diagnoses today are interpreted by many to include a wide range of presentations, some even shading into normal (see, e.g., Wing 2005). Perhaps Benjamin does not seem "autistic" because he is, and always has been, *from birth*, clearly developmentally delayed or "retarded" in all areas. His early motor milestones, for example, were all significantly delayed. This is less often found in children with autism. This having been said, I am fairly certain that there are many psychiatrists or psychologists who, following the DSM-IV, or using the highly regarded ADOS (Autistic Diagnostic Observation Schedule), would find that Benjamin met the now-much-expanded criteria for an autistic spectrum disorder, or even autism.

Given this ambiguity, it is important to state clearly the purpose of including the diary material in this book, and to identify the developmental issues and clinical groups to which it is intended to be relevant. The decision to present this chronicle of Benjamin's early years is based on three premises. The first reflects my bias that atypical social development (e.g., limitations in intersubjectivity or "theory of mind") can be found in conditions other than autism. I believe that it will improve diagnostic practices and advance our understanding of both autism and other developmental disabilities if we acknowledge this rather than diagnose an "autistic disorder" in every case in which some type or another of social impairment exists. The second premise is that the particular way intersubjectivity developed in Benjamin may reveal something about delays or disorders in intersubjectivity in certain other individuals with developmental disabilities, whether or not they have been diagnosed with autism. The third is that my experience with Benjamin has suggested interventions which may be useful in fostering the development of intersubjectivity and/or compensating for disorders in its development, in at least some atypical infants and children.

These last two are big assumptions, and they may not be correct. I suspect that there are several qualitatively different types of disorders of intersubjectivity, on the basis of which one might define a variety of subtypes both within and outside the autistic spectrum. Each, in turn, may require and respond best to a very different type of intervention. Moreover, I cannot say with certainty that the parenting practices followed with Benjamin were responsible (in whole or even in part) for his development of intersubjectivity and selfhood. It is very important for readers who are parents of autistic children to keep these disclaimers in mind.

Regardless of whether Benjamin's particular brand of intersubjectivity is the same as, similar to, or different from that of individuals with autistic spectrum disorders, the information in the diary, and the discussion that follows, may help advance our understanding of disorders of intersubjectivity. It will do so if it encourages others to identify specific subtypes along this dimension within the autistic spectrum, as well as within the broader spectrum of developmental disability, including mental retardation. In each case, one can search for the particular type of impairment in intersubjectivity and try to determine whether it can be corrected and, if so, the approach to it that is likely to work. I think that it is particularly important for us to do this now. At the same time that diagnosis of autism and pervasive developmental disorder is casting a wider and wider net, there is tremendous emphasis on earlier and earlier diagnosis and intervention. The possibility that, in conditions other than autism, there may be delays or differences in indicators of intersubjectivity in infancy raises concern about too early diagnosis of autism, with the associated risk that interventions may be introduced that were designed for difficulties with a very different etiology and course.[3]

Notes

1. Over the years, for many people, lay and professional alike, mental retardation had been viewed as more or less synonymous with Down syndrome. That Down syndrome children tend to be "social" and "interactive" may have contributed to the tendency to differentiate mental retardation from autism on the basis of social interaction alone.

2. Asperger's syndrome (AS) is a diagnosis which is now included within the DSM category of pervasive developmental disorders. Individuals with Asperger's will show

qualitative impairments in social interaction and in their range of interests (tending towards very restricted, specialized, and all-consuming preoccupations). However, while there may be peculiarities in their style of language and pragmatics (e.g., they may be overly pedantic, or too blunt), their language development with respect to syntax and semantics is not delayed or impaired. These individuals are also of normal intelligence (hence my "pun"). There is a great deal of controversy regarding whether AS is the same as or different from high-functioning autism, *and* even whether it is a developmental disorder in the first place, versus a variant of "normal" (see Schopler, Mesibov, and Kunce 1998, for extended discussion of these issues). It tends to be used, and I suspect, overused to refer to many highly intelligent people who may be somewhat eccentric or "socially inept."

3. Introducing treatments designed for individuals with autism early into the lives of children with other disabilities will also confound evaluation of the effectiveness of different treatments for autism. It also raises the risk that a more appropriate intervention will not be offered.

PART ONE

THE DIARY

~

Diary Preface

The diary entries you are about to read are transcribed as they were originally written, over thirty years ago, except that they are now divided into chapters. The chapter division was necessary to provide resting places in reading the lengthy narrative. Each chapter centers around one or another development that had seemed especially important or salient, either at the time that it was observed or in retrospect. Within several of the entries, the reader will also find a description of my attempts to understand or conceptualize what was happening at the time. Since developmental psychology was strongly influenced by Piaget in the 1970s, these attempts make frequent reference to Piagetian concepts.

Each chapter concludes with my thoughts, *today*, about what may have been going on at the time covered in that chapter's diary entry. These comments are necessary because the diary entries had been written without benefit of knowing "the end of the story." As a result, it is often difficult, in reading them, to see or foresee the potential significance of the material recorded. This might leave the reader feeling somewhat "at sea": What is happening here, and how is it relevant to the development of self and intersubjectivity? The remarks at the end of each chapter help bring the diary material into focus. In these remarks, I also raise some of the questions and issues addressed later in part II.

Piaget's theory about normal development is less in favor now than it had been two and three decades ago, in light of findings which seem to challenge the order and manner in which he believed a child comes to understand and think about the world about him. Moreover, due largely to recent advances in technology for brain imaging and for mapping processing by the brain, developmental psychology has taken a decidedly neuropsychological turn. The reader may therefore be surprised to find reference to Piagetian concepts even in the comments that follow the diary entries, since these comments were all written in or since the year 2000. As will be explained in part II, in analyzing the diary material I often found that Piagetian formulations were still useful in developing a conceptual foundation for intervention strategies. More specifically, I found that, while they may have limitations in explaining how *typical* children learn, the theoretical models of developmental psychologists such as Piaget and Vygotsky seemed particularly useful in formulating how to teach *atypical* children and in explaining why particular interventions might work with them. At the same time, recent neurophysiological discoveries also appear highly relevant to the observations in the diary and to conclusions drawn from them. "Mirror neurons," for example, have been found in monkeys and humans, by virtue of which neuronal pathways associated with the execution of an action are activated when an individual simply observes that same action being performed by someone else. This phenomenon has been studied in relation to imitation, the development of a sense of the self as like others, and the ability to understand the intentions and feelings of others (see, e.g., Hurley and Chater 2005a and 2005b)—all topics that come up frequently in the diary entries. In the comments following each diary entry, then, and in the theoretical discussions in part II, there are frequent references to these findings from neuroscience, as well. In some instances, they can even be reconciled with the Piagetian account.

~

CHAPTER ONE

"You *Should* Have Been My Kind of Kid"

Benjamin was born on September 16, 1970, with observable physical defects and suspected global delay. His first months were a time of feeding difficulties, surgery (at two months of age) to correct his cleft lip, and ongoing medical investigations of several other physical abnormalities. In addition to the worry about his physical welfare and his future development, there was also anxiety about his passivity and muted social interaction, all while trying to maintain normalcy and an enriched nurturing childhood for his two sisters. The diary entries during those nightmarish first months primarily documented my own despair and worry. Entries focusing more on Benjamin begin when he was four and a half months of age.

Diary

February 3, 1971
Something about Benjamin's style makes you float away in your thoughts when you're with him, just float away and withdraw—not get into him. He doesn't pull it from you, doesn't ask to be related to. If you do, he responds fully. But he doesn't ask.

February 10, 1971
Today, I realized something new. All I really am, or what I had been till now, I hold back from Benjamin. My "good mommy" me—involved, enthusiastic, playful, creative, vocal, verbal, "in it," child-like in the mother role—I have not felt like being *any* of this with Benjamin. In part, in large part—it is because he does not evoke that kind of response. He is all subtle, subdued, un-energetic, un-enthusiastic, relatively unplayful himself. But that's only part of it. Part must be: "You are not what I wanted. You are not the kind of baby that *my kind* of

mothering goes with. I do not know how to relate to you. I do not know how and do not *want* to do it in a different way *in order to accommodate to you*. You *should* have been *my* kind of kid."

But why can't I still play with him more than I have, even if he does not evoke a playful response from me? With my other kids, and with kids I have worked with professionally, that was my thing! My main talent! A natural, effective, stimulating, entertaining, responsiveness to children. And I expressed it with *all* kinds of kids, even unresponsive autistic kids. And my wish to get through to those kids got me to find all sorts of ways to bring unresponsive kids around. But I don't do that with Benjamin!!

March 1971

If it is a hostile act towards him, to withhold myself from him, it is a self-defeating and aggressive act against myself as well. For it leaves me without any exercise of my main identity or talent at this time. How depressed I am at the end of a day, in which I have silently cared for Benjamin, holding him, feeding him, carrying him around but without playing with him, conversing with him. Because he does nothing to request it, demand it, evoke it. But also, because it seems *too much bother*, it seems such a *tremendous* effort, over so much resistance, to work at it and draw it out of him. I cannot just respond spontaneously to a (normal) baby's cues: "come play with me, come enjoy me." Instead, I am staying home, playing mother, and not enjoying myself, and I am not using, for his sake, the best of what I am.

Whenever, for a moment, I *do* play with Benjamin and something good happens (like when I hold him high over my head while I lay on the bed, and he somehow, from high up there looking down, manages to make eye contact and smiles) I can enjoy myself. I have none of that pressure to do more, that guilt about not doing enough. I live in "the now" of it. I am my usual self, giving my usual self to him, and that is enough.

April 1971

Benjamin does not focus attention on you, not on your face, or eyes. Part of the problem may be that his head hangs to the side and down—he cannot yet hold it up and centered. But two things I have discovered help him to do it, and when he does then look at you directly, his eye contact seems normal, and for a fleeting second, he seems like a normal kid. The first: is when he's sitting in the infant seat, and I sing a musical scale, slowing down and holding off, as I approach the upper "do." His whole body tenses with anticipation of that "do," and he becomes more focused on me. Second: (as described above) holding him high up over me, as I lay on my back, so that his eyes have to look down at me. He does this and loves it.

May 1971

Back and forth: is he normal, is he not, what is he, what is he not, he's not good enough, look at the other babies, etc. Depression and panic at each indication and proof that indeed he is *not* keeping up, indeed he *is* different, weak, defective, that it's not *just* the problem of a cleft-lip and palate, but also slow development, physical, and mental. I wondered: Is he deaf? (the doctor says no). He doesn't respond when I enter the room. Most of all, there's no "self" in him, no "ego," no active-baby-grasping-at-the-world and wanting to engage it. That is the proof, the evidence that he is not right! I feel such guilt and fear—my God! He is not right, he is not normal, he is different *and* I cannot relate to him. I do not know how.

Comments

Depression and emotional withdrawal from their infants in parents of babies born with disabilities are often attributed to the experience of loss and of mourning for the perfect child they had hoped for and were prepared to have (see, e.g., Rosen 1953; Hawke 1977; Emde and Brown 1978). Others attribute parental withdrawal to the failure of the child to stimulate emotional involvement (e.g., Stone and Chesney 1978; Emde, Katz, and Thorpe 1978; Blacher and Meyers 1981). Certainly, both these themes appear in these early entries. But another source of maternal depression and withdrawal is depicted here as well. It is the loss of the opportunity to experience oneself as a good mother and the loss, therefore, of one's own sense of self and self-esteem (see also Goldberg 1977). It is also about needing and longing for feedback for the love one gives and for the effort to love that one makes, and about the hurt and anger one feels when that feedback is not there.

These first diary entries reveal that the missing "little person" in Benjamin affected my own sense of self and self-worth. His development scared me and threatened my own self-esteem because I could not feel proud of him, proud of having him, or proud of myself as a "good mother" to him. Rather than see him as a separate individual, with his own separate needs, I saw him only through the prism of *my* needs, as a baby who thwarted my need to feel good about myself and to feel like the energetic, caring mother I had been in the past. As we will see in chapter 3, it was only when my identity and self-esteem became less dependent upon the kind of person Benjamin was (or was not) that I could begin to see and to accept (or accept, and therefore see) that *different* kind of "self" that Benjamin had had all along. Only then do my observations of Benjamin begin in earnest.

When Benjamin was first born, I remember the terrible feeling of not being able to "let loose the love" that felt trapped within me. I was too afraid to love

a baby that I had been told might be a "totally defective organism." In these entries, I describe a failure to experience "attunement"—a sense of connection
and understanding of the baby. This is not a situation in which to cast blame,
on mother or child. The normal baby engages in the kinds of behaviors to which
a "normal" mother can "attune" (see Blacher and Mayers 1981 for review). On
the other hand, as we shall see, depression and withdrawal on the part of the
mother can mute responsiveness and interaction patterns in the baby (see Field
1987 for review).

CHAPTER TWO

~

Big Dipper, Little Dipper

Diary

June 1971

Today, in a follow-up x-ray, we learned that indeed, Benjamin's urine is backing up into both kidneys, into a pair of lop-sided kidneys, one higher than another. This could mean some structural (congenital) problem with the ureter system. A cystoscopy will be necessary. Another "defect." In and of itself, that notion is no longer upsetting to us. They fix everything up. Just have to take it all, one step at a time. The day to day of living through a trauma is not so terrible as its implications. We can survive his operations, hospitalizations, traumatic medical situations. The real issue to cope with is that there is yet another defect! What else will we find out!!

> Once upon a time, a baby was born
> with a birth defect
> Followed early, right away, with
> Glimmerings, all the time, that something *else*
> was wrong. His ears, his kidneys, his sexual organs,
> His mind. That something *else* was wrong.
> Not right, not good enough.
> Different, slow, weird.
> Not like babies we know.
> I panicked
> I cried
> I hid him.
> I could not love him.
> I feared him.

I could only think of the future.
What would he become.

August 1971
At the cape (Cape Cod). A last ditch effort to save the marriage.[1] I don't think it is working. Benjamin is colicky, cries a lot. But, he did do one thing that had a "self" quality. He discovered how to pull himself up on the back of the couch. He took such joy in that!

September 1971
It's been a year of medical tests, waiting for results, anxiety and terror about what Benjamin is, what he will become. But now, it suddenly seems clear! It *makes no difference* what he is or who he is! My caring for him, my love cannot be contingent on that. He is, whatever he is, but one thing is for sure, he *is, he exists*, he is here, and he needs to be loved and cared for fully, for what he is. It makes no difference who he is, *where* he will go or *if* he will go.

The returns will be different than when you love a "whole baby," one that asserts itself and has a self to relate to, but you *have* to find a way, you have the responsibility to find the best way to work it out.

December 1971
No more reviewing what's wrong with him, or horror at finding out yet another area of dysfunction. It makes no difference any more. It doesn't matter. Nothing can really shock us anymore. It doesn't matter anymore. Benjamin is Benjamin, no matter what he does, what turns up, what we find out (i.e., from the medical tests). We can't really find out that much new. We know him now.

When did I start accepting Benjamin? I think when (his father) left (in September), when I realized he had left me for real. One day, I felt a sense of exhilaration at realizing that there was an "I" in *me* that had gone through and survived all these traumas (within months of each other, Benjamin's birth and learning of his father's decision to leave)—and I had an "I" that was a continuing, surviving center that experienced these traumas but was also separate from them and not destroyed by them. Now I had to take care of myself and I had to take care of Benjamin. And me, taking on the job of taking care of me and of him, made me feel good about myself, again.

January 11, 1972
Dr. Knobloch describes Benjamin as developing at a rate of 60 to 70 percent. She never used the word retarded, but we knew that was what she meant. His brain is not right, it never will be, there's nothing one can do, he'll always be slow—but "educable," she said; "he will find some place for himself," etc. Still,

knowing for sure is a blessing, in some ways. We (Benjamin's father and I) were glad to get it over with and settled. We knew (all along) but also didn't, or didn't want to know; and now, we do. This brought about a more relaxed and accepting and even joyful attitude on my part. A "Let's get on with it!" attitude.

January 1972
(I spent a weekend away at an ashram. To take stock, revive myself, come to terms with all that had happened—Benjamin, his father's leaving. At the ashram, I went out one cold starry night. This is what happened. This is the poem I wrote to describe it.)

> I walked into the night.
> A beautiful, open, cold night.
> I saw the Big Dipper . . .
> and the Little Dipper . . .
> The Little Dipper.
> It was so small.
>
> AND I CRIED FOR MY BABY.
> I cried aloud, into that night.
> I cried for Benjamin
> I cried for my baby . . . . . .
>
> Is the crying over?
> Will it ever be?
> Did I cry for him?
> Or for Me.

I realized then that I was not crying for the Little Dipper. I was crying for *me*, for the *Big* Dipper. That is not acceptable. It is time to care about Benjamin; it is time to take care of the Little Dipper.

January 13, 1972
Benjamin has a function, a place. He will teach everyone. He has a sunny warm glow that melts you and makes you want to love, or makes you love him. People need to feel they can love—more than anything that is what we need—not so much to be loved but to be able to feel *loving*, and if just by his being who he is, people feel warmly towards him, he has helped, he has played a role. What else is there, really, to do in this world but to help each other out. Benjamin is not trying to help. His way is just to *be*; to be himself. But he brings out love in others. Benjamin radiates—something, so moving—is it his innocence?

Comments

This is such an important chapter! Acceptance of Benjamin for who he was, not for who or what he would become, took time and was hard won. But it proved to be the foundation, the sine qua non, for the success of everything that was done to help him develop. Acceptance required that I felt good enough about myself to separate my ego and sense of self, from his. Acceptance did not mean resignation! On the contrary, it allowed me to "get to work" in learning about Benjamin. And it gave him the freedom and the confidence to grow and become all that he had in him to be.

Note

1. In June 1971 I learned of events that eventually led to the dissolution of my marriage.

CHAPTER THREE

~

The "Trick"

Diary

January 16, 1972

Something very special happened today! Benjamin at 16 months has a warm, sunny smile that is easily elicited. His whole body melts with pleasure at your approach, and that sunny smile erupts. At least there has been that, and we all know, by now, how to get it from him—smile at him, lift him up, talk to him, etc. For 16 months I have been ministering to him, and working, round the clock to bring him to life. And I can do it. I can get the smile. But, except that he smiles back so lovingly to me, there has been *nothing* coming from Benjamin to help sustain my involvement. Nor has there ever been anything coming from him to *initiate* it. And so it has been very tiring to spend time with him, and ultimately depressing. I have felt exhausted, and depleted.

Feeding him, today, I asked myself, what is missing here? What am *I* missing? And then I thought, "But of course: a normal baby his age would be feeding *me*, he would be imitating me and bringing his hands and spoon to *my* mouth."

Benjamin has a spontaneous (though reflexive) movement in his happy response to others. Along with a smile, his arm raises up in tense excitement. He reacts this way to the excitement of seeing and hearing me say, "mmmmmumumum," as I feed him. So, today, I put a little bread in his hand, positioned my face squarely in the "line of fire," and made a series of vigorous "mummmmmmmmm" sounds, of the kind that would amuse and excite him. Voila! up went the hand, and into my waiting open mouth catapulted the bread!

That is the first time Benjamin has "fed" me—literally, but more importantly, I suspect, figuratively. My excitement and pleasure was *immense*, overwhelming. *And boy! did Benjamin know it.* His sunny glow erupted into a blaze of happiness. And then *he* tried it, *on his own!*—hand to my mouth, to each of my "mmmmm-mumums"—again. And again and again!!!

27

Never before had he done something that could get *such* a rise out of mommy. Never before had *he* done something that made such a difference.

January 18, 1972

Teaching Benjamin the "trick" (i.e., to offer me his food): he *loved* learning it!! He has never forgotten that movement. A "mmmmumm" from me, and he instantly lifts his hand straight to my mouth, to "feed" me. He has a little trouble with aiming it, but with help and practice, he's getting better. I have wondered if it would ever get spontaneous—or would it only be when I went mmmmmu-mum, opened my mouth, and showed that I wanted it. But now, he also does it just to the cue of having some food, i.e., bread or cookie, in front of him.

Benjamin seems to learn by association (or at least it looks that way) what in other children seems spontaneous and unlearned. That is (normal) kids don't *learn* (don't have to be taught) to offer things—they seem to imitate and identify with the other, automatically. It is different with Benjamin: he is in his own world—he doesn't connect himself with me; he doesn't seem to identify himself with me (or with any other person). Perhaps he doesn't yet have a "him-self" to connect (and identify) with a *your*-self.

Comments

This is a very important chapter. Benjamin, now sixteen months old, is able, for the first time, to "make mommy smile" through actions of his own. As we will soon see, the "trick" was a turning point in Benjamin's social development and the springboard for his learning how to communicate. How and why this was so will become clearer in the next few entries and will be discussed again in several of the chapters in part II.

The parent–child interaction is viewed by many as the "crucible in which development is forged" (Mahler 1968; see also Winnicott 1965; Stern 1985; Pine 1990). Within that interaction, strong affect will tend to energize and catalyze learning, and reinforce and consolidate what is learned (see Pine 1990; also Stern 1985 regarding RIGs (Representative of Interactions Generalized); Greenspan and Weider 1998; Emde 1999). It certainly seems that this is what happened here.

The story of the "trick" also illustrates the importance of organizing learning around the infant's *spontaneous* behaviors and of "being there" at the right time to do just that. Finally, these entries demonstrate the mutual dependence of mother and baby, on each other, for regulating each other's affective state (see, e.g., Hofer 1984). I needed Benjamin to "feed" me; he needed me to enjoy him.

In these entries, I also asked the question: *How* does Benjamin learn—does he learn differently than others? Commenting on the apparent difference, I wondered whether his learning was arrested by the absence, in him, of that which, in normal children, seems to be an inborn capacity and propensity to imitate others. This capacity, in turn, seemed to require or reflect some sense of shared identity with others—that is, the ability to perceive or experience that "I am like others" and that others are "like me."

These comments immediately bring to mind the recent discovery of "mirror neurons" in macaque monkeys and in humans (see Rizolatti 2005a and Gallese 2005, for reviews). In brief, as mentioned above, these are neurons, associated with motor acts, which are activated when an individual simply observes these same motor acts being executed by someone else. "Mirror neurons" have excited much interest and enthusiasm as providing a plausible mechanism underlying the capacity for imitation. In particular, they appear to allow for an immediate identification of a similarity between the person doing the act and oneself, and between that person's action and an action within one's own repertoire. The ability to imitate, and Benjamin's problems in this domain, will be mentioned many times throughout the diary and discussed further, along with the "mirror neurons," in part II.

~

CHAPTER FOUR

"Why Won't He *Hold on* to Me?"

Diary

January 18, 1972 (continued)
Benjamin doesn't demand *of* you, he (just) complains out loud, into the air.

Why won't he *hold on* to me? I tried to "teach" him to hold on to my legs, to help pull himself up in this way when he is trying to stand. But he wants to keep his hands closed. He seems to have trouble embracing the world. That would imply an *active*, assertive *self*. He doesn't (seem to) know he exists and can *do*.

Is he: brain damaged? Emotionally disturbed? Retarded?

I get ecstatic when he learns something, and then fearful about what it means to be "brain-damaged" (versus retarded). Who can predict the consequences and the areas of weakness? The numbers from Knobloch (i.e., the rates of development that she quoted) are meaningless.

February 1, 1972
I think Benjamin is beginning to look more and more focused, using his eyes more, getting rid of the vacancy. In part, it seems to have come along with my really trying to get into him, now, and *teaching* him to use his eyes. But most of all, it was *learning that (offering) trick!* Learning that seemed to have started something new in the way of his knowing and using himself.

February 8, 1972
The question that plagues me is: why does this child not just look or behave like a younger one and that's that. What is the *quality* of Benjamin that is "off," all about? The vacancy in the eyes and the not giving things to people? She—(i.e., Hilda Knobloch)—said he has "give and take," but I think it's *mostly* "take." Even a ten month old baby *gives* to you so *much* more than Benjamin does—

offers, calls, shows, displays, shows off, etc. Why isn't there this "give" (in Benjamin)?

What is the nature of this thing (i.e., retardation), anyway? Is it simply slower *rate of development?* (doesn't seem to be just that) with a lower *end point?* or is it SOMETHING ELSE that perhaps explains the other two?

We will find out. Benjamin will teach us what *he* is like—that is, *he*, in particular, not necessarily what other children with mental deficiency are like. We still don't know, do we, and we never will, we can never, *at any one moment* say: *this* is what he is now and *that* is where he will end up. We will not be able to understand it, anymore than anyone can predict how and where a normal child ends up, or actually "understand" what makes the normal child "give" and "be," so normally.

Comments

At this point Benjamin (now seventeen months old) appeared to me to have a delay or deficiency with respect to curiosity about his environment. He also appeared to lack an inclination to hold onto, interact with, or have an effect on the world. He did not "grab onto it," with either his limbs or his eyes. He did not seem to *make use* of things and people in his environment. This quality, apparently missing in Benjamin, is referred to by Gibson (1979) as "affordance"— that is, the innate understanding, in normal children, of the potential of properties of the environment to relate to and *enable actions* that are in the child's current repertoire. In this respect, Benjamin seemed so different from even much younger babies. He had to be "taught' the simple acts of engagement that come effortlessly and spontaneously in the normal child. Teaching him "the trick" seems to have "kick-started" some of that engagement. Still, as he approaches eighteen months of age, when the normal child is so curious and engaging, I anguish over the difference, trying to understand it. Then I decide to let Benjamin teach me about what it is like to be him.

CHAPTER FIVE

~

Sharing Pleasure

Diary

February 8, 1972 (continued)

Benjamin *does* do two new things in his high chair that are cute and kind of "ego"ish. *One*, he now *initiates*, by himself, a certain game for me to play with him. This is how it developed: when he is excited, he stretches up his head in a funny way, with his mouth open. I have lately been *imitating* him doing that. Now, *he* starts it as a game—i.e., he stretches up his head and *waits* for me to do it with him. (*Maybe that's a clue!! imitate him more in order to help him get to know himself*) [emphasis added].

Two (second "egoish" thing): He discovered how to push himself back up after he has slipped down in the high chair, and he *looks at me* to see if I saw it, to share *his* pleasure at being able to do it. He definitely gets pleasure whenever he masters something, whenever he has learned something new, like when he can stand a few seconds when I let go of him. Problem is, he learns so little that is *new* to give him that experience!!

February 23, 1972

But he does have such a clear joy in learning something new, and now, for the past few weeks, he looks to share that pleasure with another. He now appears to know that you and he *both* like it, when he does something.

Since I've taught him to offer food to my mouth ("the trick"), he'll do it "spontaneously" *if my face and the food are all roughly in the right position*. It's not *his* idea (i.e., plan) to do it; rather, it appears to be suggested to him by the situation. Would (will) it ever occur *to him*, himself, to want to offer something to me—to do it, spontaneously? That would mean he somehow was identifying with me [*note: I think I meant here, "saw himself as a person"*], not just (responding) as an association to the situation)?

This morning he had spoons in his hand. In the past, he has only offered them to my mouth. This time, I said, "give mommy," opening my *hand*. He apparently "understood" the words, *"give mommy,"* immediately, because he offered all three spoons *to my mouth*. I repeatedly had to place his handful of spoons into *my palm* and say, "give mommy *hand*" for him to learn that, too.

It seems that there is something "cognitive" that goes into building "ego" and "self"—e.g., in the ability to identify with and imitate others. That cognitive component gives the egoish "I" look that Benjamin does not seem to have—yet! (I hope).

Rollo May makes the point that the higher level often defines and modifies the lower, rather than merely being reached through starting at the lower and progressively building upon it.[1] Benjamin, it seems, is missing the "higher" from the start!! Thus, it is not just a question of his not being expected to go as far. His brain has worked differently from the very beginning—it's not just a difference in rate or destination.

Comments

In the very first "trick" entry, Benjamin shared in *my* pleasure. Just a few weeks later, he begins to share *his* pleasure, with me. He also, for the first time, does something spontaneously, actively, and, it appears, with the *intention* to affect my behavior. In this new "trick," he intentionally performs an act that he anticipates I will imitate. It appears that he does this for the sheer fun of seeing me imitate him, or possibly, just for the fun of *making me do something* (i.e., *anything!*). I say in the diary that this trick has an "ego-ish" quality, by which I mean that Benjamin seems to be intentionally directing his behavior.

In a second new "ego-ish" development, Benjamin shares his pleasure in learning how to keep from slipping down in his high chair. To appreciate the new quality, here, compare it to an earlier entry in the diary when Benjamin was eleven months old. I wrote: "He did do one thing that had a 'self' quality. He discovered how to pull himself up on the back of the couch. He took such joy in that!" It seems that feeling joy in mastery has been there for some time. The difference here, six months later, is that he intentionally seeks to share that joy with another.

Benjamin's new trick raises some interesting questions pertaining to the emergence of intersubjectivity and the development of a sense of self, not only in Benjamin but in normal infants. Benjamin behaves as if he "knows" that I had been imitating him. If so, how did he *know* that? This kind of "mutual imitation" is commonplace in normal caregiver–infant relationships. It seems to require a more sophisticated interpretation of the matching of another's actions with one's own than would be involved in being able to imitate, in the first place. And if Benjamin did experience me as doing the same thing as he was, why was my imitating him so enjoyable to him and so worthy of his making it happen again?

It might be argued that Benjamin had only learned that I would do something contingent upon his doing a particular act. If so, one would still have to ask, Why would he, and babies in general, enjoy this so? What is it about an "I do–you do" sequence that baby finds so worthy of repeating? Is it just the contingency of another's actions upon one's own? Or does the fact that the other person also experiences and shows pleasure in the reciprocity also play an important role? We return to these questions in part II.

Benjamin appears—at last!—to be *calling attention to himself*! I didn't see it coming. This is one of those seemingly inexplicable "leaps" in development—suddenly, one day, a new kind of behavior appears. Calling attention to oneself appears to relate to, and require, some sense of self. Some observers claim that chimps also "show off" in order to receive attention from others (Savage-Rumbaugh 1986), suggesting, to the human observer, some sense of self in the primate as well.

In this chapter, Benjamin does not understand the meaning of an "open hand," an iconic (i.e., not symbolic) gesture. I had to "teach" it to him. Normal babies, by this age, do seem to understand such gestures, without being taught. Understanding natural gestures and its role in intersubjectivity is discussed in chapter 47.

Finally, in these entries, I continue to ponder the question: What, exactly, is the nature of the dysfunction or disorder in Benjamin? How does the course of his development differ from that of a "normal" child?

Note

1. Rollo May (1953) an American Humanist and existential psychologist.

CHAPTER SIX

~

Learning a Gesture

Diary

February 25, 1972

Benjamin now uses the "hands-up-to-mommy's mouth" trick to request *"a plea-surable interaction with closeness,"* and he does it (his hands to my mouth) with *any* object, whether or not edible, and even *without* any substance to feed me. He also looks much more at me (i.e., at my *eyes* versus my mouth) as he does it.

He now insists upon putting the spoon to my mouth! This has not evolved from any impulse or intention of his own to offer food to me or to imitate what I did to him. Rather, it has now become a ritual, generalized from "the trick," to bring about a happy interaction with me. He now also raises his hands together towards *another* person's mouth, even with nothing in them. In a little over a month, "the trick" has turned into a greeting, which expresses a wish for, re-quest, or expectation of "happy social contact" with another.

He shows frustration and anger and dismay (this is new) if he is being taught something or expected to differentiate beyond his level.

He still doesn't imitate and I can't find much to imitate in him (mostly, he's only into throwing things now). The idea (i.e., of imitating him) would be to make him more aware of himself and able to isolate what it is that he does that has an effect.

It seems that certain tricks (e.g., the stretching neck trick and pulling him-self up trick) "fade out." The "pulling self up" was the first time he very notice-ably used his eyes for communication, appeal, shared experience. But now, any-way, he seems generally more related to me and to others. He *looks for* people. In general, he makes more active use of his eyes—e.g., he looks for things; he looks around for his food; he turns to others, he makes more use of his eyes for appeal and communication.

He is trying to pull himself up on the coffee table.

He puts his head down on the rug to go "NiNi!!!" ("nighty-night" or good-night, for sleep time) when I say those words.

Now I *enjoy* spending time with Benjamin, and teaching him. He seems to "like" me more and expect to have fun with me. It seems to have started in some way with teaching that food-to-mouth trick. Maybe this is one of the first places where he had fun, not from *me* entertaining *him*, but from *his* doing something that pleased me. I have to always be on the look-out for little things that he does spontaneously that I can show pleasure in, and then teach (i.e., shape into) new things.

Comments

As exciting as was learning "the trick," even more so was its being generalized to Benjamin's first (and for a while, only) communicative social gesture. At age seventeen months, when Benjamin wanted a pleasurable social interaction with me, he performed his "trick" (hand to mommy's mouth) to communicate that wish. When "the trick" was first learned, the action did not have the intrinsic meaning for Benjamin that it appears to have for normal babies (namely, "I am feeding mommy the way mommy feeds me"). Rather, subsequent events suggested that Benjamin had observed that doing "the trick" had made mommy very happy and excited and that this, in turn, became the meaning and purpose of the act. One must add, however, that it was not just mommy's looking happy or excited that gave the action meaning, but rather the fact that this positive response was directed to, shared with, and about *him*. In short time, Benjamin then used the gesture to elicit a positive social interaction with him, even outside the feeding situation. It served to communicate to another person, "I want to enjoy myself with you." The gesture was not a conventional one. Benjamin did not have the repertoire of conventional gestures and other forms of nonverbal communication that typical babies and young children appear to develop without specific instruction. But he definitely used his idiosyncratic gesture, repeatedly, for the purpose of requesting and initiating social interaction.

Vygotsky (1986) proposed that the infant's arbitrary actions take on meaning by virtue of the (conventional) meanings attributed to them by the mother, and by virtue of the consequences that follow from the fact that she interprets them in that way. However, in the "trick," Benjamin did not learn the meaning (i.e., "feeding mother") that I had intended to give to his "arbitrary" action. Rather, by virtue of its association with an emotional experience that he had liked, the action became imbued with a different meaning for him. He used the "trick" from then on to communicate a desire to have that "feeling" again. In this situation, Benjamin needed me to understand *his* meaning and to reinforce, by my response, the meaning it had come to have for *him*, not the one that I had intended to attach to it.

In this entry, we also see that Benjamin had learned the meaning of the word "NiNi" in the context of being prepared for bed. But it was an impressive leap that he could respond to it out of context, as well. In performing the "going-to-sleep" action upon hearing the words, was he just mechanically associating the gesture to the words? Or was he actually imitating himself? If the latter, it would be another early indication of a sense of self. And as such, although it is not noted in the diary, I am sure that this apparent "pretending" drew a very happy response from me. The observation that Benjamin seemed to be dismayed when not able to do something may also have suggested an emerging sense of self.

~

CHAPTER SEVEN

Wanting to Do

Diary

February 27, 1972

I am still trying to understand just what is the specific nature of Benjamin's problem—what exactly is it about his development that gives it a quality of strangeness—what is the pattern or lack of pattern—what are the deficits. He's not just like a younger baby. He's different—he learns differently—mainly he does not—*ever*—communicate his needs *to* someone. He may signal with a grunt or a cry to himself, but he does not actively express, proclaim, his being *TO YOU*. He does *react*—e.g., to love. He loves to be loved, but he doesn't love OUT. He doesn't seem to identify himself as a SELF *WHO* does this or that. He hardly ever imitates and he does not *initiate* acts that he has earlier imitated. If he raises his hands to be picked up—as he just did, tentatively, yesterday—it appears to be a partial automatic association—i.e., the beginning of his response to my lifting him—rather than a communication of his wish.

Still, he does now have an *"arm up" movement*, which is a signal, when I am not right there, to invite me for an interaction. The "arm up" signal is abbreviated from the "trick." It has come to mean: "Come play with me, mommy, come and enjoy yourself with me."

For some time, now, Benjamin attempts to "imitate" me when I bring two items together for any purpose. However, he does this by just *throwing* the one object in the direction of the other. For example, if I show him a pen, writing on paper, he throws the pen onto the paper.

March 3, 1972

Benjamin is almost 18 months old. In some instances, it seems that Benjamin's head (i.e., his intention) is a bit ahead of his ability to act it out. For example, he wants (I think) to put one block on top of another, in imitation of my tower, but he has trouble a) aiming the block, directing it enough to have it land in place; and b) letting go of it once it is in place. He can't really let go that easily. It's more like a *throw*, when it comes, and that defeats the placement.

However, I have now seen him *practicing* placing one thing on another. He is pleased if you help him by holding down the block and enabling him to release it without knocking it over. Release is a problem. There is a kind of rigidity, slowness and weakness in the muscle control. Motions aren't fluid; they seem choppy, immature.

In the bath tub, I tried to show him filling a cup at the tap and then emptying it, saying "wheeee!!," as water spilled out. I showed him several times. No imitation, just joy in seeing it. Then, several minutes later, he picked up the cup. I said, "make wheeee!!!" He dipped it in the water, pulled it out and threw it down. Here again, it appears that he understands that he is to repeat or imitate an act, or wants to do so, but he cannot "find" or "define" or "differentiate out" or control the appropriate movements. So, instead, he throws in a more primitive one, or one that is already in his repertoire, like throwing. The muscle, perceptual-motor stuff seems at a somewhat slower pace than comprehension, at times.

New tricks!!! This half-month or so. He can manage the milk cup himself and sometimes will take it and do so, though he still prefers and sometimes insists that someone else give it to him.

Benjamin thoroughly digs the fact that he can see me in the mirror and that I'm also someplace else. He seems to know it's me and "greets" me in the mirror with great excitement.

He likes to rotate in a complete circle in a sitting position. He does it over and over again. He likes to crawl out the door to the hall; empty blocks out of pail one by one, and put them back. I taught him to open the bread box to find a cookie.

He knows (i.e., receptively) "cookie and milk," but he still does not attempt to verbalize anything. No new sounds or consonants (perhaps r and l). Simply NO sign of his wanting to use *words*. He hasn't yet tried out many many sounds. But he definitely understands: up, down, milk, ice cream, bye-bye (he waves), and ni-ni which means, "head down." It's all very subtle, but there's a little and it needs encouragement.

Also, I do think he is imitating more [emphasis added]. He imitates intonations and tunes—sometimes, I think, he imitates hello or hi. Sometimes, he imitates—after some delay, and tentatively—hands up, banging etc. Also, he puts his head down for "ahahah baby"—I think. I think he sings "ahahaha" as he rocks (wheels) a carriage back and forth (as I have done). However, although he seems to appreciate it when I make the doll walk, he makes no attempt to do that, himself.

He *purposely* (as a game) repeats an act, to which I have (playfully) said *NO! NO!* Like throwing something on the floor, knocking over the milk carton. *He does this with a mischievous "twinkle" in his eyes which shows he knows you don't like it* [emphasis added] or, at least, that he will get a response.

He is very aware of my coming and going. He cries or complains when I leave, at first, then calms as soon as I'm out. Wary at first of sitter because he knows I'll leave.

March 8, 1972

Benjamin is missing behaviors like pointing. He acknowledges something he wants by a grunt to himself (is this the beginning of a name or label?) or a smile or he'll put his arm out towards it. This "reaching" is still somewhat mechanical in the sense that it seems to be the correct movement but without the right meaning. As if, this is what he has learned to do in this situation (namely, put an arm out) but it does not have the quality of a "reach" towards a goal. What is the quality that is missing? Partly, it seems to have to do with his control of movement. He has to think of what he wants his arm to do, and then make it do it, instead of there being an intention (e.g., to get or touch something) which then automatically initiates the proper movement. The movements should just come into play, on their own, so to speak, piggy-backing on the intention, but that doesn't seem to be what happens.

Benjamin *did* finally learn to *put* a car on a downgrade, carefully, instead of *dropping* it on. He has to control his body with effort (this was the case, even at three months old, when he first was hitting the hanging balls). You can see him trying to direct his arms and hands. Again, he can't just decide with his head and then have the motor take over by itself.

Comments

Eighteen months is a time of great strides for the normal child. There are leaps of development in representation, language, and symbolic play. Benjamin, at eighteen months, also took some unexpected giant steps. This chapter begins with observations and musings regarding his apparent lack of initiative, intentionality, and communication. Then, within just a two-week period, he appears to be doing, understanding, and communicating, so much more!!! The leaps were dramatic; so too, however, was the difference in the quality of his actions and communication, as compared to that of a typical child.

The reader may wonder why I chose to include the above entries about intentional movements, as they do not appear to have an obvious connection to the themes of intersubjectivity and self. However, when viewed in retrospect, the rocky connection between Benjamin's intentions, on the one hand, and his ability to actualize them, on the other, did appear to have significance in relation to both his atypical communication style and his difficulties in understanding the intentions of others. In Benjamin's case, the flow between the motivation to perform an action and the action itself did not seem smooth and unlearned. In contrast, in normal development, one's actions seem seamlessly connected with the intention behind them. This close connection between the intention and the motor act may render similar actions by others inherently meaningful and immediately understood by the other.[1] I wondered: If Benjamin was lacking or having difficulty in accessing inherently meaningful behaviors, would he have similar difficulty in being able to recognize meaning and intention in the actions of others?

Benjamin seemed to see the movement of the doll's legs as something interesting. Did he see it as "walking"? Matching the doll's walk to his own (or other's) walking would be quite an achievement, a reflection, on the one hand, of some kind of matching and comparing, but also, on the other, abstraction— that is, finding similarity amongst differences. Similarly, Benjamin really enjoyed seeing my image in the mirror, and greeted it, appropriately. Was he viewing the mirror image as another "me"? Or did he recognize it as an image of me? Like appreciating the doll's walking, the latter would reflect a step towards representation (i.e., something not quite the same can equal something else). Matching appears to be emerging hand in hand with imitation. Once again, imitation seems to reflect and require the matching of two souls.

At the time of these diary entries, I apparently viewed the way Benjamin lifted his hands to be picked up as different in quality from the way the normal baby requests to be picked up. I viewed it as a partial, anticipatory enactment of being lifted, a mechanical, conditioned response associated with wanting to be picked up. I presumed that, in contrast, the normal baby lifts his hands with the intention of *communicating* his wish to be lifted. But writers such as Clark (1978) and Lock (1978b) claim that lifting of the hands *as a signal* is "learned" from the response of the environment to an earlier phase, in which lifting arms was, indeed, no more than an anticipatory partial movement. Plooij (1978) claims a similar process in chimpanzees observed in the wild.

And finally, quite suddenly, a new kind of "understanding" of words emerged. Words now appeared to be associated with a particular context or consequence and came to signify it.

Note

1. How we come to understood intentions in others is a matter of debate (see, e.g., Goldman 2005; Meltzoff 1993, 2005; Hurley and Chater 2005b). Meltzoff argues that infants come to understand the intentions of others through experiencing their own intentions with similar acts. "Mirror neurons" which map the observed act onto motor neuronal patterns for the same actions by the observer may link with brain sites involved in

intention, thereby mediating an understanding of the intention of others (see Rizzolati 2005a for review of studies in animals). Matching a doll's walking to one's own requires an abstraction and generalization, but also an inhibition of any association of the action with intentions such as one's own. This is a higher-order sense of play and symbol. It is interesting that I have often found that "neuro-atypical" children are afraid of wind-up toys in which little people or animals that should be inanimate, move. It is as if, some-how, in this case, intentionality associated with perceived action is not filtered out.

~

CHAPTER EIGHT

Puppy Stage

Diary

March 22, 1972

Time passes slowly could be the motto—it's as if every second is slowed down, not just the months. That's why Benjamin appears slow even in a given moment. There's the absence of a bright, quick look of sudden recognition and awareness. Everything registers, slowly. Time is relaxed. In a way, it's pleasant, it's another world—a slow, unpressured world, no tension.

My concerns are mainly about language, both comprehension and expression. Benjamin understands certain words or commands, but appears to have no awareness of the function of language. Perhaps, he tries a bit to imitate sounds, primarily hello, which are in his repertoire, but never new consonants, and never with any sense of naming, or trying to talk (i.e., communicate with words). No babbling either. He does seem to appreciate that sound and vocalization are for communication. He also does appreciate the affective tone of language. But he doesn't seem to have the concept of "words," or of using words to communicate to others. On the other hand, he does seem to "understand" some *action* words (up, down, go ah-ah-ah baby, kiss, etc.) and he gets into position for "somersault" upon hearing the command. It is interesting that he responds to such verbal expressions, but NOT to gesture.

March 30, 1972

There has been some kind of boost, lately. He is so terribly loveable, charming, and sunny. And he seems to be doing more and understanding a bit more, and possibly trying out a few more sounds. Almost stands, for a few seconds, and then throws himself forward, onto you. Seems not to want to stand up, feels timid about it, but also excited when he finds himself able to do it unassisted for a short while. Understands "put your head down." Sensitive to being "yelled" at. Very upset by loud and sudden noises.

April 2, 1972
I think that an "I" is beginning. Why do I say so? The "I" is a kind of sad, confused looking one; one, however, that wants to be friendly, loves "to understand" and appreciates attention and play. At the hospital (trial run for his upcoming operation) he initiated a peek-a-boo game (by peeking through the crib bars) with another baby in a crib! He also brought a Q-tip to his ears, spontaneously—that's an identification/imitation kind of thing! He also brings a comb to his hair (I taught him that) though not yet on his own. He seems to be trying to feed himself—spoon to jar to mouth.

Perhaps the sense of "I" comes from the increase in self-initiated behavior, which he does when he wants to entertain another, or wants to get them to give him attention, or laugh with him. Thus, he will crawl over and put his head down to do a somersault (i.e., for us to pace him through one). He calls out Aaah! to get your attention. Or he begins patty-cake or standing up, as a signal to you to respond to him.

The other day, he pulled himself up to a stand at the coffee table, and then intentionally, tried to let go himself, on his own (usually I have to let his hands go [i.e., take his hands off the surface]). He got his balance, determined the right moment, and then let go. He also seems to carry more of his weight himself when we walk him (i.e., holding onto both arms, raised up).

What he does not do is use verbalization, babbling to communicate. He's more like a puppy that gets your attention and "communicates" non-verbally. He initiates "aah" conversations, and imitates variation in duration and expression, but he does not try "to talk." No pointing, no labeling. That's the main difference between him and another baby. He seems like a puppy, wanting and getting love, curious, getting about, into things, pretty active now, but no talking.

He's intentionally "naughty"—throws down cups, etc., and waits for your response. Laughs heartily. Adores children and laughs and laughs in their presence.

April 15, 1972
When Benjamin finds a "trick" he uses it over and over without variation. He appears to enjoy the sequence of "I do something (in particular), and the other responds in a predictable way." It's really like the Piaget level of being able to produce interesting effects—and he does it again and again. The current thing is: throwing something down *and grinning at the other*, meaning, "I expect you to object," then some expectation that the other will pick it up, return it, in order for him to throw it again. He *initiates* the whole thing himself by *calling you* (with his one and only "word"—aaaah!), getting your attention, and then "aaahing" you if you don't pick it up soon enough [emphasis added].

I'm feeling some despair lately about language development. He seems still so far from flexibly altering it. He does use N and L a bit more now, but mainly, it's the "aaaaah" chant whenever he does something. He sings along with himself. Both assimilation and accommodation seem off. He wants to imitate something but can't match the oral-motor structure. If he does match, he doesn't seem to appreciate that it has meaning—i.e., that he can use it to express what he means. Rather, it's just an association. *He does not put on it his own mark that makes it a Benjamin, an expression of and from him.*

Benjamin understands language as signal, not symbol. A word does not stand for a thing. A word or a phrase can signal a thing, but it is not "this is a that."

Along with no symbol is *no pointing* at that separate thing and no "I can talk."

Maybe "I" also presupposes being able to comprehend (detect similarity) and imitate another. Yet it may also be the other way around: imitating may require "I"ness. Imitating requires first *differentiation from*, then *identification with*, or matching with, another. I recognize that separate parts of me are the same as parts of her; (therefore) I can do what she is doing; I also do the same kind of thinking as she does. "I" involves recognition that one is like another, but also appreciation of and interest in the "I-ness" of the other. Also, only an "I" can initiate language—which rests on still another ability fueling "I-ness"—the ability to differentiate and connect a word to the separate thing.

In normal children, "I have ideas" generally is associated with and leads to "I can tell" them (i.e., my ideas). I want to tell them. "Telling" means "I have the ability to organize and relate my (that which belongs to me, is mine) ideas (something that's there to begin with before the telling)." There is a quality of "I" in the ability to organize and communicate the ideas. The feedback from being able to organize and communicate gives a sense of ME as an effective, significant person.

Here is what Benjamin's communication (or lack thereof) looks like:

I have an idea (sort of, or maybe)
I am weak in the "I" that says: *tell it!* and—
I am weak in the telling (i.e., in the ability to organize communication of it).

Imitation
Imitation reflects an awareness of self and other and the experience of oneself as like (the same as) the other. *Benjamin does not (seem to) know (reflect upon) that he exists and is like another.* He does not appear to have a sense of comparison, familiarity and empathy with the other. He does not have the sense: I can do what you can do; this in me is like that in you.

Perhaps the activity comes first, then the feedback that leads to "this is me." Then, "me" wants to do—what you can do. But what makes kids "*want to*"? What makes a kid try to act, *want* to act, like another?

Still, there *is* the quality of an "I" in his wanting to do his "tricks." So, here is where he is so far:

1. He has a desire to perform, to learn, to master;
2. He takes pleasure in doing something that he knows is liked or expected: e.g., he's proud when he stands up and he shares enjoyment with the other in his success;
3. He knows that his smile is winning, and uses it;
4. Although it is true that he is repetitive, that he repeats without variation, there must be the desire to be an "effector" in his repetition, of the same things. He wants to perform and to be active;
5. He just doesn't have his own creative self-generating capacity. He learns HOW to do something, and then, it becomes part of a repertoire of behaviors he can call upon. *This does not look or feel the same as having an intention which automatically and spontaneously translates into an original action.*

Yesterday, Benjamin found a round plastic donut. He remembered where two others (of different colors) from the same set were and went to retrieve them.

And, at 18 months of age, Benjamin *is* now sharing pleasure, calling attention to himself, seeking and appreciating the responses of others to himself. These are all characteristics that appear to be absent in autistic children, but present in normal children within the first year of life. They seem to reflect some sense of self, as separate from others, and as the object of their behavior and emotional reactions.

Comments

These entries are all about glimmerings of a sense of "I" in Benjamin. He appears to have an awareness of himself as the object of another's attention and interest. He calls attention to himself. And he intentionally behaves in a certain way towards others, to get them to respond to him in a way that he wants. These self-initiated, self-generated purposeful acts by Benjamin impart a sense of personhood to him.

Benjamin now also seems to *enjoy* the discovery that he can make others do something that he "has in (his) mind." In Piagetian terms, this might be no more than enjoying the experience of "making an interesting spectacle" last (or happen again). However, that he "grins" at the other as he anticipates her reaction suggests that something more might be going on here. Benjamin might be sharing his pleasure with the other (i.e., "I think this is fun, don't you?"), and therefore communicating across space with another. This is evidence of primary "intersubjectivity."

The "Q-tip to his ear" is a significant development that we might take for granted when it appears amidst all the other delightful antics of a typically developing little toddler. Benjamin is doing something to himself that had been done to him. Is this an imitation, or has he just learned that Q-tips go in one's ear and he therefore puts it there just by this association? If an imitation, it would also be delayed imitation, an advance over immediate imitation. And if an imitation, how did it manage to get transformed (in direction and object) from an action by another on him to an action by himself on himself? We also have to ask: How does Benjamin know where his ear is? How does he know where to put it, since he cannot see his ear, and cannot have seen me put the Q-tip there? These observations raise many interesting questions regarding normal development. How does the baby retain the *intention* of an imitated act by transforming its direction and/or object; how does one imitate using parts of the body that one cannot see?

The ability to do imitations that involve parts of the body that cannot be seen is a milestone in early infant development that typically takes place well before the first birthday. This breakthrough for Benjamin at age nineteen months did not show up again for another month (see chapter 12). In fact, in these entries, I continue to express the feeling that Benjamin is missing something that enables a normal child to imitate, and that this something appears to involve an ability to match something in one's self with something in another, and/or an awareness of a likeness between self and other. However, the matching cannot be the whole story, for, beyond making imitation possible, it does not explain the interest in and intention to perform it. What motivates a child to "want" to imitate—to even think about it as something worth doing in the first place? Here is a question that has interested infant researchers, developmental theorists, and philosophers for many decades with respect to normal development, as well as researchers and theorists interested in autism, in particular. In part II, we will return to these complex issues.

Another big step for Benjamin is seen in his spontaneously setting out to retrieve the rings to complete the set. Not only has he remembered (i.e., represented mentally something that was not present)—but he created and acted upon his own (original) action plan. Once again, this would hardly be something one might notice in the development of a normal child, in which case it might be embedded in many other acts suggesting memory and spontaneous planning, but for Benjamin it was a single incident that stood out as "a first."

In these entries, I seem quite concerned that Benjamin does not yet use any words to communicate. (Parenthetically, parents of atypically developing children frequently are most concerned about verbal communication, sometimes ignoring the importance, first, of good nonverbal communication.) The observations in this entry suggested to me, at the time, that a sense of an "I" (a "me" that is both alike and different from others) might be a prerequisite for communication (i.e., for *telling*,) but also that experiencing oneself as able to organize and articulate a communication might contribute to the sense of "I." Benjamin appeared to have a significant deficit in the ability to create words (i.e., enunciate them, spontaneously or through imitation) but also in appreciating their meaning and function.

CHAPTER NINE

~

Puppy Stage 2

Diary

April 16, 1972
Old tricks drop out—or are superseded??

Benjamin doesn't offer cookies anymore. Also, even when prompted, he doesn't do the two-handed food offer, which had generalized to a two-handed signal (arms up) for attention (although occasionally, he still does). Now, he raises *one* arm when he wants you—and reaches with it. . . . He doesn't lift his arms when sitting. Rather, he crawls to you and raises one arm, while still in the crawl position.

He now does do instrumental intentional things. For example, he has a favorite toy; he knows where it is; he goes to the place, then stands there, *and waits to get it* [emphasis added]. BUT it's that same, one favorite toy—for 6 months or more now!! When he masters something, he does not let it go.

There is still no speech that seems to say "I" want to tell you something, or show you something. There is only a call, to get your attention. It means: "look here, do what I want you to do." He has an expression: that shows affection. But he does not (seem to) do it *to* you, *for* you, for your benefit.

Here's what the difference seems to be:

1. Benjamin does not appear to have a sense of being either alike or unlike the other; it does not appear to have occurred to him, to notice, to compare.
2. In any case, he does not appear to be motivated to model himself on another (i.e., there is little or no imitation).
3. He appears either to have nothing *to tell* (i.e., no ideas) OR not to be motivated to tell his ideas to others. He appears not to be aware of having

49

ideas which may be compared to the ideas of others, which in turn might provide motivation to tell them.

So far, he seems to be consistently more concrete, primitive, perseverative, and stimulus-bound than other babies. His organization (developmental level) appears to be deficient, or there appears to be a limit on how high (or complex) it can go. Will Benjamin stay at this organizational level—even though he progresses in different behaviors? Will the organizational level be constant, and relatively primitive, even though new abilities may appear as a result of maturation?

April 18, 1972

I felt much relief when I read Stella Chess re: the behavioral peculiarities of retarded children (I.Q. 50–75). Many of the repetitive stereotypies, she says, are present in "non-psychotic autism." Also very delayed speech (more delay than predicted by M.A.) and poverty of imagination. These are the peculiarities which made me think Benjamin was more than or different than just "retarded." According to Chess, they are typical of retarded children, and that which, in the autistic child, looks like pathology, in the retarded child, . . . is more or less adaptive and more appropriately based.

(Thus, there may be a common core to the autistic child's and the retarded child's peculiarities, even if the elaboration is different and seems "psychotic" in the former. Actually, autistic children shouldn't be called autistic or psychotic or schizophrenic, any more than retarded children should be called retarded. It is a kind of atypical development—i.e., developmental, and not "psychological" or "psychopathological.")

Comments

Anyone who has experienced the joys of a normal nineteen-month-old will appreciate how different Benjamin was at this age, and how slowly he was developing. The normal toddler at this age seems to be learning something new every second, is generating his own "experiments" to find out more, is wanting to find words to describe all his discoveries, *and wants to tell you about them.* He seems to experience himself as *someone* who knows, as *someone* who can do things to find out more . . . and he wants to *tell* you about it. It is the significant limitations in ideas and in self-directed, original behavior and the absence of the "wanting to tell" that leads me to lament, in these entries, that Benjamin is still "like a puppy."

When he was nineteen months old, I presumed that Benjamin did not perceive others as like himself or himself as like others, or at least, he did not seem to be taking this similarity into account. While he could differentiate himself from others, I perceived him as not paying attention to or being interested in the similarities between himself and others (see previous entries as well). This, I assumed, accounted for the absence of imitation but also of a quality of "selfhood." Hobson (1990b), for example, writes that the baby must first develop a concept of a "person" based on his experience of others before he can identify that same "personhood" in himself. Benjamin's behavior suggested that he was not quite registering the "personhood" of others. It seemed to make little difference to him, in going about his business. This was the "puppy" quality.

These entries end with continued ruminations regarding the nature of "retardation." There appears to be a more primitive form of organization. At an early age, one can discern the absence of the usual precursors and harbingers of higher levels. Therefore, the "primitive" is not an early level of normal but rather an atypical form to begin with. The next entries represent my continuing efforts to understand this and its implications for how to help Benjamin develop. Ultimately, understanding how Benjamin processes experience will give insight into whether, and if so how, and with what kind of help, he will begin to develop into a more self-aware, self-directed, communicating little being.

CHAPTER TEN

~

Ruminating Mom (Plateau)

Diary

May 1, 1972

The relevance of the Piaget assimilation-accommodation model to the issue of so-called "retardation" and to Benjamin's "strangeness" suddenly became very apparent to me today. Benjamin is a "simpler" being and the simpler quality is there from the start. It is not the rate of development *per se* that is off—although that may be a secondary consequence. Rather, it is a question of less complexity, less differentiation, less structure, all along. What seems to be off is the assimilation and accommodation process, both aspects—which of course is what Piaget had equated with intelligence. Intelligence is the assimilation-accommodation process and the normal child has a more or less effective machine for it. The differences amongst people of different intelligence seem to be in the ease, speed and degree to which schemas are formed. This in turn relates to the capacity for abstraction, association and generalizing. That is, a schema even from the very start, involves "abstraction"—a comparison and linking of two similar, and yet different events, by virtue of recognizing or "abstracting out" the similarity or a constant association.

Benjamin, first of all, has fewer schemas (and he is slower to develop them). Therefore, when he is faced with a novel experience:

a) he does "want" to assimilate (he is happiest when he knows what do with an experience, when he knows to what to match and connect it) but

b) he has fewer schema available to him for use in responding and with which to match it. He may perseverate a previously used response. The repetitive going back to what he knows (e.g., clapping at everything) is

52

because there is still the "mastery" impulse to assimilate, but less available to which to assimilate the new experience.

Accommodation means responding to the discrepancy, doing something about it—and changing what was there before; accommodating the differences leads to new structure. Being weak in accommodation makes for that stiff, too rigid quality of Benjamin's behaviors, like when he learns "a trick" and then applies it in all situations in exactly the same way (e.g., the arms out, or casting a toy.). He doesn't make the act his own by putting his stamp on it; he does not modify it to fit better.

What is the "g" factor that determines how much assimilation/accommodation goes on? *That's what makes a child look alert and active—he's organizing (or is organized, so that he "knows" what he "sees")* [emphasis added].

Drugs like dexedrine speed up your thinking. They make the schemas fly. What do they do?—what do they work on? Maybe it's a clue to what is slowed down or does not happen in MR (mental retardation). Mental retardation (MR) should be re-named MS, or mental slowness or mental simplicity rather than retarded. It means fewer schema and slower processing.

Comments

At this point in Benjamin's development, I viewed his "retardation" as a question of *simpler*, rather than slower. Benjamin appeared to exhibit a less complex style of processing and learning than that to be found in a normal infant—of *any* age. I suspected that his style of processing and learning would remain simpler, even as new skills were learned. "Simpler" appeared to determine: 1) what could be learned; 2) what needed to be taught (versus could be expected to emerge spontaneously); and 3) how the learning would take place.

In this entry, I consider that learning and development normally proceed through the operation of the Piagetian processes of "assimilation" and "accommodation." These are the key players in Piaget's concepts of adaptation and intelligence. In his view, the infant is innately organized to accomplish adaptation through these two inborn propensities, working in tandem. Assimilation is a way of processing or understanding the world through partialing out that which is consonant with familiar past experiences (represented in a "schema"). Accommodation is the process of stretching, refining, and differentiating this structure to incorporate and resolve (i.e., assimilate) novelty. The ability to analyze input in terms of similarity and differences is therefore critical to the combined processes of assimilation/accommodation. By virtue of the spontaneous, inevitable operation of these processes, in what Hartman (1939/58) refers to as an "average expectable environment," these processes in turn will inevitably form structures of cognitive and social development. "Aliment" (the social and environmental input and influences in an "average expectable environment" upon which these innate processes operate) is necessary to enable new and successive cognitive and behavioral systems to develop. The new structures that develop will then require, and act upon new forms of "aliment," that are in keeping with their capacity for processing and integrating information.

I saw Benjamin as weak (and/or different) with respect to the normal child's natural proclivity towards assimilation/accommodation. This seemed to explain the slow (i.e., unchanging) and repetitive nature of his development. His behavioral repertoire had remained the same over a long period of time. He also tended to do the same thing (e.g., with a particular toy) over and over again. Although he had an impulse towards mastery, he seemed to lack sufficient schema (ideas, concepts) with which to recognize the meaning or potential usefulness of new experiences or observations, and the flexibility to fine-tune existing behaviors to match new contingencies.

Or so I thought at the time. Benjamin's development appeared to have reached a plateau. Until . . .

CHAPTER ELEVEN

~

Huge Leaps!

Diary

May 25, 1972

Benjamin has made a couple of great new leaps. Something exciting is going on with him! The strides appear to be roughly simultaneous, overlapping.

1. He definitely has learned the "goodbye" wave. He does it on command. But doesn't really understand the context, because he also does it at other times.

2. He has a new ritual. When he goes to sleep, he plays a little in his crib, then gets the pacifier by himself and lays himself down to sleep. He seems to have a sense, now, that "the pacifier—is—for me—to use—to go to sleep." And he does it by himself. He looks for his pacifier as his "night-time thing."

3. He is practicing standing up without holding on. He is completely turned on by his own greatness—he knows it's a great thing to stand up alone. He's ecstatic! He also *wants to come and tell!* [emphasis added]; after a success he crawls to me to share it. The kids (i.e., his sisters) scream with excitement so now he's learned a special scream to go with the standing, a combination of calling attention to himself and expressing the glee. *Definitely included is the idea of calling attention to himself* [emphasis added].

4. Finally, he now tries standing from the ground up, keeping his hands down, first, to balance.

5. Almost a week ago, he seemed to be beginning to experiment with a new sound involving his lips together. I had been making a big game at diaper change of a mmmmmmmmmm—followed by an explosive "ah!" I'd go closer and closer to him and end with a MMMMAH!! "smack" kiss. He

loves it, sometimes almost seems to be trying to imitate it at the time, but not at all reliably. However, ever since I started doing this, he's been playing more and more with "mmmm" and "om-ma—om-ma" sounds, going from open, to close, to open. I heard him this morning definitely practicing doing the oomm-ma ommm-ma sound. Now says mmma-mmma (sounds more like aaa ma—adds mmmm to his old "aah"—a lot!

6. Also when he eats, he closes his mouth, munches and chews more.

7. Very loveable, and more loving. He puts his head down on your shoulder to be comforted and to go NiNi.

8. Knows that excitement is in store if I lie on the floor, because that is when he originally started his "standing up" business—it's his cue to practice that.

9. Lying on the change table today, he began moving his hands in the "wind-wind little baby" movement (*from a mommy-infant song with gestures that I would have repeatedly sung for him in this context. I would pace his arms through the appropriate motions*). When I joined in and added the words, he seemed pleased—kept it going. When I got to "clap clap clap"—he clapped! When I continued "wind-wind little baby," he seemed to have trouble shifting back to that motion, and instead, kept clapping. Then—all by himself, without a word of prompting, he continued the song (game)—with the arms-up movement of the "ah-boom!!! di-ay" part at the end—including the several fast excited, repetitive movements that come after the first one! I didn't realize at first what he was doing. When I caught on, and expressed how pleased I was, he joined in it. He was happy too.

10. He now also anticipates the "tumble down-down" part of "This is the way the lady rides" (*song-game*) from the pitch and intonation of my voice in the preceding phrase, and vocalizes it, in "imitation" of me. He does it repeatedly in that context.

11. He imitates my singing—by doing his own "aaah" song.

12. He imitates head movements, as in peek-a-boo. Not the cloth over the eyes part, but the looking from different angles.

13. He imitates the intonations of phrases—he "sing songs" my excited exclamations to him.

14. *He now hands things to your hand, purposely* [emphasis added]. Today, he handed a toy back to me *so that* I would continue a game I had been doing with it.

15. He *initiates* conversation: He makes a little scream to begin conversation during diaper changes.

16. Benjamin had never really been put on stairs. Last week, I put him at the foot of the stairs, and he immediately crawled up with perfect coordination!!! Again, with a sense of pride in it! Next day, he did it again but in

a more advanced way, on hands and feet instead of on hands and knees. Then, he tried to go down head first!! I turned him around and in one or maybe two times, he seemed to learn that he had to turn backwards to get down, although he cannot master that coordination very well. I was struck with how quickly and easily all the stair coordinations came—compared to other coordinations. Either the timing was right— he hadn't been started too early. Or he's learning to learn—or getting better at coordination. He seems smoother. When he gets to the foot of the stairs, he then goes to a stand and lets go and is very excited with his accomplishment.

17. He definitely calls attention to himself now whenever he does any trick. He calls out "aah!! *loud*, to get attention. He looks toward the person to get their attention, to show: "I did this!!!" Same thing if he is crawling a long distance: he looks back to find someone to see and follow him.

18. Benjamin loves children. For some time now, he shows a definite love and preference for children. When he sees children, he tries to get their attention with his winning smile. He knows his smile is a winner, and he definitely puts it on to attract them!

Comments

"Great new leaps" followed the plateau! Benjamin is now *imitating*(!), calling attention to himself, and trying out more sounds. In the context of nursery games, he is also *initiating* a social interaction *and keeping it going*.

Maturation brings in new behaviors, some of which are intrinsically meaningful to Benjamin. These are in the physical realm—standing, walking, up/down stairs, and so forth. They are motor patterns that are self-initiated and self-directed but do not necessarily involve interaction and communication with others. However, they, too, ultimately appear to bind up, inextricably, with social experience. Here's how:

Benjamin has always shown an appreciation of being appreciated, of being loved. For every new development, he was given love and appreciation, and these have always seemed to be effective reinforcement. Either he has learned that praise and excitement are part of the sequence of learning a new skill (and he always enjoys having a sequence—i.e., knowing what will come next), and/or he has had, from the start, an apparently inborn, god-given tendency *to like the experience of others taking pleasure in him*. Surely, it was the latter that "ignited" the "trick."

It appears that, through repetition, structure, and routine (as, e.g., in the song-games that are repeatedly played with him), Benjamin has learned a set of seemingly "purposeful" behavioral *sequences*. Although learned (it appears) by rote and without comprehension of the purpose and role of each step, these sequences still result in social reinforcement. Thus, they can give him, again, that wonderful experience of being able to do something, on his own, that can bring about a response in the other that he greatly enjoys.

In these entries, Benjamin, for the first time (at twenty months of age!), hands something to another person, yet another seemingly simple act that we may take for granted in a typically developing young baby. But it actually is quite an important step—or rather, "leap." In it, the baby "does unto others as others have done unto him." In the Q-tip activity, Benjamin did unto himself what others had done unto him. He appeared to match his actions to the actions of another but did not change the object (or destination) of those actions. The action was also in keeping with the "affordance" of the Q-tip (i.e., Q-tips go in ears). It may or may not have involved an awareness or sense of knowing the intentions of another person. In handing things, in contrast, Benjamin not only matches the actions of another, but also modifies their destination (i.e., he does not put something in his *own* hand) so that the actions more clearly suggest the same intentions behind the act as had been the intentions of another. Handing something has the quality of the "trick," except in this case, the behavior was spontaneously generated by Benjamin, not taught.

How does the baby get to the point of giving to others? It is not present at birth. What enables the older infant to translate and reverse actions by others on the self, into actions by the self onto others? How does it come about that the infant, in doing this, is not just imitating the action but (apparently) does so with the same intentions as had motivated the act he is imitating? Again, there are competing theories, some proposing innately based equivalences of self and other, others pointing to the role of learning and the abstractions from and integration of experience. In either case, the question remains: how and why does this kind of reversed imitation arise only at this point in development, and not before?

Gray (1978), analyzing the behavior of "giving mother a toy," brings attention to the mother's "scaffolding" (Bruner 1974) an intentional act by the infant. First, the mother completes the action for the infant (in this case, taking the item *from* him) and gradually, in interactions over time, expands the child's role in completing the action by reducing hers (see also Clark 1978). Did Benjamin learn to give the ball to me, in the same way, through my initially having placed my hand in the trajectory of his movements with the ball? I was not aware of having done this with Benjamin, although it is certainly possible that it was done without my having attended to it.

Gray's (1978) analysis of a behavior performed by a normal infant is similar to how Benjamin learned "the trick." However, it does not seem to acknowledge what appears to be, in normal development, a spontaneous and self-generated capacity for *reversal of roles*—that is, intentionally and spontaneously doing something to the other that had initially been done to the self. In normal development, for example, it at least appears that, in performing the "trick" (i.e., "feeding" mom), the typically developing baby spontaneously and intentionally is experimenting with doing something to the other that had been done to himself. It does not appear to have started, as has been argued with respect to other purposeful behavior (e.g., in Plooij 1978; Clark 1978; and Lock 1978), as a random act, which only becomes shaped into an intentional and communicative one by virtue of the caregiver's response to it.

During this same time period, we see Benjamin loving other children. Does this, too, indicate that he now sees himself in others (i.e., sees himself as like them, or them like him)? Or is it an expression of a natural tendency to "affiliation"? Or merely secondary to the pleasure Benjamin feels in being "liked"? I question, in these entries, whether Benjamin's "cute" smile when with other children may be, not so much a spontaneous expression of his pleasure in them, as a means of getting an experience of pleasure, for himself (i.e., the pleasure he feels in experiencing their pleasure in him). That experience, however, could eventually lead him to take pleasure in them (because they are reinforcing to him).

Benjamin seems to have learned that he gets positive attention for certain things that he does. He appears to "know" that if he does these things (i.e., is "cute"), he will get attention. Reportedly, chimpanzees, too, call attention to themselves (e.g., by doing "razzberries") for the apparent pleasure of being the object of the attention of other chimps and humans (Savage-Rumbaugh 1986).

From a Piagetian perspective, these entries also appear to be about generalizing schema, extending and adapting them to different situations and even creating original variations of schema. What this has to do with self and intersubjectivity may become clear in the next set of entries.

CHAPTER TWELVE

~

Mommy and Me

Diary

May 31, 1972

Several nice developments this evening:

Benjamin was playing with a ball. It rolled under the bookcase. He lay down and tried to reach it. Couldn't. Sat up and cried to himself, complained, in his characteristic way. Then, he turned and *looked* at me—and cried *at* me—then turned his face away from me and towards the ball, and reached out his hand towards the ball as if to show me: that is what I want. (Better yet might have been if he had *kept* looking at me and pointed at the same time, but this was approaching that more than I had ever seen before.) He repeated the whole sequence—i.e., looked towards me, cried "at" me, then looked and raised his hand toward the ball. He was very pleased when I got the ball and gave it back to him.

Then he was playing with it. I said, "throw it to mommy" and put my hands out as if to catch it. He immediately understood the gesture!!! and threw it back to me (!!!)—with such good aim that I caught it!!! WOW!!!

In the past, he has always enjoyed a game I play of putting a toy on my head and then shaking it off. Also, if I put a toy on his head, he will shake it off his head. Tonight, he was playing with a toy while I was lying on the floor. He initiated the game (or maybe I helped him to do it once?) by trying to *put the toy on my head*!! He tried to do this, several times. Also, at my request, he TRIED (small part of total movement) to put it on his *own* head, then shook it off.

He gets such a kick out of trying to stand. He so much wants to do it. He shoves your hands away when he feels ready to try it alone. Lately, he loves crawling backwards, very fast, and pivoting around in a sit position very fast.

He has real motivation. Watching him, he seems so intent and serious and conscientious about doing or learning whatever he is doing. He seems, now, to have the same push towards mastery and motivation and pleasure in achievement as a normal child has. The only problem is that, what he is struggling so hard with, should be easy and done with by now.

Benjamin definitely imitates tonal variation of my words and phrases—when he wants to—but without any articulation.

He loves the way I shake my head to music and he repeats his no-no-no head shake whenever he hears the kind of music to which I shake my head—*even when I'm not doing it* [emphasis added].

He lost his pacifier tonight. I tried to give him an alternative nipple and another all plastic pacifier. He definitely selected the pacifier over the nipple, but then rejected it too because it wasn't his special one.

Comments

The "trick of the month" is: "toy on your head." It is yet another "reversal of roles" trick—i.e., Benjamin does to mommy what mommy does to him. He also does to *himself* what mommy has done to him. This is the Q-tip phenomenon, now returned in fuller force. For some time, Benjamin had liked my putting a toy on his head. Now, *he* is putting a toy on *my* head. How does he know how to do this? How does he connect the top of my head (which he can see) with the top of his head (which he cannot).

True, Benjamin had seen me *put a toy on my own head*. So, in this case, it may not really be a matter of his reversing something that had been done to him. But how does he know that *he*, too, can put something on my head? Perhaps he now has a "schema" of *putting things* some place. He has seen the toy on my *head*, so he, too, will *put it*, *there*. This would not necessarily involve imitation. However, the beginning effort to put the toy on his *own* head and allowing the toy to drop from his head, *does* appear to involve imitation. In contrast to his putting things into open hands (see previous entries) as had been done to him, in, this also appears to involve *imitation of parts of the body that he cannot see* since he cannot see the top of his own head (whereas he can see his hand), and therefore, in principle, cannot "match" it to someone else's. So too, does his delayed imitation of wagging his head to music as he has seen me do. How can we explain this?

From a Piagetian perspective, one might explain it thus: Benjamin has had the feeling of something on *his* head, in association with my hand and arm movements, directed towards his head. He has also seen my hand and arm go to my head. There would then need to be a bridge to allow him to integrate and cross-reference these experiences. Perhaps Benjamin had imitated only the upward arm movements. If, accidentally, they worked to get something on his head, or if I had helped him put it there ("scaffolding" again), he would be able to assimilate the visual experience of a raised arm to the tactile experience of something on his own head.

But, in normal development, does an apparent imitation of this kind come about through *such* an arduous path? It seems not. Here is an interesting thought. The Piagetian, experience-based, explanation of how imitative behaviors evolve may describe the *compensatory* course taken by individuals who have an *absence or impairment* in what others (e.g., Meltzoff and Moore 1977, and Meltzoff 1997) and "mirror neuron" theorists) believe to be *innate* processes underlying imitation. That compensatory course would, in turn, translate into the "not so spontaneous" feel of Benjamin's behavior, which seems qualitatively different from the more spontaneous feel of the same behaviors in normal children. The latter appear as if pre-programmed, rather than built up step by step through experiences, as in Piaget's model or Gray's analysis of "giving."

(As an aside: At 17 months, I had to *teach* Benjamin a "reversal of roles" trick. Now, at 20 months, they are happening, *spontaneously.* Does that mean they would have happened anyway, with about a 50 percent delay (at 20 months of age versus 10), if I had just waited for them to happen?)

However explained, here is the new development. At 20 months, Benjamin is now:

a) identifying himself as an agent (I do things); and then
b) identifying himself with the other in terms of agency (I am an agent, just as you are an agent; you are an agent just as am I)); and then
c) differentiating an "I" (as subject agent) from "me" as object (of either your agency or his own).

At this time, Benjamin's appreciation of a similarity between us is manifest as well in the first glimmerings of a true communication, from one person to another. Had Benjamin looked me in the eye as he pointed to where the ball was, that would have been an indication of "secondary intersubjectivity." It is worthwhile to stop for a moment to consider how much would be involved in what again seems such a seemingly simple act. Had he sustained eye contact with me while he was pointing, Benjamin's behavior would have suggested that he somehow "knew" or "understood" that my intentions reside "within" me and that he would need to make contact with them, to get me to do what he wanted. As well, they would indicate that he had some awareness that *he knew* something that I *did not* (namely, the location of the ball), and that he would therefore have to show or tell it to me. In this entry, Benjamin has moved a step closer to this level of communication, in seeming to recognize that I am the agent that he must somehow activate (by his eye contact) to do something that *he* knows about but I don't, and that he must therefore show me. This is a big step forward from his previous behavior in which, when he needed help, he would just cry, indicating that he was unhappy and unable to do what he wanted, but without directing his cry specifically to another. He might have appreciated that crying brought about the attention of the other, but he did not specifically direct his cry "to" the self within the other?

Did you notice too how active Benjamin has become, versus his passivity in the first year? He definitely now demonstrates a strong motivation for mastery, for doing things and being competent.

CHAPTER THIRTEEN

~

Peek-a-Boo!

Diary

June 6, 1972
Benjamin's father mentioned this several weeks ago but this is the first time I've noticed it: After I played one peek-a-boo game with Benjamin by putting a towel over his head, he repeatedly played this peek-a-boo by himself—picking the towel up, covering his eyes, then lowering it, laughing. This is not exactly imitation because I hadn't put the towel on *my* face and I still doubt that he has the level 4 imitation that would be required to imitate that.

June 7, 1972
The peek-a-boo schema is getting very mobile and active! He tries it out in all new situations—i.e., he assimilates new and different situations to it. For example, if he is under a chair, he will move his eyes up so that he can't see me through the rim of the chair, and then lower his head so that he can; then I will join in the game, and he laughs. Also—lying on his back with a (toy) record in his mouth, he finds he can flip it back over his eyes so that he can't see me and then he flips it back down. This definitely was also a "peek-a-boo." Because this time, he added a vocalization with the "peek-a-boo" rhythm—aaah-ah-aah. He does this more and more now—i.e., he vocalizes with the correct rhythm and intonation.

Benjamin sings perfectly "aaha aaha, baby" in the rhythm and tune, but no letters, no consonants. He does seem to (try to?) imitate my mouth movements, but I'm not sure it's intentional: You just see his mouth opening along with his eyes. He won't (can't?) *imitate* an "mmmmmmm" sound (i.e., versus making it spontaneously). He imitates banging movements, head and hand movements, etc. but *not mouth/lip* positions and sounds. He can imitate pitch and rhythm. I think he has not yet gotten to level 4 with respect to his mouth (i.e., being able to imitate mouth movements that he can't see on himself).

Some thoughts, again, on Piaget's assimilation/accommodation model and mental retardation (MR) and Benjamin: At times, I have thought that what is wrong is that there *isn't* an assimilation/accommodation process—that assimilation is just not there so that whatever progress and learning goes on is by some other process. An alternative hypothesis has been that assimilation/accommodation *is* there but that some other higher level function is missing. That function (or precursors) has been missing since the beginning. This higher level has to do with a capacity for abstraction and integration.

This has interesting ramifications regarding how to encourage learning or reaching optimal levels:

1. If one accepts the first explanation (i.e., that the assimilation/accommodation process is missing), one would then expect the child to learn by some other process and therefore attempt to teach him by that other means. This might mean, e.g., not expecting that the child will progress, more or less on his own, through the Piagetian developmental sequence. Rather, one might instead train and condition, etc., the correct responses, to reach the same ends.
2. The second interpretation (i.e., that assimilation/accommodation takes place, but that there is a weaker ability to perform the abstracting required) allows one still to follow a Piagetian training model. Specifically, with respect to assimilation:
   a) There has to be appropriate "aliment," just as there must be appropriate aliment in normal development. In the case of MR, the aliment (stimulation), if it is to be appropriate, must be less complicated so that the judgments (as to similarity) can be made more easily. MR will have more trouble catching on to the similarities so the similarities must be made more obvious, less hidden. Presumably, the cognitive structure of persons with mental retardation is not so deficient in the ability to abstract that only complete likenesses are perceived (at least Benjamin is beyond that). But it might be necessary to make the similarities easier to find, improve the discerning. Cut out weeds, and excessive elaboration etc.
   b) There also needs to be a lot of stimulation (aliment), though always of a certain clear sort. The child then goes about learning by his own methods—e.g., repetition, associating.
   c) Then we get to the notion of ceiling. Obviously, the ceiling (or potential) will be reached faster and more easily if the right stimulation (kind and amount) is provided than if the conditions are such that, even if the capacity for assimilation/accommodation is there, it cannot be

exercised for want of appropriate aliment. This means that two kids with the same problem might achieve very different levels, depending upon the extent to which appropriate aliment has been provided. Even with the most perfect aliment, however, the "top" will never be the same as the level reached in normal development. This is because of that original higher order deficit.

What is it that is present from the beginning and all through the child's development that allows the infant to generalize and grasp? Are there certain qualitative structural leaps that the child cannot make because of this lack—or, is it possible that if you worked long enough and sensitively enough, feeding the appropriate aliment to the (presumably intact) assimilation/accommodation function, you could move it?

Comments

In past months, I had put a towel on Benjamin's face, then removed it, to play "peek-a-boo." The "peek-a-boo" experience appears to be intrinsically enjoyable and rewarding to babies, no less for Benjamin. Now, in this entry, he spontaneously plays peek-a-boo *on himself*—once again, as in the Q-tip phenomenon, being both the object and the agent (subject), where before he had been only the object/observer. He brings a towel over his eyes, and then removes it, to play "peek-a-boo." The same questions arise with respect to how he had come to do this, as were raised in trying to understand how he knew to put toys on his own head. When I was the agent, Benjamin would have felt the towel on himself, and then felt it being removed (by me). How, then, did he "know" that he, himself, could reinstate the feeling of "towel on my face," through raising it up, himself, over his eyes (the location of which he cannot see)? How did he know that he could reinstate the pleasure of "peek-a-boo," through removing it?

What is new in these entries is Benjamin's engaging in *novel variations* of peek-a-boo that he appears to have discovered on his own. Whether or not he engaged in the towel peek-a-boo through imitation, imitation alone cannot explain his now seeing "now you see it, now you don't" potential in other situations. This kind of creativity and spontaneity is quite unusual for Benjamin at this stage. (It is interesting that these peek-a-boo games first appeared while he was at his father's house—i.e., in my absence. The psychoanalytic interpretation of the child's pleasure in the peek-a-boo experience is that it represents separation and reunion. Perhaps, in this particular instance, a strong emotional "cathexis" gave a boost to Benjamin's cognitive capacities!)

Benjamin's novel peek-a-boo games seem to reflect a very nice, spontaneous development with respect to generalization. Still, there is something missing in the realm of generalization that, at the time, continued to concern me. In these entries, I consider the possibility that the degree of "retardation" or of otherwise atypical development (as in autism) is a function of the degree to which the individual can abstract (see also Cowan 1978; Morgan 1986). At the end of these entries, I raise the question: Can we feed and expand existing schema to the point where a leap is made to a higher level of abstraction? Or can we, should we, try to *teach* generalization, directly?

The issue bears on that ever-nagging question: How and why, in normal development, let alone in atypical development, does the "leap" to a new level of organization, a new conceptual level, or new "theory" (Gopnick and Meltzoff 1997), come about? Since it may not come about spontaneously in his development, do we have to find ways to foster or invent "leaps" for the special child? ("Leaps" and interventions are both discussed in part II.)

These entries are about generalizing schema, extending and adapting them to different situations and even creating original variations of schema. One must read on, in this diary, to see what this has to do with self and intersubjectivity.

~

CHAPTER FOURTEEN

Imitation/Limitation

Diary

June 10, 1972

21 months: How's this: Rather than do an imitation *himself,* Benjamin imitates *on* someone else—i.e., by getting *the other person* to repeat the act, or by moving the other person's body to repeat it (e.g., by clapping the other's hands). If I put a cloth over my face, or a toy on my head, he tries to put it back there (on *my* face or head), rather than try to do the action on himself. In this way, he makes interesting spectacles continue, but he still does not (or not as much) try to coordinate schema from others, with schema from himself. Is this perhaps why he has limited facial expressiveness and "human-ness"? He doesn't identify and match those schemas on others with possibilities within or on himself (so he's still not through Piaget's stage 4!).

He *does* imitate banging, etc. The problem seems mainly to be when he must imitate using parts of his body he cannot see (lips, head, face). Just over a week ago, however, he *had* seemed a little inclined to try to perform, on himself, something I had done—i.e., put a toy on his head. How was that possible? Perhaps, one has to start building in the "match" for him by using mirrors. Or, in keeping with earlier conclusions, if that doesn't work, then just wait for the leap.

You can see the whole schema differentiation/accommodation process more clearly in Benjamin because it is so much slower. Like how long he keeps the same movement to cover many situations.

If autistic kids develop normally, then stop, and don't progress beyond some early, pre-symbolic stage, then we have a very different situation there than that which I have been assuming with MR. And it poses new questions: In MR, the *slowness* (lack of development) may be due to the absence of the potential for a higher order cognitive integration. The absence is there from the start; the precursors or early forms of the higher order thought are not in evidence. If autistic kids are OK up to a point, however, this means that the early forms and precursors of the integrative system may have been there. We are then faced with having to explain an arrest of development, or blocking and regression in that system. (Perhaps this is how the "emotional" disturbance hypothesis got started.)

Comment

In this chapter, I conclude that, after all, Piaget's level 4 imitation (imitating with or on parts of one's body that one cannot see on oneself) is still out of Benjamin's reach. Instead, Benjamin's "imitates" *on the other,* where the parts are clearly observable. I viewed this as an instance of making an interesting (or enjoyable) spectacle last, through doing something to the other to recreate it.

Benjamin seems to do best with "imitation" games in which, initially, his own body had been passively involved (e.g., "wind-wind little baby," or peek-a-boo with a towel on *him—see previous chapter).* The sensory input from his own body and movements may help mediate the matching of experiences. This is different, however, from being able to reproduce the precise actions of the others through observation alone. Some "pre-existing" template of "the other" in oneself seems missing (those "mirror neurons" again?). Hence, my considering a mirror strategy.

~

CHAPTER FIFTEEN

Effectance, Self-Awareness, and Kindred Souls

Diary

June 17, 1972: 21 Months

There is something new and good happening. Let me try to capture it. Benjamin has been showing that HE wants something of ME. There seems to be something about his appeal that has been growing for a while (see, e.g., the hidden ball incident) that suggests a) that I am experienced as separate from him and b) that he has to watch to see if what *he does* will affect me (the other). He seems to wait to see if the result he seeks will come about. *What is really different* today is the look in his eyes that seems to me to express "WOW! I am *aware* of *me*. I am someone who does something; I am one who waits to see where it goes." I would emphasize in the sentence the WOW!—i.e., his pleasure in this. I would swear he seemed to want me to know that he was onto something new and really digging it!!!

The apparent awareness of self seemed to come from the experience that "he" had the power to initiate actions that could affect others. He seems so gleeful at the prospect. This is subtle and hard to describe. He seems to know, e.g., that he can be cute. That there are things that he does which get a response. He LOVES to be kissed and loved. He puts his head back over and over to get a kiss. He has become increasingly affectionate—or rather (or in addition), he is interested in getting affection, and doing something to get it. He comes over and buries his head in my lap to get it, climbs on me and lays his head down, etc.

Practicing the M sound again. He very consciously tries to hold his lips together—the top one doesn't seem so flexible. He knows I like it when he tries that sound. Still, he doesn't tend to use it in imitation—does it later, practicing it. But loves best aa aa aa aa-baby—sometimes combined with M.

Does "wind-wind little baby" by himself now, on request, and anticipates the next move. Uses "no-no" a lot now, often appropriately. But it is also for fun, to tease (?). Also, I think, he motions "no-no," when he hears music, in an apparent imitation of the way I often waggle my head in time with music. Loves music, goes over to speakers, sometimes waves body or arms to it.

Today, on his back, while changing him, I sang, "here's a ball for baby," encouraging him to do some of the movements.[1] I thought he almost had the trumpet idea himself, I'm not sure, but I put his hands in position and he seemed to understand he was doing it. Then, on the "peek-a-boo" part, I tried to get him to cover his own eyes, on his own (that is, without my putting his hands over his eyes). I think he had some understanding of WHAT was wanted but he could not do it. Then I did put his hands on his eyes and did the movement over and over. He got a great kick out of that—then tried it on himself—first, his hands ended up on his mouth, then on head, then on ears. I think he might have finally gotten it tentatively, but I have to try again.

Definitely, now, seems to want to imitate and emulate same-sized creatures who do more than he does. Like Aaron and Tanya. Wants to stand like them, tries, interacts by trying to get their attention, touching, climbing on them. Recognizes them as kindred souls!!! [emphasis added]

Comments

At twenty-one months, here is what is new: *"What is really different today is the look in his eyes that seems to express, "WOW! I am aware of me!"* Benjamin has seemed, for some time, to be aware that certain actions have an effect, and that, through initiating these actions, he can get a desired response from the other. The "wow!" here refers to a new quality of self-awareness, a greater awareness of "himself" as the one who can generate and execute these actions, and a sense that this self-awareness is, in and of itself, enjoyable.

I have noted before that it seems to be intrinsic and preprogrammed that Benjamin (and other babies) like positive (social) feedback, just as it seems preprogrammed for him to feel pleasure in the mastery of his body (i.e., in achieving motor milestones). A positive feeling in the response of others appears to cement learning (see Pine 1987 regarding "moments"). According to Savage-Rumbaugh (1998), chimpanzees [in captivity], like children, also appreciate, seek, and are rewarded by the laughter and positive affective response of others to their actions. In Benjamin's case, his pleasure in another's pleasure in himself was not apparent, until "the trick"—that first occasion in which something that *he* had done had made another person take pleasure in him. He then used it (i.e., his arm and hand in a particular motion) as a tool to reinstate that pleasurable experience. This extension of "the trick," however, had the quality of a conditioned response. In contrast, in this entry, Benjamin takes pleasure not only in the behaviors that he has sought and effectively brought about in others but also in experiencing himself, and being aware of himself, as the one who could do that. This, at least, is what appeared to be conveyed by "the look in his eyes."

If Benjamin waggles his head to music, it is in imitation of me. That would be imitating that which he cannot see on himself. In Piaget's model, that would be a level 4 imitation, only first appearing in older infants. Meltzoff and Moore (1989), in contrast, report imitation of head movements in neonates. But, at twenty-one months, Benjamin still does not know where his facial features are, and he cannot connect them to the facial features of another. Thus, for example, I tried (unsuccessfully) to teach Benjamin a "hands over the eyes peek-a-boo." Within a Piagetian model, then, something appears to be "out of synch." Perhaps, "hands over the eyes" was not close enough to an existing schema for him to assimilate to his other "peek-a-boo" experience, or there had not been some other input (e.g., words) to mediate the assimilation. Or, as in Meltzoff's model, he just didn't have the (presumably) constitutionally given capacity to do these imitations.

Still, Benjamin seems now to recognize other children as kindred souls. He does seem to identify himself with other small children. How did this come to pass? It also seems "out of synch" with his continuing difficulties in imitation.

Note

1. In contrast to "Wind Wind," in which mother moves baby's hands, in the "here's a ball" "baby game," the mother does the hand actions for the baby to look at.

~

CHAPTER SIXTEEN

I, Thou, and Communication

Diary

August 1, 1972

Lots of good new developments, especially last week or so, or so it seems. Since we're home, he's looking very fine and together.

He seems very turned on to the world now. *All* the time. There is no longer any of the early-late (in the day) dichotomy in his interest and activity level. He very actively runs after things, full of vigor; no more flat, foggy look. Goes after people and things with enthusiasm. Always grunting his complaints about being restrained—in high chair, crib, etc.—wants to get out and go. Lifts hands to be taken out so he can be on the move. Sometimes crawls very hard and determined, head down, like a bulldozer.

He is very self-motivated now. Of course, this is something that must have been developing for some time. It must be a long time since the days that I would write that he had to be stimulated if anything were to happen. But, even if it is true that he has been steadily increasing his self-motivation, there recently seems to be such a spurt in it that it now really stands out. He is on his own and has a sense of what he wants to do (!!!) Does it, and insists and does not wait around for someone to show him. Somehow he does seem to be getting to know who *Benjamin* is and I think he likes the idea. He knows *he* can entertain other people, and he can enjoy them. He laughs out loud very heartily, big belly laughs—just on his own (i.e., without being tickled or played with). Finds things to laugh at. He makes funny sounds with his mouth for the fun of it and for other people to hear.

That's one of the big changes—a change in the quality of his sounds. The sounds themselves are not that much different, although I think there are more of them—more L's and N's (M dropped out again, needs a lot of stimulation) but he says them, now, not just to himself or as an accompaniment to an activity, but, at times when he is trying to express himself *to you*. He seems to realize he can enhance his communication by vocalizing it. It's getting closer to words to tell you something or at least, to emphasize something.

He also tried to imitate my saying HELLO although he seems kind of self-conscious about it—he doesn't try when you know he could. But he makes an almost Hello sound and when I repeat it, many times, making my mouth movements very visible (i.e., opening wide for the H and showing my tongue and rounding my mouth for the second part), he watches carefully and clearly tries (or does part of the same motion) to *imitate*, especially the open mouth part. *So, he has finally gotten to where he can identify and coordinate parts of his face (invisible to him) with parts of yours—LEVEL 4 imitation in Piaget* [emphasis added].

That's very interesting, because I was going to comment on the increased motility and expressiveness of his face. He has more facial expressions now with which one can empathize. In other words, and this is exciting—he must be at a point now where he is more able to see himself as one of "them" (us)—and in some way, he is taking in and integrating what he sees on others ("us") onto himself. And I have been having the feeling, lately, that he seems so much more like the *typical* little baby—in his interactions—picking up on facial cues, and making his own that you can pick up on—and doing things for your enjoyment or to see what you'll do if he does it. It all is coming together. The crucial observation here, I think, is the Piagetian one about being able to imitate movements one cannot see on oneself.

He adores children and people. He goes over to strangers on the beach to play with them. He loves just to sit in the middle of a bunch of kids. He likes to play ball, and has a good sense of the whole game. Tries to stand up all the time. Knows it is exciting for others and it is to him, too. He is very proud of himself when he does it a long time. He wants to be walked around.

Susan (mother's helper) said he put *her* hands over *his* eyes to make her play peek-a-boo with him (!!) Tries to do the same to himself, but sometimes misses—i.e., has hands on his ears, or forehead!!

Couple of weeks ago, he wanted to play, "here's a ball for baby" and indicated that to me by putting his hands up in the "ball" position, perfectly!!!! Imitates, I think, the hammer part too. Completely anticipates all parts of that song and does it. He probably could make more of the movements than he does. He's shy.

He is *positively loveable and beautiful*. His face has gotten more beautiful with the extra motility and expressiveness.

Everybody LOVES Benjamin.

He is eating lumpier food.

Susan said he tried to feed himself.

Tries to stand up little toy animals.

Remembered from before the summer that he could see me in the mirror in his crib, as I came in his room.

Comments

At twenty-three months Benjamin's flat, foggy look is gone. So is his passivity. He seems self-motivated and "on the go." He also seems to be more aware of himself, as BENJAMIN.

At twenty-three months, Benjamin also demonstrates (Piaget's) level 4 imitation, which appears in normal development at about age nine months. It appears that he is now able to match his face with my face. This, in turn, appears to have made his own face *more expressive.*

At twenty-three months, Benjamin engages in *intentional communication,* using parts of himself identified as the same as in others.

And finally, at twenty-three months, Benjamin now definitely identifies himself as "a member of the human race." This is especially so with *little* people. He is one of "them."

All of these developments seemed to happen simultaneously. Are they connected, and if so how?

The core development appears to be Benjamin's newly manifest (and late arriving!) ability to imitate facial features that he cannot see on himself. This would appear to involve some process of matching "self" and "other," and therefore, by implication, some developing awareness or conception of "self." The appearance of *communication,* and an interest in communication, appears intimately connected with this appreciation of "self" and "other" as separate but similar beings. Moreover, the more (it appears) Benjamin identified himself as "one of us, and indeed, began to look more like one of us (through adopting similar facial expressions), the more Benjamin becomes "endearing." Looking like one of us, in part because his face became more "expressive," seems to have been an epiphenomenon to the ability to imitate facial features.

Do normal babies also develop expressive faces that way? That is, do their faces become expressive, or more expressive, only when they are capable of level 4 imitation? Imitation of facial expressions has been reported in neonates (Meltzoff and Moore 1977),—that is, well before level 4—although it is questioned by others (e.g., Anisfeld 1991). Neonatal imitation, however, tends to "drop out" in any case. Most writers, along with Piaget, do place true imitation of facial expression relatively late in the second half of the first year (e.g., Stern 1985; Guillaume 1971). However, babies' faces might start becoming more expressive even before that. Eibl-Eibesfeldt (1979) reports that even congenitally blind and deaf children display the facial expressions of normal children. If so, imitation cannot be involved. Yet it is interesting that Annie Sullivan describes Helen Keller's face, when she first met Helen, as flat and expressionless (quoted in Hermann 1998). Fraiberg (1977b) also describes the faces of blind infants as relatively lacking in expression as compared to normal infants (except in response to mother's voice and physical contact). Fraiberg attributes this, however, to the fact that the babies do not have the faces of others to *stimulate* their own facial expressions (i.e., rather than that the infants are denied opportunity to *imitate* the others). Cicchetti and Schneider-Rosen (1984) reviewed studies which revealed a delayed, dampened, or limited range of facial expressiveness in Down syndrome and other groups of neurologically compromised children. They query whether cognitive competence, deficits in information processing, arousal modulation, and/or impaired neuromuscular functioning may be responsible for this. They call for more research on atypical populations to determine the factors that may cause irregular or deviant patterns of emotional expressions. Would limitations in the ability to imitate parts of the body that cannot be seen on oneself be a possible candidate, at least for a limited display of emotions beyond those of smiling and crying?

How do we understand the entry: "[Benjamin] tries to stand up little toy animals." Is this delayed imitation? He never did this movement before, he would not (it seems) have known how to do it on his own, and it was not learned hand over hand. Benjamin must have had a memory, an expectation, that the figures should be standing up. He apparently was then able to coordinate enough action schemas to re-create this state of affairs, on his own, on his own initiative, through an original, novel act. *What a leap!* What made it happen now and not before?

It is so hard to understand the leaps!

CHAPTER SEVENTEEN

~

Frustration and Limitation

Diary

August 28, 1972

Several changes. Benjamin is very insistent and demanding—through a repetitive loud grunting-cry, hands pointed generally in some direction, and he just sits solid and points and grunt/demands, sometimes looking at you, sometimes still somewhat more to himself, until you discover what he wants. It may be that he wants the kitten to come out from under the couch, or a ball to come out to where he can reach it. It may be that he wants you to turn the box of toys over, *but he won't budge and won't try it himself.* He just demands till you come. He seems to start off with a feeling that he can't attempt it himself—would fail or gets frustrated—but he now puts all his energies into getting what he wants by *demand*, rather than by attempting himself. This is all taking place during a very cranky, unhappy period, largely due, I think, to teething. He cries when I get up from the floor if I've been playing with him, cries and complains angrily, when I say goodbye. Wants someone to stay with him and play with him. He is very irritable and cranky.

It seems as if he is feeling limited where he is. *It seems as if he should learn either to walk or to talk.* He's getting more differentiated in terms of *what* he wants, but he can't say what he wants to say and he can't always DO what he wants to do. That is a theme of many things.

1. He stands better and longer but still doesn't trust he has full control. He does it best in the tub, with water, with the faucets to hold onto.
2. He has gotten the idea in his head of walking. He realizes what must be done. One day, he actually took three steps—though more often, he takes almost one. But it seems still to be miles off. He is excited at what success he has. But he won't try it as often as he could.

3. He enjoys taking rings off a pole. He wants to put them back on but just aims in the general direction, and hits the pole. He can't coordinate or inhibit, as necessary, the movements needed to aim and place. I THINK he has somewhat more of an idea of what is necessary—aim and place—than he can execute, but I'm not sure. Maybe he has only "figured out" that a movement connecting the pole and ring is involved. He is enchanted by my showing him that the pole comes through the hole, but I don't know how he understands the connection.

4. He is clearer with blocks. He understands that he must place one block on another—that one must try to control and slow down the movement, but he still has trouble aiming and placing accurately enough.

5. He loves the cat and picks it up, scrunches it, by back and neck, drops it. Possibly would like to try mouthing, "smooching" it, with his mouth.

6. If the cat goes under a chair, he tries to pull it out. He reaches under the chair after the cat is out of sight to get it. But if the cat disappears, goes out another way, he doesn't seem to understand about looking for it somewhere else. He doesn't seem able to anticipate and imagine its new whereabouts, or perhaps, he doesn't have the idea that it will *have* whereabouts which he, Benjamin, might then try to discover. He doesn't understand that *he* could do something, actively, to find the cat, so he will get frustrated if the cat is not here. If you say, "where is the cat," he will look for the cat in several ways. He looks in places, currently visible, where the cat had been before (e.g., on the floor) and where he'd have just been when Benjamin saw him. But he does not go looking for him in other places. It's out of sight, out of Benjamin's having to (or knowing how to) search for him.

7. It is the same with respect to me. Does Benjamin come to look for *me* when he's upset? NO. Does he go from room to room looking for me? I don't think so. It's out of sight, out of Benjamin's having to (or knowing how to) search for me—or the cat.

So—is he really still that primitive in his object permanence? He knows, e.g., that the ice cream is in the freezer, and he knows to open the freezer to find it in there. Perhaps because that is a constant, he has learned that association. Maybe the option of doing something about it will only come after he recognizes that I (or the cat) can have other whereabouts.

Comments

At just short of two years of age, is Benjamin feeling frustration with respect to what he can do and what he can say? Frustration would suggest that he is motivated to do and say more than he can. Loss of faith in his capabilities would be devastating to Benjamin, in whom a sense of self has seemed, thus far, so tied to feeling effective. Wanting to do more reflects an "I-ness." The entries at this stage suggest that, sometimes, Benjamin appears timid and lacking in confidence because he senses that he cannot do what he wants to do . . . and, at other times, because he simply does not know what to do. In particular, he still seems so limited in taking action when the object of the action is not present to trigger the action.

Thus, for example, Benjamin does not look for me when I am not in front of him. Is this simply a matter of primitive object permanence—that is, does he not have a mental concept of and memory of me when I am not in front of him? This does not seem likely. He cries, and seems to want me, in my absence. And recognition of absence indicates that there is a concept of the object (me) independent of its (my) presence. But Benjamin does not (appear to) have a representation of what I might be doing or where I am, when I am not right in front of him, and therefore, of what he can do, or should do, to find me. Why has he not learned that? Surely, he has followed me around and therefore has seen me in different places, and knows the route to where they are. Is it that he "knows" my various whereabouts only when he is there to see me in them?

In Piaget's theory, children at level 6 can know where to look for an object when they see that it is being hidden (i.e., they observe the hiding process) but the object itself is not in view as it is being hidden—for example, if it is in a closed fist. Curcio (1978) found autistic children could pass object permanence tests at level 5 (the object is visible as it is being hidden, as, for example, by having a cloth placed over it) but not at level 6. Level 6 is associated with the ability to *represent* internally (i.e., remember) what is not there to be seen. However, Benjamin does remember "objects" that are out of sight and knows where to go to find them. For example, he knows where his bath is, where his toys are, and how to get there. He also has a representation of me (it seems) and recognizes me as the same, in different situations, in different contexts. I am a constant. Why then does he not look for me (as he does his toys) in places in which he has seen me before? How does one explain that he can know (recognize) me in different situations but not know to go and look for me in each of these situations? In like manner, autistic children usually perform adequately on simple object permanence tests though they too may not search for a person who has left the room.

Perhaps it is because toys in his room, or bathtub in bathroom, or ice cream in the freezer, are constant in relation to their environment. They appear, and reappear after his absence, in the same place. My comings and goings, in contrast, allow for too many changes in my context. When I leave Benjamin, he has only himself as the constant. So Benjamin waits where he is. Or perhaps, not looking for me is a function of neither object permanence nor representation but of something separate, related to initiation, activity, and executive function.

CHAPTER EIGHTEEN

~

"Sneaky Eyes"

Diary

August 28, 1972 (continued)

Meanwhile, there is increased appreciation of word meaning. Benjamin understands certain words as signals: cat, cookie, ice-cream. He knows bath (or water, splash). I think he knows "out" (e.g., from bath) and "in" (e.g., put something in . . .). Once, I told him, put something IN a large box (emphasizing IN), and he tried to get in, himself.

The other day he found a long blue velvet tie and put it around his neck—i.e., tried to "wear" it. Not as a *tie*. I don't think he has that concept yet. But somehow, he saw it as something "to put on."

LEARNED "SNEAKY EYES": I look at him with my head down, eyes looking up against the direction of the movement of the head, expressing questioning, as in "are you sure?"—a look of disbelief, etc. coupled with affection. He imitates it (!!) He puts his head down and looks askance. He laughs, I think, *at realizing he is imitating* [emphasis added]. I named this action, "Sneaky Eyes." He seems to recognize the words: "Sneaky Eyes" as the signal to perform it. I say, *"Make Sneaky Eyes!!"* and he does!!

He is beginning to experiment more. The other day, he clasped his hands to each other, lifted them over his head, and then watched them carefully as he brought the circle down again. He repeated this with interest. He also tries to feed himself—i.e., spoon to food to mouth. Likes to stick fingers into faucet to watch changes in the water's flow. And finally, possibly the very beginning of something closer to expressive babble—a kind of continuous changing "talking" with his very limited sounds.

Comments

Approaching two years of age, Benjamin is making more progress on the verbal front. He is beginning to recognize words as representations. He is also now imitating the patterning of the sounds of speech. Because of his oral-motor problems, he has the tune but not the words; he can match intonation but not syllables. This is his version of expressive babble.

The "sneaky eyes" trick was so endearing. In it, Benjamin was imitating a facial expression, and in particular my eyes, and thus, once again, a part of the body he could not see on himself. So, once again, we can ask: How could he do that? If there is an innate association between the visual representation of facial features and representations of one's own facial features in the motor area, why has it taken so long to assert itself? Perhaps "peek-a-boo" was a scaffold for "sneaky eyes," as follows: Benjamin had already shown an ability to imitate my head movements. Perhaps he had imitated my head down (causing me to leave his sight) then looked up to see or find me. Then, once again, the action became consolidated through my enthusiastic response to this. Along with the rest of the family, I remember being ecstatic about this new "trick."

~

CHAPTER NINETEEN

"Two Years, Two Weeks Old and Lots of New Developments!"

Diary

September 30, 1972

Two years, two weeks old. Lots of new developments.

Walking: Benjamin has taken up to 13 steps, but usually either 3 or 4, or 6 or 7.

Very proud of himself: He doesn't do it to show off. Rather, he appears to do it *in tribute* to a favorite person. Often doesn't take time enough to get his balance and then takes off too soon. If he gets his balance, he is good for several steps. Cruises a lot, wants to walk from place to place. Some days, tries a lot, other days not at all.

Rings: Suddenly has mastered the placing of (graded) rings on a spindle and now, nothing can stop him! He loves to do it, and does it constantly!! non-stop with very good aim. As usual, once he gets into something, he repeats it again and again, and again and again.

Peek-a-boo: He now plays this himself—puts things over his face and pulls them down and laughs heartily. He has that incredibly hearty laugh. He really laughs TOO hard.

Words: Lately, he seems to understand more and more words. He knows ice cream (points to freezer), shoe, cup, flower, splash splash. If you ask him if he wants to go "splash splash," he lifts his arms eagerly to be brought to the bathroom. I made him a book of pictures of things for which he knows the words. Very *ecstatic* about the book, but mainly, the turning of pages. Loves to turn the pages, FAST. First time around, he *tried to take the things he saw, off the page*.

Tongue sounds: Makes his own gurgly or tongue sounds for fun and keeps it up to amuse himself. Not sure whether he'll imitate back when I do it.

Eating preferences: Definitely has hit upon baby food cottage cheese as a favorite. Recognizes the jar, and refuses all the others. Has to be blue with checkered field, etc. Very excited when sees it in the supermarket. Also knows and loves yogurt containers. Re: ice cream, if you ask, do you want it, he motions towards the freezer. Thinks the cottage cheese container is ice cream.

Blocks: Builds a tower of three, sometimes 4 blocks. Usually knocks it over with the fourth, but the placing is especially careful. He "realizes" he has to do it slowly and then let go.

Interest in learning: He really seems to like to learn "tricks" with toys—e.g., the Playskool box (putting things "in"), and also the nested barrels. If they are inverted, he enjoys taking them off successively.

Social: He is very playful and sociable. Loves to laugh with and at others. Loves babies. Seeks out the other children and cries if they lock him out. Getting closer to hugging and clinging (to) me more actively and spontaneously. Still refuses to kiss me (!!) but kisses Susan (mother's helper).

Music: His response to music is very strong and clear. He "dances" by bouncing his feet up and down to music he loves, while sitting. He absolutely adored a Kabalevsky Piano Concerto.

Comments

Benjamin is doing so much more. He seems more confident and experimental. He still appears to use his mastery and effectance as a gift to a loved one, but he also enjoys his increasing competence and seems to be "turned on" by learning. Perceptual-motor mastery involving coordination of schema—in fine and gross motor acts—appears to be developing at the same time as words have begun to have meaning. This is as it should be in Piaget's scheme.

~

CHAPTER TWENTY

Cleft Palate Surgery— Progress in All Spheres!

Diary

October 14–21, 1972

Benjamin has done so well post op. By 36 hours, he was drinking from his cup again, and now, 48 hours, it's non-stop, with no liquid coming through the nose.

This note is because of the new development in his speech, which came so fast upon the operation. Yesterday—i.e., 24 hours later, he was, for the first time, clearly saying ma-ma, and today, mommy—and he seems to use it *for* mommy. He also seemed to imitate "mill" for milk. Plus, all kinds of new babble and combining consonants with the "aah." He started with nananana—then mamama—later, b and d. I think.

His voice and laugh and cry sound different—deeper and more mature.

He is still pretty down-faced (post-op), but is playing more and crawling more.

November 10, 1972

Benjamin has been home (from the hospital) for two weeks, today. He seems to have developed so much since before hospitalization. Even with the misery of that, plus an awful cold, he seems not to have had any set-back, except for walking which dropped out for a week or so after he came back, and now has come back stronger than ever.

He has walked as many as 22 steps in a row, with occasional turns and shifts in direction. But he is very uncertain. Even though he walks, he doesn't seem to have his balance yet, hasn't found his center. He walks and has to find his balance with every other step. But he wants to walk—does it spontaneously when he sees someone to show it to. *Even sometimes walks without anyone there as an incentive* [emphasis added].

84

He got a toy telephone and a jack-in-the-box in the hospital. He discovered himself how to bang the jack-in-the-box to get the jack to pop. Then he showed that he understood the necessary sequence of the toy—by next learning how to close up the jack-in-the-box before beginning to bang it again to get it to pop up. He also hands the mouthpiece of the telephone to the adult or child playing with him—he doesn't put it to his own ear, but does, I think, at least some times, say "aah" as if to say the hello.

The other day, he put a pair of sunglasses on himself.

There is a drawer of toys that he has learned to open by pulling the ring. He also knows that to turn on the TV (which he loves), one must turn the knobs and he "does" it. After the drawer is open, he empties it all out, one toy after another, looking around for an adult to see, and calling attention to himself, *with a roguish naughty look.* Likes you to yell at him. The more you (pretend) you are angry, the better he likes it, laughing roguishly.

Benjamin has always had, or for a long time, an incredible sense of rhythm. He even sometimes crawls in a 1, 2, 1-2-3 rhythm, humming ah-ah-ahahah to himself, as he goes. He can imitate a rhythm like that with his hands. Clapping, patting. He loves music and any rhythmical things—bounces his legs and arms to them.

When he came home from the hospital, *he pointed, for the first time*, with his arm to the house [emphasis added]. Since returning from the hospital, he is now very direct and intense in his demands. He sticks out his arm with a "Heil Hitler!" ferocity and directs with the whole arm in the direction of what he wants. He also now lifts his hands for "up," very clearly. His eyes are very direct and focused and he also is mischievous with them.

There seems to be a more communicative quality, all around, and especially with his language. He almost "babbles expressively." That is, sometimes there is something (slightly) more imitative and conversational about his "talking." He is using a few more syllables, I think, although NaNa is still his favorite. Also maaw. *I think both are beginning to be words.* That is, they are beginning to be understood as meaning something, or at least, as making something happen. Maaw—may sometimes mean milk or more, or open up. NaNa is used to call to someone else (including nana) to look.

He made a lively "intelligent" game with me the other day on the changing table. He strained to pull himself up and then imitated himself doing that several times and laughed. He gives real belly laughs if you look up his nose or mouth (to see the palate correction). It strikes him as very funny.

He once seemed about to say, tried to say, "ice cream."

Comments

At twenty-five months, Benjamin had an operation to correct his cleft palate. The entries immediately following his surgery document a dramatic increase in communicative, conversational, expressive babble; representative language; and initiation of interaction. Did the surgery free up physical capabilities required for these developments? Or were these developments the natural unfolding of a predetermined sequence or the next steps prepared for by the developments documented in previous entries?

In the normal child, the communicative quality appears much earlier. Was Benjamin held back in this regard, because of physical limitations affecting his ability to form words? If this is so, it raises the question: If the intention is there but not the mechanisms for execution, what happens to the intention? Does it atrophy? Leading then to an apparent lack of "self" (because intention signifies a "self" as the executor, separate from action)? What is the subjective experience when there is no possibility of executing an intention?

Benjamin's use of the toy telephone and jack-in-the-box shows how far he has gotten through Piaget's sensori-motor stages. He bangs the jack-in-the-box to get it to pop ("secondary circular reaction") ; closes it to prepare it for banging again ("coordination of secondary schemata"); hands the phone to the other to use it, recognizing the other as an agent (causality, at the level of tertiary circular reactions); and he says "aah" for "Hello"—delayed imitation (level 6).

What should we make of the mischievous look in his eyes, his "roguish look"? Is it merely a reflection of his pleasure in being able to control the behavior and/or emotions of others? That is, "I can do something that predictably will make someone look and yell at me, these being 'interesting spectacles' that I can make happen, again?" If so, what makes these responses of the other person so intrinsically "interesting"? Or does his "roguish look" reflect satisfaction and glee specifically about being "naughty"—that is, not just about "knowing" how to make a response happen again, but about doing something that he "knows" the other person does not want him to do? This implies so-called "mind-reading" (i.e., viewing something from the perspective of the other). Or is it something that goes beyond a mere expression of his pleasure in either of these scenarios to being, instead (or in addition), a communication to others about what he is doing, and a sharing of his experience in doing it, with them? All of these possibilities are pregnant with implications regarding intersubjectivity, each progressively reflecting more awareness of the internal world of others and an interest in connecting with it.

~

CHAPTER TWENTY-ONE

Development with a Difference

Diary

January 19, 1973
Initiates goodbye as he leaves living room. Initiates peek-a-boo looking over ledge or wall. Helps set the table by handing me the dishes to be distributed. Demands things—e.g., cookies in bakery. Knows what he wants.

January 20, 1973
Instant imitation in bathtub ("doggy splash," "dolly splash"). More understanding of words (e.g., "take bath"). *Takes me to show me things; GETS me (finally!) and points.* I feel he has a greater appreciation of language. *I feel I can start using words* [emphasis added].

January 24, 1973
Attempts to imitate "mommy"; *spontaneous imitation of my facial expression*; focuses on my facial expression, eyes and mouth for the imitation of sounds.

Very excited with his own power (mainly since starting to walk outside). Points to playroom and TV—waits for me to follow.

When I "read" a book to him, he gets tired: Is it too great a demand?

Feels warmly towards animals.

Enjoys knowing he has done something that is liked. Shows enjoyment in knowing he has done something that is liked and repeats it. The quality seems to be something other than repeating an act simply because it is reinforced by "the other" taking pleasure in it—i.e., because he likes the experience of the other's pleasure. Now it seems like Benjamin has an awareness that he is being liked, and it is that, in particular, which pleases him. In like manner, there is dismay if yelled at. (I'm not really yelling or upset because he is not really naughty, but I pretend to be angry.)

Says "ahaha" with rocking things.

Once, a spontaneous hello kiss!! That is, more typically, he imitates a kiss, but it does not seem to be associated with or emerge from a feeling of affection within him.

January 25, 1973

He loves animals.

He's picked up that it's naughty to go off the curb, and does it with a laugh.

He seems to be trying so hard to make a *true emotional contact.* He uses his eyes mainly. He's recognized the "eye to eye" thing (i.e., eye contact).

His kissing (open mouth on your cheek) and hugging are becoming more spontaneous *and* associated with affection. He now seems to be *feeling affection* and associating the act of kissing with it. It often happens when I come home after a long day.

BUT still no use of words (except, maybe, "la"? na???). He has the language-less quality of a mute child which even pre-language babies don't have, because he doesn't have his own vocabulary, his own imaginative word play.

Benjamin has a difference in style, not just in level of attainment. He always has been less differentiated, less focused. His imitation seems different. He doesn't assimilate this to this, doesn't make the relationships.

He'll never be "imaginative." He might learn to push a truck along by copy-ing someone, but not because he's playing out the larger on the smaller. He doesn't have the idea of representing one thing with another. He doesn't seem to know he has ideas. He doesn't seem to have ideas. Does he "think"? How do deaf (language-less) kids think?

He seems frustrated not being able to express himself to either himself or an-other. He seems gagged.

It is time to teach Nim [Benjamin's nickname] ONE word!!

Comments

At twenty-eight months, Benjamin's imitation has improved. He also now points to show things to me, as I have to him. He is feeling affection for others and initiates acts that express it. There is also a subtle change in the quality of his enjoyment of social interaction. He does not just bask in the pleasure that others take in him, but somehow, seems to experience or recognize that they are liking him—that is, that there is within himself a "him" that is the object of their affection—and this sense of himself, as the one who is pleasing to others, gives him an added pleasure. These developments reflect a sense of being like others, and an inclination to model oneself on others, but also, a sense of one-self as different from others. The latter is reflected in Benjamin's apparent grow-ing awareness that he can do things that will either please or displease others, and a sense of himself as an object of their attention and affection—as they may be of his.

In normal development, these developments in the interpersonal realm are soon followed by symbolic play, language, and imagination. And yes, in these entries, Benjamin is now appreciating that words have meaning. However, he appears to learn words in context, through repetition and routine. I wonder about the missing symbolic play, language, and imagination. Indeed, at this point in the diary, it was my impression that Benjamin would never be imaginative. He seemed to be following a normal developmental sequence—but with a difference. (Yet he did say "ah-ah-ah" with things that rock! Wasn't that "symbolic play"?) I then suspect (project?) that Benjamin feels inhibited and frustrated because he cannot express himself. I end by promising "to teach Nim [his nickname] one word."

~

CHAPTER TWENTY-TWO

How Do You Know
What a Feeling IS?

Diary

January 27, 1973

Benjamin is becoming affectionate, even clingy. He couldn't have been affectionate earlier—somehow he only now has been able to *differentiate* within himself an emotion of tenderness and love (and identify it with what goes into *my* hugs and kisses). He can only match his emotion with mine if he "sees" mine but he would only "see" mine when he had differentiated (experienced) something of his own like it.

What normally helps differentiate the emotions? *Is* it really through different expressions and consequences in the environment? Or, aren't they there to begin with, to be expressed and responded to, differentially?

It's a depth I cannot get into.

Benjamin can only imitate sounds he can see. That is, he cannot imitate "inside the mouth" ones. This is BECAUSE he doesn't make those sounds to begin with—so he cannot connect them to their *sound* as made by someone else. Why doesn't he experiment with sounds and with his lips—is that connected with the mouth trauma and absence of sucking?

What do other cleft lip kids do?

Benjamin does NOT understand *my* non-verbal language (even pointing). Nor does he have a language (non-verbal or verbal) that he uses to *tell* me something. He has learned to get me and let me know he needs something, but he doesn't appeal to me by showing the want directly *to* me (e.g., combining pointing with eye contact). He just signals *that* there is want. *He does what he has learned will work to get it*, but he doesn't ask me. It appears as if he doesn't tell me something because he doesn't seem to know yet, see in himself or discriminate yet, something to tell, even hunger: He just calls my attention by groans and eyes. Maybe he sometimes does do part of the action desired and points, but he doesn't *direct his communication to me, personally.*

Comments

At twenty-eight months, Benjamin is becoming more affectionate, giving hugs and kisses with apparent feeling. At this point in his development, however, I believe that his display of affection has come about through a process that is different from that underlying the affection of normal babies. I assume that Benjamin has learned by imitation and association that which, in normal babies, comes spontaneously and unlearned, as a natural concomitant of emotion (see also the January 25, 1973, entry).

I attribute Benjamin's show of affection, first, to his only now being able to identify or isolate *a loving feeling in himself*. Being able to discriminate a loving feeling in himself, I reason, has emerged from his repeated experience of a positive emotion, within himself, upon receiving hugs and kisses from others. His own loving feeling is then associated with the affectionate behaviors he has observed and experienced on the part of others. The bridge might be either an (inborn) ability to experience and empathize with the loving feelings that are in others (as in Hobson's theory) when they hug and kiss him and/or the loving feelings he naturally feels when hugged and kissed by others.

Is there a more spontaneous and unlearned development of affectionate behaviors in normal children? In typical development, emotions appear to be innately and universally connected with certain observable gestures or facial expressions (Ekman 1993). Therefore, the child will express his emotions in familiar ways, without having to learn how to do it. Or the child, having a natural empathy with the emotions of others, may early on match his own emotions with theirs, and then, adopt the gestures that he has seen associated with them. However, although I have found a great deal about the universality of facial expression and even vocal expression in relation to emotion, I have not been able to find much discussion about emotion-related gestures. Do babies in all cultures cuddle? Don't babies in different cultures learn different expressions of love and affection (e.g., the nose-rubbing of the Inuit), on the basis of how their caregivers express it to them?

Although at this point in Benjamin's life there is appreciation of the other as a causal agent, he still only notifies others of his needs, with the apparent expectation that they will do as he needs them to do. Notification must be contrasted with *appeal*. In the latter case, Benjamin would be asking for help, with an appreciation that the other may have some say in the matter. Theory of mind analysts would say that, in simply signaling his wants, he is operating without a "theory of mind"—that is, without an awareness of (or taking into account) the mental experiences of the other. Perhaps, but haven't we seen inklings that Benjamin is beginning to be aware of the inner world of others? Well, let's see what happens next.

CHAPTER TWENTY-THREE

~

Appeal

Diary

January 29, 1973

Today I realized there is a great deal more "appeal" in Benjamin's approach to me! He has also been "refueling" like mad. He also comes with one demand after another—usually, *catching my eye first*, and then signaling what he wants [emphasis added]. He is very cute, bringing things to me, showing me the door to go out, etc.

Still, his absence of language is frustrating to us both!!!! I was trying to get him to repeat "Lydy" or Lily" for Lydia. His response was to make his (new and favorite) "mmm" sound. He apparently associates the idea of trying to imitate with that sound, the first (and only) sound he has learned directly from and through us. He remembers "mmm" as his "attempt to imitate words" and this is set off by what he recognizes as my desire to have him learn a sound. Even this is something! He "reads" that that's what we mean when we say, "Nim, say ____." But he doesn't "remember" the sound of the "mmm" lip movement, just the idea of making a special lip movement.

He plays the piano very well—goes up the scale and down with a rhythm. He actually "makes" music.

The next step has to be to understand why, how, the jump takes place between sensori-motor intelligence to preoperational intelligence, or, within the sensori-motor stage, from tertiary circular reaction (trial and error experimentation, trying several methods) to mental operations ("thinking about" the effects he creates and how might they be produced—i.e., planning). Consciousness of one's actions. What keeps Benjamin at the kind of assimilation/accommodation characteristic of the sensori-motor level? This somehow interacts with what he is capable of emotionally.

Benjamin's assimilation methods are *primitive*—sensori-motor, concrete. Are they also different? Whether children like Benjamin are at a lower level—longer—or are even different at that level is important for determining interventions. Should one change the *level* of the input or its *nature*, in order to accommodate, and provide more appropriate aliment. Also: is there some way to push, permit, encourage them onto the next level or can one only feed into the current level—and assume that they will learn, albeit, differently.

(He does learn differently. When I am showing him an activity, such as putting in pegs, he imitates or remembers just the very first part of a movement or technique, rather than the whole gesture as defined by the function it is to serve. It takes a while for him to build up enough of the segments of the whole to become a meaningful, functional act, to catch onto the necessary movement in its entirety.)

I have to reread Piaget to find out why that leap takes place. What do the psychoanalysts have to say? What happens in autistic psychotic kids when they do make that jump to spontaneous speech—what frees, permits, elicits it?

PLAY, absent in both autism and Benjamin, equals flexible assimilation.

Benjamin does not play. The assimilation tendency is inherent in the biological organism. It's a given, and it IS the rudimentary "ego" which changes its character as a result of the interaction of assimilation with the environment and the qualitative leaps (the stages) which result.

Comments

Just two days after I comment on the absence of appeal, I am recording "appeal" and bringing and showing things. These are indications of "secondary intersubjectivity"—at last—at two and a third years. They reflect an apparent appreciation of two "minds," the need for communicate between them, and an interest in doing so. If correct, my assumption, in this entry, that Benjamin "recognizes . . . my desire to have him learn a sound" when I present a word to him to imitate, also suggests that I believed that he was now interpreting behavior as reflecting the motives and intentions of others. This would be in contrast to just responding to it in a way that had been taught or conditioned.

This development appears in association with "refueling." This is Mahler's term for behavior in the older infant that, in her theory, is the child's way of managing anxiety associated with the process of separation and individuation (Mahler, Pine, and Bergman 1975). The baby takes off to explore his environment, on his own, and then comes back to mom for a "fix" of cuddling or attention. Is this separation necessary for appeal? In Mahler's theory it is. This is because, according to Mahler, appeal, not observed in autistic children, requires the subjective experience and recognition of two separate people, versus a merger of self and other as (she presumed) was the case in the very young infant and in "symbiotic psychosis" (her term for a form of autism). Mahler's theory of autism and childhood psychosis and her description of normal infant development have been discredited by infant research. Yet, in Benjamin's case, as in normal development, refueling and appeal did appear to emerge, hand in hand.

It has been reported (Plooij 1978) that nine-and-a-half-month-old infant chimps in the wild look into their mother's eyes when whimpering (called "begging"). Dogs also whimper, with eye contact. Would this behavior, in animals, be considered evidence of a fledgling "theory of mind"? Or, in both infants and animals, does it come about because the eye contact is for targeting and "holding" in place the individual who the infant has learned will react to its pleas?

CHAPTER TWENTY-FOUR

~

Little Buds

Diary

February 27, 1973

Seems like it's been a relatively static period, with illnesses possibly a factor—with much repetitious, rigid behavior, and no advances in language. Benjamin almost seems bored himself with where he's at! He is dependent upon me to "play" with him, and he doesn't seem to know what the next step is. Yet also, some new things lately plus good examples of his contemporary learning style.

1. *Raggedy Anne doll*: Takes pleasure in her face. Gives her tentative hugs and kisses. Responds to my making her perform (sit, dance, walk) by doing the same. Clearly (I think!) he seems to connect his movements with hers—that is, he appreciates (I think) that the doll is doing the same kinds of things he can do.
2. Benjamin puts his head down on the floor and cries, after a loud reprimand or "no no!!!" from me. But today, he (we) made it into a game. First, he did it "for real" in response to a NO NO!!! from me. Then, I playfully imitated him crying. Then, I playfully said an angry NO-NO to him—and he "caught on"!! That is, he seemed able to recognize that I *didn't* really mean "NO NO" and then playfully pretended to be crying. He then wanted me to repeat the same, over and over again. Would call out his "aaah!!!" to me to get me to pretend "NO! NO" and anger, and then he pretended crying!!
3. When he hears piano music on radio, he goes to the piano to play his own. Connects the word "play" with piano.
4. Points to high chair, then to piano (!!) to show me to set him up (i.e., at the piano to play). Yet he doesn't seem to comprehend (my) natural ges-

96

tural language—e.g, "come here." Perhaps he is *beginning* to get the idea of following a point—e.g., when I say, "look, look here, or there."

5. If he has made an association, he gets very rigid and frustrated if it's not allowed to be completed—if, e.g., the word "play "comes up in a different context, and he wants to play piano in response, and for some reason, is not allowed to, he gets very insistent—he is very insistent and rigid about following through not just his wants, but any "connection."

6. Once when he seemed to feel "warmth" between us, on the floor, an affectionate interaction, he immediately insisted (through aah's) upon getting the book I made for him, because I think he associates reading the book together with times of closeness.

7. *The "drawer"*: insistent, repetitive, taking stuff in and out of the drawer, handing it to me, and taking it back. It drives me nuts! Lately, he's always insisting on my "participating" in his taking-things-in-and-out.

8. Loves music, always dances, beats rhythm with his arm (in imitation of my conducting?). If he's excited and feels related to me, he might lapse into a "wind-wind little baby" routine—again, through the association it has with emotional contact and feeling good.

9. He likes to be chased; also, running into your arms; also running the length of hall, after backing all the way up to the wall first.

10. Puts his *head* (!) down on a diaper laid out for him "to help" out in the diapering (!).

11. Associates his father's coming (access visit) with my leaving: waves goodbye to me as soon as he picks him up.

12. Knows to put things on his head for "hat" (I think). Pretends to put something on his head when he hears the word "hat."

13. Very clingy, demanding of me.

14. Likes to get dizzy—expects to.

Comments

It is hard, isn't it, to keep track of all that is happening, in these entries, to see connections and understand the sequence of development. Although dated a month later than the last chapter, these entries describe developments that had taken place, in some instances, just days apart. And I have described Benjamin's development as being in "slow motion"!

So, what *is* going on here?

When Benjamin is twenty-nine months old, the diary entries suggest the beginnings of representation and symbolic function. Thus:

—Benjamin recognizes Raggedy Anne's (two-dimensional, stylized) face as a face;

—He matches the doll's movements with his own;

—He engages in "pretending."

So it appears that symbolic function and representation had emerged, right on the heels of the signs of the "intersubjectivity" recorded in the previous entries.

Still, there is a perseverative, ritualistic quality to Benjamin's activities and "play." His play lacks the creativity and variety that one would expect, in normal children, at this point in development. Rather, for Benjamin, it appears that repeating the same thing, over and over and over again, is play. Older infants or toddlers go through a phase of enjoying this kind of repetitive play, but it is short-lived and/or it is not so pervasive—that is, other kinds of exploration and experimentation also take place. Benjamin's activities, in contrast, were overwhelmingly repetitive at this time.

Although Benjamin is now pointing, to communicate, he is only beginning to understand pointing when others do it. This is another big difference between his development and that of normal children. Benjamin did not appear to understand gestural communication by others, and his own was extremely limited in range, and he had a "learned" rather than spontaneous quality. On the other hand, he did now, for sure, recognize the movement of the doll's legs as "walking"! He seemed to match its movements to movements of his own.

CHAPTER TWENTY-FIVE

~

"Make Nice, Mommy" and Play

Diary

March 5, 1973

More and more spontaneous loving. That is, Benjamin seems able to identify in himself the experience of feeling loving and warm to me. He takes on a special glow in his eyes and face when that happens. Then he associates certain things to do when he feels that way. He puts his face to mine for a kiss; sometimes puts his lips together in an "mmmm" for "kiss"; has a kind of "wanting to take me in" tension and excitement in his arms and face; puts his head in my neck, affectionately; cuddles up for me to pat and say, " aaaaha"; cuddles up very close and is very happy (I think as much with himself for having performed the "right" responses—as shown by my great pleasure—as in liking to be cuddled). It's "spontaneous" affection, but it still has some quality of being learned and associative, rather than "organic." He has first to differentiate the emotion in himself, and then attach the learned response. This is *instead of* a situation in which the emotion automatically stimulates certain behaviors, which are seamlessly connected with the emotions, rather than merely associated to them, as in Benjamin's case.

He continues to do "wind-wind" with his hands when he wants to make playful, happy contact with me. It means: "I like you, I want to play with you; I want you to play with me"—friendliness, feeling good with someone. Also it means sharing in something with someone, making you laugh WITH him.

I lay down on the floor, tired, and said to him: "make nice, mommy." He smoothed his hand on the rug (in response to "make nice"). I repeated and emphasized, "make nice MOMMY." He still didn't do it "right," though he stayed near me and was very interested. Then Lydia did it to me (i.e., stroked me) a few times and he immediately imitated her!—with much enjoyment.

Then, Lydia lay down. I said, "make nice, Lydia." *HE DID!* This time, without a model! Then he crawled up in my neck for affection and looked lovingly.

Makes toy cars move and also all other small moveable shapes (e.g., a piece of bread). He "moves" them like cars on the floor or table. Thus, he makes his own toys—i.e., he plays. He tried to copy my block arrangement (rectangle on bottom, square and triangle on top). He placed the triangle on top of the square, then "discovered" that it could be moved about like a propeller, and repeated the spinning movement spontaneously, several times.

When he wants me to come and do something with him—e.g., play at the block drawer—he now brings me a block and then goes back to the place where he wants me to be and "demands" insistently. Certain "games" or interactions with me, or certain previous responses, are irrevocably attached to certain stimuli and the association must always be repeated—or else he cries. It's a kind of rigid S-R bond. He doesn't just remember the previous connection; he just HAS to complete and repeat the S-R connection. There is a tension in him until it is completed by the appropriate action.

Puts toys on his head as "hats" that fall off, because he loves when *I* do that. Usually puts it too far back. Does it now by himself, without my doing it first. A strong example of delayed imitation.

With his diaper off, and in the nude, he went to bathtub, predicting a bath. Is there something like this going on?

The stages appear in order, though slowly, but the behaviors at any stage are still always less differentiated than normal (maybe that's why the stages are at a slow rate—it takes longer to make the critical connections). The assimilation goes on, but there's a problem in differentiating the aliment. There is less frequent assimilation because it is harder for Benjamin to find similarities between novel or elaborated situations and familiar ones. When it's finally done, it is still off, because it is over-generalized—i.e., there is insufficient accommodation. You can't make finer associations and accommodations if there is weak analytic ability and insufficient schema—i.e., conceptions, and groupings—to apply to each situation. If you feed in smaller and more familiar chunks, you may enable a connection but then there is still the problem that the associations are too rigid and concrete. The schema do not allow for variation. Accommodation requires that you respond to the difference and still incorporate the little changes. Benjamin just repeats, without incorporating the changes.

—Raises car seat guard when car stops.

—Adores music, dancing, being held while I dance in rhythm.

What has to happen, for him to desire to use words to communicate? [emphasis added] He does say NiNi, however, and he picks up the telephone, puts it to his ear, and seems to "say" "Hello" or equivalent.

March 8, 1973

He moves his body up and down for the "aaaah *boom* dee ay" part of "wind-wind, little baby." More delayed imitation (e.g., he picks up his brush and puts it to his hair). Is really trying to eat with spoon. He seems to have more sense of where he's at and wants to go. He takes off his clothes, and goes straight to tub. He is trying to make kissing sounds with his lips, using, however, the same "mmm" as with momma. Knows Lydia's name, Jean's, and Anny's. Sometimes imitates "mmmmm" followed with open mouth, *without* putting in the vowel sound.

Comments

These entries begin with observations about Benjamin's particular brand of affectionate behavior. It is my impression that something is off in his ability to express (but not in his ability to experience) emotion. The emotion appears to be there but not, it appears, the natural pathway to expressing it. Benjamin appears to need to "learn" which behaviors to perform in the context of an emotion. They do not seem to be seamlessly tied to the emotion.

Once again, I ask: How did Benjamin learn that certain behaviors go with certain feelings? How could he learn how to behave when he felt a particular emotion? Before being able to imitate the appropriate associated act, he would have had to match his own feelings, first, with the same feeling in the others. This is how I explained his learning to "kiss." But on what basis could he make the match? There is some neurophysiological evidence that in normal individuals neuronal patterns associated with engaging in facial expressions may be activated when one perceives these expressions in others, at least in adults (Dimberg, Thunberg, and Elmehend 2000). In keeping with the assumption of an innate and universal association of certain emotions with certain facial expressions, one might hypothesize that the observing individual then interprets the observed facial and gestural expressions through the emotions associated with them within himself. I presumed, however, that the foundations for this "natural empathy" did not exist in Benjamin and therefore wondered how he could "learn" how to behave when feeling a particular emotion. It seems that Benjamin must have had *some* ability to sense the similarity of emotion, after all.

Benjamin learned the meaning of "make nice" in the context of a heightened emotional contact, a "moment," as described by Pine (1987). He did not understand the words in "make nice!"—at this stage, his understanding of the phrase was like the baby's understanding of "all gone!" when the plate is cleared (Gopnick and Meltzoff 1997). He also did not have a spontaneous understanding of the purpose and function of the "make nice" gesture. But he seemed to learn its meaning, very quickly, plus the words for it, through imitation, in the context of "a moment."

Words are still not used for communication. But the concrete objects and actions, about which he might wish to communicate, are used. Thus, he uses the objects themselves (e.g., the block) and/or actions associated with his wishes to make the point, to communicate his point to the other. This is not verbal language, but it is a language of sorts, a nonverbal, prelinguistic language and the beginning use of signs (in this case, parts of the whole) to communicate about the whole. It's on the way to language and communicating. The block that he brings is like a word representing the activity he wants to tell me about. It has a shared association.

Benjamin is developing, through repetition and predictable sequences, a repertoire of behaviors and sequences of behaviors that he can use again and again (e.g., undressing and going to the bath; raising the car seat). He can count on them, he has them now as his own to do, and he is able to initiate them or anticipate parts of them. This gives his behavior a more active, engaged, "with it" feel. This shows the importance of routine, and consistency, especially for children like Benjamin, because establishing routines for him appears to stimulate and support a capacity for self-direction and initiation.

There are now many more signs of symbolic function in his play. For the first time, Benjamin uses things *as if* they were something else. Using something as if it were something else reflects an emerging capacity for representation and language. Something equals, can stand for, something else. It is interesting that, in Benjamin's case, the strengthening of symbolic function and communication is happening at the same time as Benjamin appears to be more loving—as well as somewhat more able to show and express his angry feelings. He seems now better able to differentiate the feelings within himself. I do not know how this capacity relates to the emerging representational ability. But in a sense, Benjamin's method of expressing his emotions (through "learned" acts) might be said to reflect as well the emerging capacity to have something stand for something else.

CHAPTER TWENTY-SIX

~

Wanting to Say Words!

Diary

March 18, 1973

There are definite new and parallel developments in language, imitation (delayed), playfulness, intelligence, and affection.

On language front:

—He says "ah ah—ahah-ay-ee" (ah-ah-ah-ah-baby) and "ni-ni" more or less in connection with realizing it's time to go to sleep;
—He plays telephone—picks it up and says "Hello" (aaa). His articulation is completely off but his desire to be "lingual" is ahead of it;
—He tried to imitate "flo-wer": ah- ah, accent on last syllable;
—He tried, spontaneously, to imitate, the sound of the car, by making a br-rrm sound. He did it with his new pressed "m-b" lip formation which he can do better now, but he still has to *place* his lips, to control the lip portion, and he still is not sure of what sound will come out of it—sometimes no sound.

On delayed imitation:

—Goes to phone, takes it off and says "hello" (a-ah);
—"Brushes his own hair" (and is now more tolerant of me doing it);
—Picked up "eency weency spider" quicker than usual; tried some finger movements.

On affection:

—He "knows" (better than before) the *looks* and *sounds* and softening expression in the *eyes* that indicate it, and he can both recognize it in others and do it himself;

—He puts his head down to cuddle, makes "mmm" soft sounds. Loves it. Loves to be loved and to love.

On intelligence:

—He knows his way around the apartment, the elevator, outside;

—He gets in the stroller himself;

—He goes to the door, when he wants to go outside;

—He got my attention to the backpack (that I carry him in); tugged on it, then went to the couch and climbed up to be put in it. When I brought it to the couch, he tried to get in it himself.

March 22, 1973

Definitely, at this point, *Benjamin is wanting to say and imitate words!!* But he absolutely seems not to have a memory for language sounds. Thus, to hypothesize:

1. (Normal) child makes sounds, lip movements, etc.
2. Child hears sounds, sees lip movements, etc. on other.
3. Child connects 1 and 2, so that upon seeing, hearing, the other, he "remembers" the patterns in himself that evolve into the same (auditory) response.

Benjamin is deficient in both 1 and 3. His problem in 3 is not only a function of 1. The "memory" or integration of past and present experience is off, even with sounds he CAN make. His attempts at imitation despite his handicaps are very touching, noble, courageous!!!

For example, he sees my mouth movements for ice cream (open mouth for "ice," parallel lips for "cream"). He imitates the visual part (i.e., he opens his mouth wide, then closes his lips, "mmm") but without any sounds from within. No sound comes through. Same with "mom"—first closed lips, then round mouth, then closed lips. He attempts to imitate *visible* mouth movements without the sounds (the exception is the *single* sound, "mmmm").

Also, as previously reported, he associates the recently achieved great triumph of closing his lips for an "mmm" sound with *any* attempt to learn a new sound. Trying to imitate sounds sets off the "mmmmmm" motion (just like wanting to have fun, enjoy the contact, play games, sets off the "wind wind" motion [from the baby game]).

He is so sweet with his "mmmmm." He offers it, whenever you try to teach him a sound.

He is definitely imitating intonation:

flower—ah *ah* (accent second syllable)
cracker—ditto

Comments

At exactly age two and a half, Benjamin demonstrates an increased interest in talking (i.e., in using words *in association* with a situation) although still not (necessarily) for communication. His difficulty in developing a verbal language seems due in part to his perceptual-motor deficits. He cannot make aural-to-oral associations because (it seems) he does not (cannot) make the sounds to begin with. For the same reason, he does not integrate visual presentation of sounds (e.g., lip movements) with aural inputs. But there is a problem as well in integration of the making of sounds with meaning. Benjamin seems motivated to talk—that is, he wants to initiate and imitate vocal sounds. But, it seems, he has not yet grasped that the sounds have meaning and that they are used to share that meaning with others ("ah-ah ah-ay ee" and "ni-ni" are the exceptions). But look what's coming, *just one day later!!*

~

CHAPTER TWENTY-SEVEN

Communicating with Words—
and Without

Diary

May 23, 1973

Today, he got the "I" sound—a bit, and on a few occasions, sequenced it with the closed mouth, for the "open mouth–closed mouth" sequence he needs to sign for ice cream. Better still, he did this *when* he wanted *ice cream*—as he pointed, he made the movements (!) I think this development met with TOO much enthusiasm, because he didn't repeat it. It almost *seemed* as if he knew I wanted him to do it and was resisting.

When I said the word "flower" to his father, in the context of telling him about Benjamin's verbalizations, he (Benjamin) responded to hearing the word *by pointing to the flowers* on the table (!) He definitely now is using (or can use) NiNi or "aha a" to TELL ME that he's tired. It is *communicative*. It *is language* (!)

Re: the "mmmm" for all "learning to imitate sounds" or "wind-wind" for all "fun with mommy" etc.: it is not that Benjamin does not generalize from one situation to the next, but that he generalizes too much!—as today in the following:

He successfully "got" the idea of filling up a cup at the faucet in the bathtub. Most often, he has gotten it, with a bit of help and much hooray from me, but then, he also puts non-vessel things under the water, as well, and says his "hooray" (AAAH! with correct intonation) for that, too. He hasn't analyzed out the crucial factor of the *open* container. Similar in one respect is similar in all, but it isn't the "right" respect. He doesn't know which part of an act you are reinforcing, and so all of the act becomes strengthened.

May 30, 1973

Several new tricks:

He has finally coordinated—though still with some difficulty—filling a cup from a faucet and emptying it out. Also took a tentative *sip*. The hard part of the coordination for him appears to be tipping the cup at enough of an angle to reach the water. He tends either to tip it all the way to the bottom or half way to the side. He knows where he has to aim it and you can see the muscle strain in his arms and hands as he tries to orient it!

I think I would like to write a book as psychologist-mother, re: Benjamin's birth, development, and my reactions etc. for the first three years [!! emphasis added].

Comes up to me more and more frequently with *something in mind* that he wants me to do [emphasis added]. Looks at me and waits for me to follow him, looking back as we go, with pleasure-filled anticipation as I follow him, then takes me to where or what he wants—e.g., the bathtub. Gets in the bathtub himself. Lately, comes and gets me to play with his records, brings the record to me, and then goes into living room to piano, phonograph, etc. Wants me to dance with him to music; gets his hand in position to hold mine.

Turns light on and off by pulling a switch.

Can pull a pull toy at his side.

Musings: B needs to have simpler, less complex, more discrete presentation of input. There needs to be less "noise" to allow for assimilation to begin. *Plus,* the assimilation itself requires greater similarity; in this sense, it is less playful and there is less generalizing.

It seems you cannot just wait for developmental progress [emphasis added]. You need to restructure the environment to allow whatever assimilation is possible to occur. Otherwise, there is apathy and flatness. In turn, building up units, schemas, will allow for more growth, because there will be more categories to use the next time with which to recognize, organize, assimilate stimulation.

There is an intense, uncompromising quality to Benjamin's assimilation: that goes with the *low* degree of accommodation. Thing have to be *exactly* the same. The Piagetian model seems helpful in conceptualizing the nature of MR (mental retardation). Based on the way Benjamin *does not* develop speech, I would guess that *speech requires:*

1. spontaneously emitted sounds;
2. the ability to "remember" the connection between the sound and the physical coordination used in producing it (so that hearing the sound, one can repeat it);
3. the ability to reproduce with one's own musculature, movements visualized on another. This requires #1—that is, the movements must already be one's own, in one's repertoire, just as the sound must already be one's own;
4. hear the sound, "recognize" it as familiar, "remember" the muscle pattern associated with it;
5. ability to register the connection between the "sound" and a visual stimulus (e.g., position of other's lips) so that one can "imitate" the visual, without being able to see it on oneself, through reproducing the associated sound.

The primary problem for Benjamin is his extremely limited spontaneous array of sounds (#1). How can B imitate a sound he has never made? He does not know how. Yet he DOES know how to imitate *rhythms* and phrases and *intonations*(!?) These were NOT originally spontaneous (though perhaps, varying voice tempo and pitch were). He cannot say "cookie" because he doesn't know any consonants he can't see. He tried to imitate it today by picking up the "pressure" quality (i.e., the forcefulness of the "c" and "k.") This he associates with making a B and M. He confuses B and M because they look alike (i.e., on the lips of others)—he wants to say "bath" but says "Maa" instead of "Baa." He, of course, cannot imitate the TH.[1]

Do normal babies learn sounds the same way? That is, do they also specifically copy the physical appearance of the mouth? I think not. Rather, they have a kind of empathy with the speaker. Or they first have all the vowels and consonants in their spontaneous babble, so they can then "remember" the sound/musculature association when they hear the sound in a social situation. *Blind* children don't see the lip and tongue movements of the other. Clearly, they don't learn to talk through the visual images. But Benjamin needs to *see* the model to learn how to do it.

June 6, 1973

Today, he seemed to use his words (e.g., Muh for milk, maa for bath), to *ask!!* for these things. However, this is very new and tentative. Most of the time (99 percent) Benjamin demands by grunting and will not say the word.

Occasionally, he says the word AFTER he gets or sees its referent, but the word is not used to ask for the referent. That is, he *labels* it when he sees it but he does not represent it, in its absence, with the word.

How come he can imitate *rhythm*??? (Good question!)

During the last week, Benjamin clearly is using his 1 or 2 words (mainly muh = milk) for asking. He has to see it, but at least it is used *when he wants it*, and in order to communicate wanting it. It is not yet used without any visual experience. But maybe "bath" (maaa) is.

The only consonant Benjamin knows is "m" because he can see it (and we could teach it to him). Any attempt to teach him a new consonant elicits an "m" formation, because "m" stands for any words and sounds I want (him) to learn or imitate. This is because "m" is the only one he has been able to learn or imitate. Obviously, P and B elicit M, also F and V, but so does C for cookie. He tries so hard!!! He definitely tries to say "cookie"—i.e., to use a word to represent it—by offering an "m" word. It's not that the "m" word is the word for everything, as with the toddler's first general words, but rather, that the "m" lip formation is the *only* articulation possible for him, and therefore is there for *all* attempts to form a word.

When he imitates, as in "ma" = more!, there is the quality in its tone and tempo of deaf speech. That is, he seems to form it without a sense of how it is going to come out—so it takes careful and conscious control. He plans it as he does it, and his concentration gives it a very unspontaneous feel.

Comments

At thirty-three months, Benjamin's vocabulary continues to increase (but not his articulation). And, on a few occasions, he now does seem to want to talk for communication. However, in my notes, I express doubt that an appreciation of the representative and communicative function of words has truly consolidated. I note that Benjamin does not yet understand that words can represent things that are not there, and that you can use them to communicate about those things in their absence. On the other hand, would he, at this stage, have any inclination, need, or reason to share thoughts about things that are not there? Does he *have* thoughts about things that are not there? The exception is his "bath."

"Ni-ni" and "aa-ah" (as in aa-ah aa-ah ba-a-by) have communicative value, whether or not so intended. Like his use of the word "ice-cream," they are associated with a need or want and are repeated in the presence of the person required to satisfy that need. Even if they are (only) associations to this situation, they become a "representation" and a communication by virtue of the response given to them by his caretakers. This would be a Vygotskyan interpretation, and it seems to apply here. But is it really the way that the words of so-called normal babies are endowed with meaning and communicative value?

Benjamin is initiating interactions and activities with me. He has (seems to have) these activities and interactions "in (his) mind," but he does not yet have the words to get them into my mind. Or he does not yet know to use words to get them into my mind. So he waits for me to follow him to do or see what it is he has in mind. The initiation and self-direction are now here. Coming up to me and waiting seem to be the beginning of communicating; and his use (in the presence of a listener or receiver) of words and/or concrete items that are part of or associations to the whole do reflect an emerging use of representation in communication.

Benjamin's communication ability seems to parallel his ability to produce speech. The latter is so difficult for him. Both his speech and communication seem very self-conscious—that is, he has to work so hard on them. His talking and communicating do not seem to be as automatic and spontaneous as in a normal infant. *But such determination and motivation!!!!* (How could you not love and admire a kid who tries so hard? And everyone does.)

At this point in the diary, the answer to my ever-present question, Do you wait for development, or try to train it in? was this: in the normal child, you can wait for development to proceed, as long as the child is in an "average expectable environment," such as will provide the proper nourishment for maturing structures and capacities. But in the case of children with weak internal structures, one must alter and optimize the environment to fit these weak internal structures. On the other hand, one *can* wait for development, along more or less normal lines, once one has adapted the environment to match the child's capacity to process it. And the more this (adaptation) goes on, the less altering will be necessary because that many more structures will have been made. However, since environmental and developmental demands increase with age, the child will never catch up. As well, accommodation is weak, so there is a constant tendency to relative rigidity and perseveration.

I state here, "The Piagetian model seems helpful in conceptualizing the nature of MR." I then wonder, however, whether it is as relevant to development with normal children. Perhaps not. Perhaps the Piagetian model about the origins of intelligence and about how schema are formed, and the implications of that model for intervention, do work well for kids, like Benjamin, who have neurological deficits. Or maybe the model does apply to normal infants and toddlers as well but, in their case, processing along Piagetian lines happens so fast, most of the time, that we do not see it happening.

Note

1. The reader may wonder whether it would have been helpful, at this point, to use a mirror in trying to teach new sounds to Benjamin. Although I do not mention it, I am sure we tried it. My guess would be that the mirror image would not have solved the basic problem—namely, that, at this time, it appeared that he did not have the necessary lip/tongue formations in his repertoire. This, combined with his extremely weak imitation skills, would probably make the mirror exercise both fruitless and frustrating.

CHAPTER TWENTY-EIGHT

~

"What's a Parent to Do?"

Diary

June 22, 1973

Many reflections after reading *A Child Called Noah* (by Josh Greenfield). It is so easy to get caught up in the cuteness and lovability of Benjamin and forget how very different he is, and how behind. Also, there is the recent problem, recent in the sense that I only lately have given it much thought again, and the Noah book reinforced it. And that is: how much should one wait for development—spontaneous development—to bring him to the necessary milestone (not just the purely motor ones but ones like eating by himself, toileting, etc.) and how much should one teach it, program it in. The latter approach (program it in) is based on the supposition that this is not just a slowly evolving child, but a *different* kind of child, one with a different kind of brain. He can LEARN, what in normal children spontaneously evolves and develops, but only if the environment is arranged so that he can. The stuff must be fed in, and learned, in a Skinnerian conditioning sort of way.

This particular question—i.e., which way to conceptualize Benjamin's development—and the fact that the two possible answers lead to entirely different ways of dealing with him—is tied up with the following considerations:

1. That it is possible that it doesn't really make any difference how you approach him, as long as you have some *confidence* in yourself, and in the way that you feel inclined to work with him; half or more, or maybe ALL of the "success" of any technique is that the parents feel that they know what they are doing, they have some light to guide them through this unknown (and it IS an unknown, even more so than the challenge, say, of a first child, because there is less of the familiar, the expectable feedback

111

that helps make it second nature to know what to do). In Greenfield's book, you feel that a large part of what was working with the vitamins and conditioning stuff, as Foumi (Noah's mother) says at the picnic, is that they felt they knew what to do; they felt less baffled, and that made all the difference;

2. That one could probably line up an equal number of experts arguing for each approach—the developmental versus the training and;

3. That maybe each has a place in different areas. The motor milestones came when they were ready and they couldn't have been forced in any earlier. Perhaps, however, other kinds of behaviors are less maturation specific and require cognitive and perceptual skills which the child will never be capable of acquiring on his own (but would he compensate on his own??). Yet: Benjamin held his cup when he wanted to and was ready, and you couldn't force it earlier. With the feeding now, he is ABLE to feed himself, but doesn't yet want to—because it is still too hard?? because he is not ready to, on an emotional level?? if you try to train it into him now, he balks, and becomes very upset. Which leads to these considerations:

   a) *Developmental/psychological point of view*: Why introduce stress (especially into eating) and perhaps produce secondary interference with the developmental process?

   But on the other hand:

   b) *Pedagogic point of view*: why not teach him "reality" (i.e., that he must grow, that he needn't be as much of a baby as he presents himself), even if it means frustration?

Same with talking. Benjamin could be refused the food he wants until he asks for it with the words he has—but he gets extremely upset when you do this. Should one acknowledge this as a sign that HE is NOT ready and therefore, not push it OR should one persevere in the demands, and teach him that he cannot fight us off with his tantrums?

Perhaps an answer here is that one introduces frustration only at that point and to the extent that the child can handle it. The problem here is: you don't know the progression of this in an exceptional child. You don't know about this particular aspect of his or her development any more than you know about whether the thing you are trying to "get in," in the first place, might not happen anyway, on its own, if you leave it alone.

I remember the part in Noah when Rimland's wife said that what she did was listen to nobody but just do whatever she could—teach and teach and teach, however she could. The trick is to know *how* to teach: how much to push ahead; how far to push at the point where the new, the to-be-learned seems too frightening, too challenging, and the pressure leads to regression instead of progress.

Benjamin is so loveable where he's at. On the other hand, there are also a few places where he's unbearable. That's perhaps another key: you can (and should) begin to frustrate and impose and insist upon progress (and be able to persist) only when you feel strongly about it yourself—when it really matters. You have to be able to weigh out your own "right" to a reasonable life against what is important for him, if he is to grow and change. He's unbearable now when he "aahs" repeatedly, non-stop until he gets something he has decided upon—usually, a bath or ice cream or "outside," and he *won't* accept a "No"! He simply does not understand, "NO!" and/or the reason for the NO (he does not yet have the concept of "reason"!!) and he cries and feels hurt and frustrated. I usually give in, although somewhat less lately. I used to try to distract him. Now I think I'd like him to learn instead, simply that NO means NO—though, I'm not sure he's ready.

At lunch today, I tried to insist that he feed himself his ice cream. No success. Then I tried to insist that he, at least, let me assist him to bring his hand with the spoon in it to his mouth. But he got VERY upset—cried, got all tense and miserable. He does NOT WANT to feed himself yet—just like he didn't want to hold his own cup, even when he could.

He insists upon ice cream. He goes to the refrigerator, points, SOMETIMES says "I-Mm" but more usually, "mmm," the sound which he still relies on as his "speech." Or sometimes, it seems he cannot process anything else out quickly enough. "Mmm" is always there, on tap, to use when he tries to speak. It is usually for ice cream, first thing in the morning, and at the start of every meal.

Sometimes, he wants baby food—and even the jarred meat—when he's really hungry. He still positively REFUSES to try anything other than pureed/ smooth food—and crackers, cookies, and one day, HALVAH!! Here's another area: does one force or wait? He won't try whole fresh fruit, meat, vegetables, bread, cheese, etc.

Comments

This chapter speaks for itself. Some thirty-two years ago, in raising an atypical infant and young child, I worried and pondered, as do parents of young autistic children today, about whether to take a developmental versus training approach to help him develop and progress. The controversy rages on. Does the parent of the young autistic child use "ABA"—applied behavioral analysis, such as in the "discrete trial approach" developed by Lovaas (1987) to train in adaptive skills— or a developmental-relational model, such as the "floor-time" approach of therapists like Greenspan and Weider (1998)? Proponents of both approaches claim success. Both require that the parent spend many, many hours doing it. In these entries, with Benjamin now thirty-three months old, I conclude, after reading Josh Greenfield's book, *A Child Called Noah*, that what matters is not what you are doing but that you have confidence in doing it. Confidence, in a sense, is an epiphenomenon of either approach. This is because, in what experimental psychology calls "cognitive dissonance," one will tend to feel confidence, and would need to feel confidence, in any approach to which one must wholeheartedly commit so much time, energy, and, in some cases, money. To the question: Do you "force" in the adaptive behavior that isn't there, or wait, while looking for a readiness in the child, to help a bud blossom? I answered: You (try to) "force" it in, *only when it really matters to your own quality of life.*

CHAPTER TWENTY-NINE

~

An Idea of His Own

Diary

July 18, 1973

Since we arrived at L.A. he is "talking" a great deal, more than ever. But the problem is that with all his INTENT to speak, and ability to mimic intonation and rhythm, he still cannot articulate any consonants except "MMM." He can't do p or b, and he is frustrated, because they look like an M. He is getting better on the vowels, however. He mimics many remarks and words in rhythm and pitch. He also imitates many things—movements etc.

He has a pretty good "Old MacDonald" routine and "what does the pussy cat say?" routine (pussycat—meow; dog—uh uh (throaty); duck—ah ah; cow—mmm; car—aaaammmm) although, in the latter, he does not comprehend the meaning of the question—he just has the associations. Thus, at the refrigerator today, as he "aahed" for ice cream—I said, what does Benjamin say? (meaning, what do you say for ice cream, and expecting "I-MMM"). He responded, "meow"!

But he sizes up situations better, and sometimes, responds less concretely, more spontaneously, less robot-like. For example, we all sat down to dinner with guests, at a big table with many chairs. *Benjamin got his own little chair (which he had just gotten to know—we had only been in L.A. a few days) and brought it over so that he could sit at the table too! He wanted to join in.*

He loves the pool. He is quite relaxed in the water when I hold him. He likes me to jump up and down, etc. He kicks, loves to play with a boat in the water. He runs all around with a ball. He goes up to people, says "Hiya." Friendly, playful.

He is trying to get two words together like "Hiya Nana" (or Lydia, Anny or Mommy). He rarely can get it. He can't coordinate that sequence. If he can artic-ulate the first part, the "Hiya," he can't keep going and remember (or whatever) the second. Usually, he gets only the first syllable of the second word (e.g., "Hiya Na; Hiya Li." He also tries "Bye-Bye "(without the B, of course), followed by a name.

He has learned to kiss—in that he can now close his lips and makes some kind of "t" sound behind them. Interesting, it's again a palate sound substituted for a lip sound. He does this without contact, that is, as a thrown kiss, rarely when in contact with your face. He's very affectionate or at least wants to be. But his *spontaneous affectionate* kiss is an open mouth, excited, as if rooting, with loving eyes. He hugs a little—but that, too (like the "t" kiss), has the "learned" quality. Both the hug and the "t" kiss appear to be learned, rather than natural, spontaneous love expressions. Nevertheless, they are now full love expressions for him. They are not empty rituals. It's just that he had to be taught the vehicle for expressing the emotions. He definitely has the emotions and it appears to me that he is thankful to have been given the form through which to express them. Somehow, he is not able to evolve it naturally. But *snuggling is* spontaneous, putting his head in your neck, and giving those loving eyes.

He is very loving and happy and basically content. At times, he plays a long time by himself—leafing through a book; throwing and retrieving or bouncing a ball; moving cars along; emptying things out and putting them back etc.

It's time to teach him a new coordination toy, like the rings.

He loves space—running down long halls, large rooms, open areas. Learns his way around quickly. Good spatial memory. Learned my mother's building, elevator, way to pool, etc., very quickly.

He laughs uproariously—with Anny and Lydia. But it still has that opaque quality, that thick clogged sense. I think that what I am responding to is the sense that things get in, and get responded to, he's open to them, he wants, enjoys, receives and reacts to the stimulation—BUT much much less comes *out* (spontaneously) and certainly, no "ideas." He's mute, not only with reference to words, but with respect to *ideas*. It's as if there are none in his head. Even when he does *initiate* something, when he does begin an action or interaction, on his own, it appears reactive. It has been set off by something outside—it is cued. An exception is *bringing the chair over. That was fresh. That was a new act that he had never done and which never had been done for him. He "thought" of it. It was his idea, brand new. It wasn't just an association* [emphasis added].

It's not that (generally) nothing comes out, but rather, that something original and new does not come out.

He loves to flatten himself against the door, then run forward, wildly, after first saying, "on your mark, get set—go" (vowels only, but in proper rhythm). He repeats this game a thousand times. He helped set up that game. He loves any game, anything that CAN be repeated, again and again. He is anxious to learn new things to do, but he's dependent upon others to feed them to him.

He responds to "give it to mommy," when I present an open hand. But he won't respond to (or he doesn't understand), the request, "give something" to someone else. (Like, "give this to Lydia.") Is he only understanding "give" in the context of the one who is saying it?

Pretty good catcher.

Calls Lydia and Anny (especially, Lydia, I think) from across distances.

Always happy to see you. Feels hurt if yelled at or rejected. Loves kids, wants to join in and be included. Is friendly to strangers, always says Hiya. Again, however, Hiya has that tacked on, learned quality. The impulse (the emotion) to greet is there—*completely*. The spontaneous, natural connection of that emotion with certain words is not. You can *teach him* the words and he'll use them appropriately. The affect is there but it is somehow still separated from the language. He uses the word to inform, as a vehicle, to signal his ideas and intentions, but the words do not seem to have an intrinsic connection to them.

Comments

While visiting his grandparents, Benjamin brought his chair to the table "in order to" join in with the family. This was his first foray into creative problem solving—the first time we had seen evidence of Benjamin imagining a goal, and creating and self-generating novel behavior that would be instrumental in reaching it. True, he may have seen others pull his chair over to the table. But, in this vignette, he is not simply imitating the act but intentionally creating one, in a situation that he has never before encountered. Keep in mind that we were not at home at the time, and that the situation involved a different set of people (e.g., grandparents), a different room, a very different dinner table, and very different chairs than those to which he was accustomed. Here was Benjamin wanting something (namely, to be included in a social situation!), "thinking up" (planning) a way to make it happen, and then setting out on his own to do it. The enterprise had a whole different feel from the usual Benjamin who, at this point in his life, while self-directed, was not creative. He typically did not initiate and engage in new acts.

Still, it seems to be an exception. I lament in this section that Benjamin generally does not seem to have "ideas" or at least know that he has them and want to express them. Generally, at this point, Benjamin still has to be taught what to do. We had to teach him a repertoire of activities that he would then initiate and engage in on his own. He had the capacity to play by himself, but we first had to teach him what to do.

In these entries, the quality of Benjamin's communication is still that of learned associations and signals. It does not have a spontaneous, self-generated quality. The entries about his language are reminiscent of comments made when he was younger, about his movements: "It does not have a quality of being his own, of flowing automatically from his intentions." Similarly, he does not use natural gestures. He clearly seems to have deficits in the oral-motor integrations needed for speech. And, although he seems now to want to share his feelings with others, he appears not to have (or be able to access) natural channels to express and communicate them, either.

At just two months shy of three years of age, Benjamin seemed to understand "Give it to mommy," in the context of my presence and my open hand, but not "Give it to Lydia" (i.e., to a person other than the one who is speaking).

My attitude towards Benjamin at this point appears to be one of acceptance and interest in who and what he is, as he is. I am interested in, even appreciative of, and take pleasure in how he is different. It seems that I have not (for a long time) been afraid to see that he is different.

So—what does all of this have to do with intersubjectivity? I describe Benjamin's communication as thwarted in two ways—in his inability to articulate the various sounds and in the apparent absence of ideas to tell. Also, although there is evidence of the intention to speak, there appears to be limited or no awareness of the role of words in communication. In saying that Benjamin has an "opaque" quality I am referring to the fact that the meaning of the words of others just doesn't seem to "get through." They may be correctly responded to as the stimulus in a stimulus-response sequence, but he does not appear to register their meaning. These characteristics add up to something atypical with respect to the sharing of ideas and intentions across the interpersonal space. Benjamin is almost three, and yet there still does not appear to be a "meeting of the minds."

~

CHAPTER THIRTY

Almost Like a "Real" Kid

Diary

July 27, 1973
Many new changes recently.

1. In the past few weeks I had decided to insist upon self-feeding. After 4 or 5 days of semi-successful work, I went away for four days, during which time the spoon bit was abandoned. Then, upon my return, Benjamin immediately associated with me the requirement that he feed himself—and showed extraordinarily good (in relation to previous attempts) co-ordination PLUS voluntary, enthusiastic participation in it.

   In the earlier attempts, he clearly refused to consider a spoon AT ALL. Then, when forced to at least touch the spoon, as I fed him ice cream, he acquiesced. Then, he was willing to hold the spoon if I guided the movement. It stayed there a while, and that probably helped pattern the movement for him. Then, at least with ice cream, he was willing to do it himself—and, at times, even insisted. When I returned from my trip to Berkeley, he (even) indicated a) that I take the baby food out of a jar and put it in a bowl so that he could eat it himself and then b) proceeded to do it himself. Now he is clearly able to feed himself but his motivation varies. Sometimes, he even insists, other times he refuses. Partly it's the food. If it's ice cream, he'll always do it.

2. Yesterday, I couldn't find the (training) cup. I tried to offer him milk in a glass. As always, he totally refused (he has in the past even refused a training cup that was different from the one he had learned on). I forced him to taste melted ice cream in the glass. He became interested and accepted it. I brought out chocolate syrup for the milk. I let him taste it on a spoon.

Then mixed it with the milk as he watched. Spoon fed a few spoonfuls from the glass. And he was willing—indeed eager—to pick up the cup and drink himself!! Now, he is very in love with the new skill. At times, he insists upon a glass!! (a little glass cup with a handle) He drinks it down gulp gulp gulp—spills a lot—not yet regulated—and also he "bites" more than draws, but it's on its way.

3. Yesterday, he went to the refrigerator when he saw it opened, took out his baby food jars, put them on the table, then went to the silverware drawer to get a spoon and put that too on the table. *This has the quality of his new level. He communicates better by actively doing and getting or imitating what he wants.* Brings his chair and sits down when he's hungry etc.

4. Imitates *so many* things now. E.g.:
   —Lydia slapped me in anger two days ago and I yelled at her. Benjamin immediately came over and started slapping me too, waiting for a response (done very playfully, of course).
   —Saw Nana yelling down to someone from the terrace—immediately went out there, yelled too.

5. He is playful and teases; he knows what's forbidden and does it while watching for your reaction and laughing. For example, he is very good in the pool. However, he has fallen in twice. He insists upon teasing me and being naughty by going to the tippy edge—then he slips, accidentally, and falls in—and he WON'T learn not to go there.

6. Knows "HOT." He says "Ha," goes over to the oven, or to a cup of coffee—and tentatively approaches, saying "Ha." Knows to be afraid of it.

7. Saw a chandelier with candle-like look in Morris' house. Began to sing "Happy Birthday to you"!!! (Ha-a-aa-aa- a-a, with right tune) in response to it, then ended by saying "Hooray!" (i.e., for the blowing out of the candles). Was overjoyed and obsessed with that. We had to turn on the light, sing Happy Birthday, then turn it off and say Hooray!! over and over again. On return to Nana's house, he looked up at the light, hanging over *her* table and, although it is circular and does NOT have the candle quality, he sang Happy Birthday to it, too!!

8. He "swims"—on command, by the word, whether in or out of the water. Out of the water, he puts his head down, and does a dog paddle. He loves to kick, holds on the side and moves around. He's *very* relaxed and at home in the water.

9. Extremely friendly and spontaneously affectionate with his "t-n" kiss (palate and tongue click) and open mouth, and hugs (still stiff and not connected enough with the feeling, but *spontaneous* nonetheless).

10. "Reads" books constantly. Favorite activity: leafing through big (adult) volumes.

11. Dances to music with more variation—hand movements and turns, hops and jumps. Brings record over to be played, directs me to the phonograph to put it on.
12. Extremely loveable, less kvetchy, very large and sun-tanned.
13. Places his shoes near his feet as if to try to put them on.
14. Still refuses solid food other than cookies—although since the cup, I sometimes think he's getting interested in the idea of trying the food that he sees the grownups and other children eating. He was interested in Anny's peach, took it from her, but was not willing to put his mouth to it.
15. When he's tired, he comes up to you, lays his head down, and says "ah ah (b) a(b) ee!!"
16. *Saw picture of a baby on Gerber's label—took the jar up to his shoulder, and cuddling it up to him, sang "aaa (b) a (b) ee!!"*
17. Fake "cries" to manipulate or play. Puts his head down as if in total misery.
18. "Hoorays" himself for all kinds of achievement—even non-achievements.
19. Says "Hi" and i-i (bye bye) with wave. Always appropriately, and in context. Even waves goodbye to dogs he passes, and when leaving places he was at or liked.
20. Categorizing (!)—toy cars go here, animal toys there, etc. (as I have taught him).

Speech is same hang-up: he tries to imitate *everything* in sound and rhythm, but *absolutely cannot* find the articulations. Everything (consonants) comes out like an M. The vowels are differentiating a bit (i's and a's) but a long way to go.

Comments

These entries appear to document a tremendous leap forward in Benjamin's capacity for "imitation" and delayed imitation; for *representation* of himself; and for self-generated, playful spontaneous behavior. And there are also cognitive leaps.

In the "Gerber's baby" example, Benjamin comforts the baby on the baby-food label, as he himself has been, "doing unto others what others have done unto him." This appears to indicate a cognitive advance in representation as well as the development of a concept of one's "self." Benjamin may recognize the picture as "baby" because similar pictures, in books, or even on jar labels, have been so labeled for him; he himself may also have been labeled "baby" (e.g., while looking in the mirror). The verbal label "baby" may have helped him to bridge the two experiences and, possibly, to recognize the similarity. Having apparently identified baby-ness of this picture, he then treats it as he himself has been treated. In so doing, Benjamin appears to have some representation of himself, and some ability to match himself with others.

Benjamin's pretending (such as his "fake crying") also seems to signal some representation of himself. That is, the ability to imitate himself suggests some memory and representation of what he is like and what he does. He says *Hooray!!* for his own achievement. This, of course, is in imitation of our response to him. But once again, he is imitating with respect to himself, and therefore, there is not only an "I" that is the subject but also a "me" that is an object. *I* applaud *Me*. And in the same time period, he has begun to sort things into categories. He is perceiving and abstracting out underlying consistencies.

In all of the above, Benjamin is now acting (finally) like a baby moving towards the end of the sensori-motor period (fifteen to eighteen months), rather than the three-year-old that he nearly is.

Also, at this time (i.e., at around age three), I wanted Benjamin to feed himself. He seemed able to do it and was at a developmental age when it should be happening. However, it wasn't (happening) or rather, he wouldn't. At the time, his not wanting to feed himself seemed to be a function of both the difficulty of the task for him, and motivation (which may, in turn, have been influenced by difficulty). I used a graduated training procedure with tempting foods to try to work through his resistance. At the same time, I was aware that feeding himself and drinking from a cup were difficult for Benjamin. He may have been ready, from a developmental point of view, to feed himself, but his oral-motor and motor planning handicaps might have made what he wanted to do, and was ready to do, difficult to perform. (Eating difficulties persist in Benjamin to this day. See part III.)

Routine and repetition in our interactions, activities and play with him, have given Benjamin a repertoire of behavioral sequences which he can apply, through generalization, and use in different situations. He therefore now appears to "initiate" appropriate behaviors in any given situation, through delayed imitation of the routines he has learned.

At thirty-five months of age, Benjamin showed an apparent failure to understand expressions of anger by others and the implications of "aggressive acts" (i.e., slapping). As with affectionate gestures, it appears that he has to learn emotional gestures, and learn to associate them with the feelings. With affectionate feelings, he seemed able to "read" and respond to affection and loving feelings in the other. It is interesting, however, that, in contrast, he neither appeared to *have* angry feelings nor was able to *recognize* them in others (although he did find the loudness of an angry response noxious).

Singing "Happy Birthday" as an association to the chandelier indicates another big new step. It is, as well, a delightful example of the value and joy one can find in deficit functioning!! I would not (did not) for a moment consider "correcting" it. Benjamin's "assimilation "of the chandelier into his birthday cake schema was quite poetic. He had created a metaphor. More important, it was an association, self-generated, that was all his own, and something in which he appeared to take pleasure. He seemed excited and happy with his "discovery" of the "sameness" of these two events and with his ability to name it.

~

CHAPTER THIRTY-ONE

Words Don't "Get Through"

Diary

August 1973

(The diary entries at this time consisted of my musings [omitted here] about right and left brain contributions to language and cognitive functioning, a topic which was very much in vogue in the early 1970s. I used my limited understanding of brain functioning to try to explain problems in the comprehension of meaning in the so-called psychotic children I had worked with at Master's Children's Center, and in Benjamin. The right-left brain references are most likely not correct, but the description of the phenomena still seems valid. So, with some embarrassment, I am transcribing here some of these entries.)

August 16, 1973

There is a "thick" quality to Benjamin's reception, like you're not getting through; the feeling that words don't strike through (even if they are responded to), the words don't seem to cut through the medium. There is a feeling of density—as if there is some "deafness" or partial "deafness" in him. From the very beginning, even before language, the normal baby has the quality that makes others feel they are *getting through*—with words, and other communications—even before language is understood. You don't get that feeling with Benjamin.

Benjamin, for example, has never been responsive to non-verbal communication like pointing, and natural gestures (e.g., "over there," "come here," "go," etc. These gestures do not *get through*. They are registered perceptually, they can be recognized and remembered and matched up, later, with a context, and anticipations can be built up in a S-R way (conditioned response) around them. But they lack intrinsic meaning of their own. Words do not have a clarity, and "pointedness." They do not have a significance that shoots home—a significance that comes through being appreciated in a time dimension and with conceptual meaning. Words should *tell* the other person something; they talk to the other, and try to get something to and all the way into the other's center. There is a line that pierces through.

With Benjamin, words don't seem to pierce through; it's as if the medium does not conduct. It blocks the message. Is this an inactive left hemisphere? His "thickness" is not really like that of a deaf person in relation to language, because the deaf are missing only the percepts, but not the potential ability to interpret them and to understand the meaning of words.

Imitation, as parroting, or photographic memory must be strictly right-brain. When, however, the content is identified with the other's intent and purpose, and is then associated with one's own intent and purpose (as in communicative use of delayed echolalia) is it becoming a bit more left hemisphere?

How can you bring conductance to the Left?

Should one try to stimulate the Left, or is it out of commission?

Comments

Benjamin seemed to have a "deafness" for the meaning (semantic) versus signal value of individual words. What seemed to be missing was semantic comprehension of language, verbal or gestural, versus words and gestures as signals.

In this entry, I ask: How can you connect words with meanings if there are neurological deficits interfering with the development of semantically meaningful language? But let us see what transpires in the following entries. Benjamin did, eventually, develop a spontaneous and (more or less) semantically correct language system (more or less because now, in addition to the correct use of words, he often borrows expressions, clichés, and proverbs, which may approximate his meaning, but with varying degrees of closeness of fit).

CHAPTER THIRTY-TWO

~

And Now Words DO "Get Through"!

Diary

September 16, 1973

3 YEARS OLD TODAY! ADVANCES IN LANGUAGE AND COMPRE-
HENSION, and constant imitation!! Benjamin now uses the following (21)
words, in context, appropriately, spontaneously. He also uses the asterisked
words, to request or communicate. (*It is the instrumental quality that is new*):

Hello, Hiya, ByeBye, Lydia, Anny, Mommy, Ice cream*, Milk*, mmmmm
(food)*, cookie*, open (new)*, no more*, hot*, Jean, Outside*, Ni-ni*,
Aaaababy*, flower, Ha(ppy Birthday), Hi-ya (Lydia, and Anny), and Daniel
(anyuh).

He responds appropriately when asked for the sounds of:

cat, dog, cow, duck, car.

He *understands (in context)* the following prepositions, nouns, and verbs:

(put) in, (take) out, open, close, sit, stand, run, sing, sleep, cry, hand, foot,
head as "put your *head* on mommy's lap," shoulder, put back, bring me (something), dance, model (i.e., showing off what you are wearing), jump, down, all
better, give me your hand.

September 19, 1973

Benjamin seems to be making dramatic leaps the last week or so. It is notice-
able in:

1. An ever-present readiness to *try* to repeat just about anything. He seems
   to want to say (and learn) *words* and they are snowballing;
2. Today, a willingness at least to try (to explore) *new* sounds in the course
   of attempting to repeat something. He is aware that something new is

126

called for, and though he is unable to hit upon the correct one, his effort and mistakes at least signal a broadening of his repertoire of sounds. Thus, e.g., for "shoes": he makes a nasal, breathing ("hn") sound, before the "oo," in trying the repeat the explosive "SH." He adds an "n-y" sound in his attempt to say Daniel.

3. He picks up every tune or inflection he hears. He wants to join in with other children who are talking and singing, and there is immediate repetition of their intonations. His ear, his pitch is perfect. He repeats and sings everything, and captures the inflection patterns of the sentences that catch his attention.

4. He picks up words (comprehension and/or use) in one trial or so.

5. Memory: He remembered the nursery rhyme, "1, 2, buckle my shoe." I had said that 1 or 2 times the week or so before. Then, when the word "shoe" came up in conversation, he repeated that tune. Shoe was the link and the whole tune came in.

6. Today, in the car, I overheard him rehearsing to himself names of the children we were on our way to pick up: Anny, Lydia, Daniel, etc. He really knows "Anny" and "Lydia" as names of people.

In short:
B seems more open to language and one has more of the sense that one can talk (use words) to him. He seems to have discovered that words have their own meaning—not just through a context or as a signal. When I say, "we're going to the elevator," stressing *elevator*, I know he knows that the word "elevator" refers to something in particular, and he is able to grasp in one trial what it is.

Thus, words now *do* "seem to get through." They have that pointed, piercing quality of "getting through the medium" that I had felt was lacking.

It seems that, in atypical children, you can have any of the following:[1]

—semantics without syntax
—syntax without semantics
—syntactical inflection without semantics
—syntax plus semantics without syntactical inflection.

Comments

Three years old, and here comes language and comprehension after all!!! Just when I was struggling to capture the quality of it not being there.

Toddlers whose language is just emerging will apply to a new situation a word which corresponds to one component of a similar (to the child) earlier event. The one word appears to stand for the whole situation, and might not be semantically correct. This is because the word, in the child's developing lexicon, stands for the entire situation, not just the specific component that was named. For example, a child says "BABA" when she sees again a cup that her grandfather had been drinking from, although this time, BABA is not there (see Simon 1969; Werner 1940 regarding holoprasis; and Schur 1966).

Benjamin is now getting this "syncretic" kind of meaning. And his receptive language is increasing. And he is now using words to communicate his needs. He shows an interest in learning and understanding words and in trying to explore new sounds. These developments have been emerging over a period of two months. What sparked them? How much had his oral-motor dyspraxia held him back?

In this entry, I claim that Benjamin is using some words to communicate his needs and wants and that he appears to understand the meaning of words that he hears. The shared understanding of the meaning of words opens up (but does not clinch) the possibility of connecting minds.[2] Moreover, subsequent entries will show that my sense that Benjamin was truly understanding the shared meaning (versus the signal value) of words may have been a bit premature.

Notes

1. This list referred back to descriptions of the different language styles of the children at Master's Children's Center (omitted here). At that time, the children were referred to either as "autistic" or as having a "symbiotic psychosis."

2. This can be done, without words, too, through comprehension of gestures and expression, but Benjamin is especially weak in his use and understanding of gesture.

~

CHAPTER THIRTY-THREE

Integration

Diary

October 6, 1973

Benjamin is very loving and affectionate. He initiates hugs. You can see him experience a "libidinal rush" for you, and he then "marks it" by a hug or an open-mouthed kiss.

Benjamin appears to be very un-physiognomic!! That is, emotions are *not* seamlessly linked and merged with acts and perceptions. Everything is too separate, too rigid, which leaves little room for generalizing, as e.g., through an associated motor or emotional response. His thinking is concrete and associative, not physiognomic. So: is physiognomic *really* so primitive? Isn't it rather a cross-modal integration that is a harbinger and bedrock of a later ability to generalize?

Benjamin responds to and can *imitate* prosody. But it (i.e., the variable intonation) is not intrinsic to his *own* speech. It is not integrated with it. He seems to add it in. It sounds "tacked on."

Comments

The seamless integration of emotion with actions is there from the start in normal babies. Its absence in Benjamin marks his development as not just delayed but atypical. Benjamin's prosody (i.e., the "music" in expressive language) was (and is) also atypical. Then (as now) he had a capacity to hear and imitate changes in inflection but this variation did not appear in his own spontaneous language, which was, and remains, somewhat monotonic. That's odd, isn't it? He could hear (recognize) inflection in the speech of others, and even imitate it; he could imitate changes in pitch, perfectly, even sing (then and now) with a perfect tune. But inflection as a reflection of his own changing affect and meaning was absent in his spontaneous speech. Clearly, Benjamin's language development was not only delayed but different.

Still, he was beginning to "talk." This carries and captures so much of the sense of self-hood. It helps establish the "I" with whom one can interact.

~

CHAPTER THIRTY-FOUR

Decalage

Diary

December 3, 1973

Recent developments:

After a bad (cranky, regressed) period, due to illness, there are a number of new developments:

1. Though he does not love it, Benjamin will now eat any evening table food (including steak, chicken, hamburger, etc.) mashed together (not blended). He has to chew, but would rather not—or perhaps more correctly, he does not seem to have the hang of swallowing so he often chews too long, unless you stuff something in that is very soft and slips down, so that he swallows. He still will not pick up anything except a cookie or cracker to eat by himself (peanut butter sandwich on cracker is also OK). He generally refuses to feed himself.

2. Usually, Benjamin (still) cries instead of "asking" me to do something he wants (like to pick something up or pull a string). I have often insisted that he say "*Mommy* . . . (pull, get, etc.)." Now he "says" it—"NaNa" (mommy) plus some grunt sound. The inflection and emphasis is an exact replica of mine. However, it does not sound like he is "spontaneously" calling, asking, *me* (NaNa) and knowing that that is what he is saying. Instead, it is a password that he uses effectively. Sometimes, in his crib, in the morning, or after a nap, I *think* he is calling "NaNa" as if he is really calling me. I am not sure—but it seems to be on its way. However, while the *verbal* appeal is not (yet) spontaneous, and self-generated, the motoric and facial one is. That is, he *comes and gets me, turns to me, looks for me, appeals with facial expression, etc.* [emphasis added]

Sometimes he seems to use Lydia's name as a spontaneous communication—when he wants her attention, and she is nearby, but this too is at best very tentative. It's still more like a password, a signal he knows will work. It's an amazingly subtle difference yet it's unmistakable. It's in the tone, voice quality. He repeats the words because he knows that doing that will work as a means of getting her; but he does not seem to recognize that it is intrinsic to the words themselves that *they* call her, that they are a direct translation of his intentions.

3. He is very interested in airplanes. Always looks up.

4. He imitates (versus generates) two-word sentences, or 3 or 4, now, and I think that at least in the 2-word (noun-verb) he knows there are two words—i.e., he's aware of two referents and what each means. E.g., if I say, "see the birds," and then, when the birds fly, "Birdies, flying," he repeats the inflection with, I think, some understanding.

5. Always "singing" to amuse himself. It's his form of spontaneous babble!! Sings "Baa Baa," "Happy Birthday," "Here's a ball for baby," "Firecrackers," "Pop Goes the Weasel," etc.

6. Increasingly affectionate. Hugs, warmly. His hugs still lack some strength and that "from within" quality. They still have that signal quality—i.e., this is what I do to express what I am feeling (rather than this feeling is intrinsic to the hug)—but he appears to be experiencing the *feeling* VERY strongly. He really feels a lot of love towards me, Anny and Lydia. Also Jean (i.e., his nanny). And he wants to express it. It is expressed in his frequent parroting "I love you" (in vowels only) with emphasis.

7. Still virtually no consonants, only vowels and inflection. I am looking into speech therapy.

8. Does more things for himself and engages in more instrumental acts. If he wants to eat something, he brings his high chair over to it. He brings his chair to the drawer at which he likes to sit. On his own, he removed all the cushions from the couch to prepare for a game he likes which the girls have played with him. *This was spontaneous. He set up the game and played it.* [emphasis added]

9. In the bathroom, he reaches for the water, gets his hands wet, and licks them (and repeats sequence) to get a drink. Then, he dries his hands and face on a towel, as he has seen the girls do.

10. He helps in taking off his clothes and putting them on. He removes his socks and shoes if you give this an initial prompt.

11. He likes to sweep. He takes out a broom, in imitation of me, when I am sweeping. He brings out the dustpan. He put the dustpan down on the floor for me, appropriately. Picks up some dirt and *puts* it in the dustpan (!) Reaches for me to get the garbage down, so he can empty dustpan into it. Brings dustpan back to closet and reaches to hang it on the hook.

12. In the playroom (building community room), he goes down the slide backwards, by himself. He goes up the slide, himself, and down (frontwards), almost by himself.
13. Laughing, joking, jovial. *Feels good about himself.* [emphasis added]
14. He likes form perception toys. He recognizes that the forms are different. He can do simple form boards, without difficulty.

Comments

Benjamin has learned many sequences of behavior. He strings together, through imitation, actions he has observed in others; he remembers and repeats the sequences of behaviors that have been done with or to him. These now become his own plans, his own property; he likes them; he initiates them; and in this way, he has become more active. It would appear that engaging in organized and repeated behavioral sequences plays an important role in development of self, partly because they set the ground for differentiating out the sense of self as agent and partly because the child now has a repertoire of activities that he can reliably put into play that help define who he is and what he can do. For some of these sequences Benjamin still needs a cue to get started (e.g., when I am sweeping). But he also now engages in instrumental behavior, means to ends, where the ends are of his own devising, and the means to them are spontaneous and less ritualized (see, e.g., the L.A. chair story, chapter 29).

With respect to language, Benjamin, at three, is something like a child of eighteen months to two years. In Piaget's scheme, the means-end behavior he is now displaying is at level 6, also at about an eighteen-to-twenty-four-month level. At about this time, as well, toddlers can do simple puzzles, and indeed, Benjamin is now doing form boards. However, there also were important differences in the pattern of his development, specifically with respect to the emergence of intersubjectivity and its relationship to language. Piaget (1952) termed these irregularities in levels and realms "decalage"—that is, different levels in different realms. For example, in normal development, both use and comprehension of gestural language precedes verbal language. Benjamin, however, seems to be developing verbal language while an understanding and use of natural gestures is still not there at all. Requesting with eye contact, an early indication of intersubjectivity, is now present. Typically, it would be associated with appreciating the meaning of words. In Benjamin, however, at three years of age, appreciation of the meaning (versus signal value) of words apparently is still questionable.

~

CHAPTER THIRTY-FIVE

The Laundry Basket
("A Mind of His Own")

Diary

February 1974

At 3 1/2, Benjamin knows about and enjoys putting his clothes in the laundry basket, when they are taken off him before his bath. One night, Lydia was in the bathroom too, preparing to take a bath with him. When she removed her clothes, I suggested she give them to Benjamin since he enjoys the laundry basket routine. He returned them to her, and "showed" her where SHE should put them—pointed and grunted towards the laundry basket. He did this with the air (rare, for him) of "one who knows"; *he* was *telling* her what to do. This was something different in Benjamin: he seemed to have a little "self" that could, and KNEW it could, affect others.

"Mommy" is still "Nonny." But, his second speech therapy lesson appears to have reinforced the idea that lip sounds are desired, and he now lets you put his lips together. After a little manual manipulation and stimulation of this kind, he will repeat a string of Mamamama—and even keep it up, a bit later, but it then dies out. You need to prime it all the time. Once, he ASKED me to put his lips together. He likes either the feeling or the applause he gets for successfully "mmmmmmmm"ing.

Though he is loveable and the girls, especially Anny, really love him, I have been feeling somewhat discouraged and exasperated with him lately. Partly, he seems even more demanding and clinging than ever. My back is in bad shape from lifting him so much. I've made the decision to stop that. This is just one of a couple of "Hard Lines" I have begun to put into effect, which, in turn, could account for some of the extra difficulty with him. I have wanted to demand more of him. *The discouragement I think comes from seeing how little he is able to accommodate my demand for growth in him* [emphasis added]. Clearly there is a good reason for the infantile patterns he follows. He is (still) infantile, and really remains unable to be otherwise. It is not just a function of my being too soft with him. Anyway, the whole thing leads to more anger and impatience with him than I have felt in the past. It is tempting to give up the whole thing and say, let's go back to the easier interaction of me accommodating him (versus asking him to accommodate me). Problem with this is:

1. I would likely feel discouraged and resentful;
2. Probably, it *has* to be difficult, at first (i.e., to insist on growth), and perhaps, to give up is to cop out. It would be me, unable to stick it out because of his understandable and expectable resistance.

Still, some of the unpleasant consequences (of demanding and expecting more of him) are making me want to reevaluate it. For example, I have tried to insist upon his eating more solid foods. Holding out, expecting him to get hungry and then, therefore, to eat them, doesn't work. If you force it, he gets upset and chokes and gags on the food anyway. *Could it really be impossible for him to manage them?* [emphasis added] Plus, he has become generally suspicious of the table, now, and of what I feed him, so that eating has become an unpleasant thing for him. So I give in, and want to make it pleasant again, which means giving him his usual soft foods.

He won't eat by himself, and if he does, it's only pureed food. So I have to decide between "chewing" versus "self feeding" as a goal. I've decided to go with self-help—hold out on feeding him until he's really hungry, so he'll eat the pureed himself. Then gradually, I can put in the lumps. A real problem is his limited generalization. Even when he has been able to eat some new finger food, it extinguishes very quickly. A few days later, it's just another unacceptable solid food, which he won't touch. Only cookies. Also, he does not generalize to other pick-up foods. He learns one at a time.

Toilet training seems very far away. I'm trying to get him to *tell* me he needs a change, by bringing me a diaper. So far, he only brings me a diaper when I tell him too. He does not specifically complain of a full diaper, though possibly, he displays an increased demandingness and irritability when he has one. In a way, he's been more negative, and more "two-year oldish" which is probably good and OK. He is "naughty." *He does all the things he knows will make me angry* [emphasis added], like throwing all the records on the floor, and I've been getting angry (I never used to).

He turns to Anny a lot. He knows she is always on his side. He has strong affection for her. He clearly loves both Anny and Lydia. *Puts his arms around them affectionately.*

March 1974
He does seem to be growing up, and is more willing to be independent now.

Learned "No" with headshake. Says "No" and shakes his head appropriately for refusal. (However, cannot say and learn "Yes," and sometimes uses "No" but *without* the head shake!! to mean yes.) Gleeful, happy about being naughty. However, if you yell at him and get really angry, he cries instantly. He's very sensitive to anger and yelling (he cries when anyone screams, even at someone other than him).

He really likes to walk outside now. He doesn't want to be carried, unless he is very tired, and even rejects the stroller. The reason is his new-found love of cars and trucks. He wants to watch them, and stand and clap in excitement. Trouble is, he won't move while he's watching, so if you're in a hurry, you must pick him up after all.

More about continuing efforts to learn, practice, MMMM sound:

I gave him a mirror, and he likes to look at himself, trying to say Mmm. Says "Hi Ninny" (Nimmy, his nickname) and watches lips for MAMA. It is still a conscious effort, one has to place his lips together and he sometimes loses the placement.

He had his first day of school, trial day, at Kennedy's Children's Center School. He responded to the teachers as teachers—i.e., he went to them for assistance or to show them something; he interacted with children. Ignored me. Seems to like and understand the place, probably because of his (earlier) playroom experience. Will he accept my leaving? I am determined to help him get through the separation, because it looks like such a good deal for him.

Comments

The Laundry Basket story: it appears that Benjamin experiences himself as "one who knows something" and as one who is able, and can decide to, communicate what he knows to others. He is *showing*, and *telling*! This seems to be the first manifestation, not only of some kind of self-knowledge (which would be special enough!), but also some awareness of and ability to reflect upon the internal state and knowledge in the other. For it appears that Benjamin shows the laundry basket to his sister because he somehow seems to understand or presume that she does not know about it. In this example, the first manifestations of both "having a mind of his own" and awareness of the "mind" of the other appear to come at the same time.

This measure of meta-cognition, of knowing about what he knows, may be seen as well in Benjamin's efforts to overcome his dyspraxia and in his asking for help in learning to make certain sounds (i.e., "I know I can't do this, you help me"). All of these instances involve motivation, intention, an awareness of self, but also, again, in his trying to do something that is wanted by others, some recognition of the internal world of others.

Benjamin's two-year-old kind of independence, asserting a "mind of his own," and learning to say "'No" all suggest some growing awareness of self, with a fledgling awareness, as well, that the other has a self, too, insofar as the other's wishes are experienced as different from his own. His being "naughty," on the other hand, may still be an extension of "making an interesting spectacle (i.e., mommy getting angry) last."

Also coming in now, too, for the first time, are specialized interests and personal preferences. The interest in cars and trucks is Benjamin's idea—he has selected these, on his own, from all other options.

Some of the unevenness or unusual ordering of Benjamin's development is a function of specific neurological and structural defects, which hold back development in certain areas. For example, language seems held back by dyspraxia affecting his capacity to form the words. Part of his relative immaturity in feeding himself is a function of his impaired oral-motor equipment and function. Unfortunately, I did not know that then, which is why I decided to present here all the entries about "should I insist—should I not" with respect to his eating this or that food. In retrospect, it became clear: you can't force development in such situations, without first helping the child to compensate for or overcome his deficits.

So now—from whence and how did the new "little person" quality emerge? In Benjamin's case, these signs of selfhood, intersubjectivity, and communication had arrived, more than two and a half years late, when, just a few months earlier, they were not there at all or, if there, only in muted forms. What had to have happened to allow them now to emerge? Though I was there all along, was with him everyday, the "laundry basket" took me by surprise! No amount of observation seems to help explain or "dissect" the leaps.

~

CHAPTER THIRTY-SIX

School Days

Diary

April 24, 1974

Loves school. Has made friends, knows the routines, and participates. Has already seemed to grow and learn from it in three areas: social, skills and language. E.g.:

In "social": Benjamin's really gotten the idea of relating to other children. He immediately starts up when he sees a child (any place). He goes over, says Hello, and tries to engage them in some play. Shares a toy with them. Babbles to them. Tries to show off what language he has (!!) Greets old friends with a beginning hug and kiss.

In "skills": He knows how to use new materials, such as beads and string; can climb up a slide and get into position himself; walks down stairs, one foot at a time (holding on).

In "language": This is really picking up again.

1. He imitates everything immediately; there is a little more of the quality that he knows what is being referred to;
2. He is beginning to make two-word or two-phrase "sentences"—e.g., Hi, (name); NiNi, (name); No more. . . The latest, and most exciting: first, (in vowel sounds only), the phrase "I like you" (with some attempt to purse the lips for "u"), then "I like" combined with an object. Today he said, first, with prompting, "I like school" and then, when he waited for me to give him milk, "Mommy, I like milk." (!)

The "I" and the "like" don't yet have separate meanings and referents—"I like" is like the "I want" that I often try to get him to say. But the exciting point is that he spontaneously experimented with a new combination, and a relatively original one. I think he thought he was saying, "I want" but I'm not sure. May just be that he caught on to the invariable stem followed by a variable word format, after I introduced the "I like school" phrase.

When he's in a good mood, as after a school day, he really lets fly with the "mmmmmmmmmm's."

Comments

Benjamin shows off what he knows to other children. He continues to express "selfhood" in his awareness of his repertoire of skills, as evidenced in his intentionally putting them into play. On the other hand, his social interaction with other children is primarily in his showing and doing *his* thing, rather than responding to them (or theirs). He wants and knows how to get their reaction to him. As I recall, there was little give and take insofar as he did not take in and respond to what they had to offer, separate from their response to him.

The quality of Benjamin's selfhood continues to rest upon and/or coincide with the building up of a repertoire of skills, which he then initiates and with which he experiments. In language, he is making two- or three-word sentences. This requires and/or reflects some kind of "executor"—that is, a central activator that attempts, puts into play, the formulation and expression of an idea. I have wondered whether the ability to do this has been slowed down by his dyspraxia. Again, we must ask: Which came first: an "I"ness which focused and directed him to work on the dyspraxia OR improvement in the dyspraxia which gave him more verbal competence and, therefore, more opportunity to experience his "I"? Or both?

I taught Benjamin the stem phrase, "I like" and in this context, his use of the word "I" does not yet refer to a separate "I." "I like" is just a label for his feelings. But having an ability to identify and label one's inner states *is* part of the development of the sense of "I" (Cicchetti and Beeghly 1987).

When he appears to be feeling good, and proud about himself, Benjamin practices language. This looks like an "I" activity because it requires motivation, intention, self-direction, and "conscious" effort.

CHAPTER THIRTY-SEVEN

~

Understanding "NO!"

Diary

May 26, 1974

A bit of a slump about Benjamin, but this is likely to be the aftermath of some very big strides. The issue around which the slump comes is discipline, and wanting him to "shape up." I experience a kind of discouragement that probably previous records will show has come up periodically. It is about finding the technique that will work for allowing me to create and control changes in him. In other words, most of Benjamin's great gains are developmental—one just suddenly notices them come about on their own. But if I'm really impatient with a certain kind of behavior, or wonder about its future implications, and therefore try to shape it, or extinguish it, etc., the situation becomes very frustrating.

There are three kinds of frustration or negative side effects when I try this:

1. It doesn't work on the specific behavior, so that it persists, along with whatever it is about it that made me want to get rid of it in the first place;
2. I get a general anxiety: why does it seem so impossible for him to understand—or rather, not why . . . but just, that it seems beyond him to *understand* the usual kinds of discipline or shaping techniques; and
3. He gets unhappy, feels hurt, for he is aware he is arousing my anger but he does not understand how or why.

He is *very* sensitive to my feeling dissatisfied with him. Actually, my feeling angry with him is very new. "NO" *without* anger was not working. I thought that perhaps if I felt and/or expressed anger he'd learn from my "no's" and my discipline, instead of just thinking it was a game. Then, when even expressing anger (really only half-felt) didn't work, I *did* really feel angry (out of frustration and anxiety: *will anything ever work!*).

The issues right now are:

a. throwing things (a problem mainly because of the people downstairs, but now, secondarily, because it has become, on his part, a game—an attempt to get a big reaction from me, and he is throwing pretty terrible things at people, such as a large glass bowl, shampoo bottles, also heavy blocks);

b. Stuffing toilets with paper and other things (part of the throwing things and also part of copying us throwing toilet paper in the toilet). At first, the toilet stuffing was an attempt, as Benjamin is always doing, to comply, to do what is right (i.e., put toilet paper in the toilet); only when his excess in this regard created an uproar did it then become something to do to get the uproar;

c. *Less clear and focused a complaint: his general refusal to take "no" for an answer, and the ensuing screaming temper—he is all or nothing about crying and temper. Any frustration tips off the whole slate of hurt and temper. He wants things his way re: cookies, outside, attention, getting certain toys; not eating "dinner" etc.*

If you get angry when you say no, Benjamin gets hurt and also WORRIED; because he doesn't seem to understand the connection between anger and what he has done. He does seem to understand: *If* I do this, then she will get angry, but *not*: this is WRONG (no concept of right and wrong) and *therefore* I shouldn't do it, and that it is *because* it is wrong that Mommy gets angry. Moreover, anger does not function as a deterrent or punishment for him. Rather, if you get angry with him, he seems confused and upset, as if he anticipates that he's going to do it *again*, *anyway* and therefore has to go through the anger again.

So I shouldn't use anger. It only adds to hurting his feelings. It doesn't mean to him "don't do it" so he knows he is going to bring about that unpleasant situation again. He does not know how to avoid it. Sometimes, he's not sure whether it's a game or not. Or rather, he picks up that somehow this game is not always *fun*. This is because he DOES feel, naturally, intuitively, that anger towards him is sad, bad, and no good. And it worries him, especially because he doesn't understand that there is something that he can DO about it (namely, not do the behavior that brings it on). For him it seems to be just an awful fact of life that that unpleasant stuff (i.e., my being angry with him) has become part of the game of cause and effect. Benjamin does something, mommy reacts.

He is really pathetic when you get angry or punish him. He just doesn't understand it, and his eyes plead to get things back nice again, and for me to be not angry. I melt, and two seconds later, he is doing it again! He says "NO" but still does it. "NO" is now just part of the game.

It's probably better not to get angry and punish, but to remove the temptations and distract him. However, this takes more time and effort than I have to give. Distracting means work for me and doesn't he eventually *have* to learn confrontation and "NO!"?

A little bit later: DaDa!! signs of NO becoming meaningful!!—He is beginning to *inhibit* something which has been "No-ed" a lot!!

I'm sure we'll get there, eventually and I know my getting angry is not all that effective. But *throwing blocks etc. at people*!! That MUST be stopped! How???[1]

If you hit his hand, he tends to hit himself in imitation. But he also pushes me away. (That's fine.)

Benjamin is also learning (at school): "hit others" (back). However, he does it when angry as an associated act, NOT because he feels impelled by his anger to hit. That is, hitting has the same quality, as do his kisses when he feels affection. It is something he has been taught to do, in association with a feeling.

He now uses a whole series of "I want . . ." "I like . . ." phrases appropriately. "I want" and "I like" are a base stem, he uses them correctly to signal his feelings and flexibly changes the other parts.

When he accidentally broke the mirror on Orchard street (market), and the man got mad, B recognized this, went up to the man, and sweetly repeated, "I like you."

He really wants to be good and is upset if he isn't loved.

He "talks" a lot. I can't understand certain new words. He gets a little frustrated but keeps trying.

Comments

This chapter is relevant to "theory of mind."

It appears that Benjamin, at age three and three-quarters, does not understand that there is a connection between the anger of "the other" and something that he did that apparently provoked it. Thus, discipline that involves an angry response to something undesirable is not effective. Benjamin does not like the anger (it is loud, not friendly) but, it seems, he does not understand that I am angry *at* and *because of* something that he did. Nor does he seem to understand why I would be angry. Since he does not make a connection between what he did and the noxious experience of an angry response, there is nothing in this situation that would indicate to him that he should stop doing what he was doing.

This would not be surprising were Benjamin a baby (one generally does not or should not try to "discipline" a baby with angry disapproval and one would not expect a baby to understand *why*, versus only *that*, one is angry). But Benjamin is now nearly four, and even talking in little sentences. Yet, like a baby, he does not seem able to take the perspective of the other. Even if he perceives and can anticipate the temporal sequence, and therefore, what preceded the unpleasant response, he does not seem to understand the meaning of the sequence: He does not understand that it is in the nature of things that one person's behavior might elicit anger in the other and that the anger is intimately a function of the nature of that eliciting behavior. He does not see a connection between anger and the object of anger. He does not seem to understand that anger has an object.

How does a normal kid translate mommy's "No" into a concept of bad or wrong, or even just learn that he can prevent mommy's anger by not doing the eliciting action again?

Not liking mother's anger or even her "No!" seems to be an innate response. Benjamin seems to have that part but he does not seem to have what seems to be (in a normal child) an equally innate tendency—namely, to inhibit behavior that has been given a negative response. But here is a paradox. In contrast to his response to anger, Benjamin does seem to be "innately" reinforceable by positive affective feedback.

The following observations seem relevant.

—Benjamin appears to have an innate aversion to the expressions of anger just as he has an innate attraction to expressions of love and approval. But he has a capacity for and demonstrates positive, affectionate feeling, while he has not so far shown anger at or directed towards someone. He does not get angry at you, he does not yell at you, he does not spontaneously hit. One would anticipate, therefore, that he would have difficulty understanding the connection of anger and object in another person.

—Benjamin had to be taught the gestures that typically accompany feelings of affection (hugs and kisses) and he had to be taught how to express the feelings to another (see chapters 24 and 25). In the case of anger, he again does not have the gestures (and would have to be taught them); he also does not seem to have, and/or have the inclination to express, the angry feelings with which they are associated.

—If Benjamin is to learn from my anger, I would first have to teach him to recognize that *he* is angry and that it is *at* someone (or something). The problem is that he does not seem to feel (get) angry, to begin with, and hence, the whole problem.

—When Benjamin does not get his own way, he has a (little) temper tantrum. This is his only "anger" but it does not have the quality of being angry at someone or something. It is not directed towards anyone. It seems to come about because he does not understand that there are other ways (besides his own) to have or do something. It is an expression of frustration at being thwarted in what seems to him to be the only way.

Note

1. I wonder, now, why I didn't just take away the blocks? It appears that I might have missed the obvious in spending too much time trying to "understand" it.

CHAPTER THIRTY-EIGHT

~

Parenting

Diary

June 17, 1974

The past two weeks I have noticed (school-related) improvement on perceptual-motor tasks. Language has hit another plateau, I think. It is higher than it had been, but there seems to be a drop in Benjamin's attempts at articulation. I think he must sense his failure here (that is, in articulation), though not on the building of vocabulary. The latter keeps moving.

He has the concept of a nest of cubes. He rearranges them himself, and self-corrects. It is not all there but the idea of smaller into bigger definitely is.

He paints in school. He has the right sequence—brush, held in right hand, paint.

Also, he has learned how to make a collage: take the picture, turn it over, paste, turn again, and pat down. He builds with blocks himself, constructions somewhat more interesting than a simple tower. He can construct an incline for cars to go on.

He is still mainly interested nowadays in throwing things, especially paper into the toilet, but we've started with the potty chair. He will sit on it, and if it's there to come, it will be made there. Also, he can be overheard to say, "No No!" when doing it in his diaper. He will also ask to go on the potty again, AFTER he has made in his diaper, and expects the ritual of being read to. He gets the book for me to read. He appreciates the "hooray" when there is success. But no evidence yet of his going to the potty himself before having to go. Perhaps, also, some resistance now to going on it—i.e., intentional holding back (which implies some control).

June 19, 1974

Re: programming versus allowing and "feeding into" spontaneous development: You *have* to "program." Partly this is because without the responses you teach, these children would fall further behind. But also: in their spontaneous development, they learn the "programmed" way, anyway. That is, in respecting the child's spontaneous development and keeping within the child's style, one could be following associative learning and conditioning anyway. Because that is the (only) way they learn.

Versus the normal child's way of learning from experience which is two-tiered, involving: 1) the basic "learning theory" method; and 2) the "comprehension" method, which is based on the match between the child's organization (structures) and the stimulus (assimilation). The retarded child can proceed to the comprehending match only (if at all), by virtue of the "altered input" system. But often, that still comes down to a programmed approach.

June 21, 1974

It is not appropriate to explain the child's demandingness by attributing it to "infantilizing" by the mother—i.e., the mother gives too much and hence, the child becomes spoiled and demanding. Rather, the demanding reflects (as does the behavior that precipitates the "infantilizing") the child's deficits. Lacking the ego structures for modulation and delay, there is an "all or none" quality to the expression of need and feelings. Apparently, the ability to experience or interpret gradations of feeling requires some resources unavailable to these children. They are demanding, not because they are given into too much (though they MAY [have to] be given into because they are so demanding) but because there seems to be no way to get them to experience and respond less dramatically. This may then get reinforced and continue. Thus, a primary, biological defect which affects the child's ability to interpret emotional factors or to modulate their expression (rather than the child's interpersonal history) results in the demandingness, which, of course, is then compounded and may be reinforced by the way it is responded to.

This being the case, if demandingness is to be reduced, there needs to be "altered input" to reduce the risk of the child feeling frustrated or deprived. However, at the same time, you need to deal with demandingness when it does appear in such a way as to effect modulation, through behavior modification techniques—i.e., reward and extinction processes—in the hope of approaching the type of modulation that, in the normal child, evolves spontaneously.

Demandingness and infantilization can evolve in a normal population out of a particular interaction history (as they may too, as secondary phenomena, in atypical populations). In a "normal" child, the ego structures necessary for modulation may not evolve because of a particular psychological history, etc. In contrast, in the MR population, it is more likely to reflect a biological base—the "ego structure" cannot or does not emerge, even when the developmental history deemed necessary for its emergence is present.

June 27, 1974

Benjamin continues to talk a great deal. He is always trying to say things, and there is the added difficulty now of understanding him, since he does not use consonants. He is saying many more words but (without consonants) they all sound alike! It is hard to know which of three to ten words a particular pattern of vowel sounds stands for. He is trying to round his mouth more—beginning to approximate lip movements a bit, like for B and P. That is, he does try to alter the vowel sound by changing the shape of the opening of his mouth.

He appears to comprehend gestures for "where is . . . ? and "show me . . ." He can point to facial features on request. He loved a "NiNi" ritual I introduced one night (saying "nighty-night," as in *Good-night Moon*, to various objects), and has since initiated it several times himself, saying NiNi to just about everything he can name.

The other night, it really did seem that he was trying to "make conversation" from his own head, although he was frustrated in not having the words or phrases he needed. He said *"No aha aha baby,"* as I prepared him for bed when he did not want to go. Definitely a spontaneously generated sentence, not one taught and learned as a sign of the event or just learned in association with an event and parroted at an appropriate time.

Comments

Seems like Benjamin is becoming a bit of a handful, a late-blooming "terrible two." Was it because I was being too laissez-faire? At this point, I decided, no, that's not it. At the same time, I acknowledged that waiting, watching, and respecting that which spontaneously evolved might not be enough. I had tried for some time to resist the zeitgeist of "training in" what was normal and desired. But, I concluded, even parenting that respects the child's developmental level and allows it to evolve also requires teaching. Normal children do not "just develop"—they mature in an environment that provides varying degrees of stimulation, information, structure, and teaching. Respect for and faith in the child's developmental potential does not preclude teaching contents and methods, as long as they are in keeping with his or her cognitive style and capacities, at that time.

In the case of the atypical child, too, one must certainly teach and program. Certain capacities, "ego structures," are necessary to form the bedrock for further development. Development will decelerate unless efforts are made to help the child develop them or compensate for their absence. For Benjamin, providing consistency, support, and repetition; encouraging imitation; teaching verbal labels; and creating situations of mastery helped create structures with which he could process and/or adapt to his experiences and helped develop feelings of agency and effectiveness that contributed to his sense of self.

In short, I concluded, there is room for, need for, both a developmental and a behavioral approach, and each must be finely tuned by consideration of the other. In the next chapter, we will see a need for even more fine-tuning than that.

At forty-five months, Benjamin is displaying, in certain realms, more executive function. His perceptual motor skills are developing and he is progressing in toileting. Best of all, at three months shy of four years old, he composes his first self-generated sentence! The three words, "No ahahaha baby!" culminate his progress thus far. Here is the sequence:

First, he imitated language in the context of an emotional "high" (in himself and in the interaction with another person);

Second, he used words ("ahahaha" baby) independently as an association to and label for an action;

Third, he began to see that words have function—i.e., to communicate;

Fourth, and, perhaps contemporaneously with the "third," he differentiated "ideas" (e.g., the Laundry Basket) and feelings within himself; and

Fifth, he found reason to communicate these feelings, in words, in order to assert himself.

In these entries, too, suddenly, finally, Benjamin is able to read some natural gestures. Was this learned (through, by now, years of experience) or has it just emerged, as programmed developmentally?

CHAPTER THIRTY-NINE

~

Predictability

Diary

July 4, 1974
Musings regarding the nature of autism had been recorded in the diary notebook on this date, and are omitted here.

August 5, 1974
Two weeks in Cape Cod with his father, sisters, Grandma and Grandpa, and Yvonne (father's girlfriend). While away, he apparently did very well. Came back, looking great. Very affectionate upon seeing me. Seemed to remember, and happy to return to, everything, But very attached to Anny, and *very concerned about comings and going, appearances* and disappearances. Did not like it at all if separated from Anny. Constantly talked about "no more"—i.e., his comment on the disappearance of things and on not wanting things. It seems he is working, constantly, on the question of changing persons in his life. Now in Vermont, there is a new group—Nana (grandmother), Morris (my boyfriend), me and the girls. The girls are the only constant and for the first few days, he could not tolerate their leaving, and their not being home. We had to help him a lot with getting their names straight and with their comings and goings. There was much emphasis on verbal "bye-bye," "come back soon," "who's home," "where is everyone," etc.

He manages to communicate a great deal just through NO, YES, MORE, NO MORE. These can be used to indicate: present or not present; want or don't want; stay or go away; continue or stop.

He can now say YES in answer to a question (HOORAY!) and indicate "more" and "no more." (Previously, all questions were answered NO.)

He announces "uh oh" for BM (and also pee, I think). He goes to the potty-chair and sometimes, he goes! He definitely is getting the sequence better now—i.e., 1) urge; 2) announce verbally; 3) go to bathroom; 4) go on potty chair. Sometimes, he gets 1–3, but not 4, until after the event; sometimes does only 1 and 2, and sometimes (still!!) step 1, followed by going in his diaper, and then step 2.

I worry about the fall (i.e., my going back to work). Will he remain so insecure about my coming and going and why shouldn't he? I really do think it was "wrong" for me to have left him for two weeks, at this age, when he could not comprehend that I would be coming back. Given all the shifts he has experienced of late, it shouldn't be easy for him to shake the fear that a separation may be another long one, and to be insecure about the stability and permanence of what he has.

He is happiest now in Vermont, when there is a routine. This is understandable, given all the recent changes. He loves the playground. He has made great progress in the last few days, by virtue of our going there regularly every day— e.g., from a fear of the rubber (u shaped) swing to getting on it and handling it well. He can do a great deal more than he is willing to acknowledge (e.g., on the slide and seesaw).

Answers "what your name?" Ninny!!!

Can point to himself, his chest, when asked, "Where's Nimmy?" [emphasis added]

Has sentences with the stems: "No more . . . ," "Bye bye . . . ," "More . . . (request)," and imitates "I want . . ." and "I like . . ."

In the fall, check out his tonsils which are very enlarged as to whether that has been interfering with the eating of solids with which there has been so little progress!!

I think I'm moving *away* from the conditioning approach (not that I ever was fully there) even though I keep it with the eating—but only because I know that he knows he is "being conditioned." That is, it's more like a bargain between us, a deal, and he understands the deal: if you eat this, then you'll get your ice cream. And since he likes rituals, routines, he accepts the arrangement. But for the rest, I cannot approach him that way.

August 18–19, 1974

Now calls "Mommy!" when he wants me and I'm in another room. (Is it a true calling me, or a learned signal?) Tried to say: "my toy" (mm toy).

Re: his adjustment to Vermont: that he never really did adjust became clear when we finally arrived back in N.Y. Here, he is completely comfortable, and my comings and goings from room to room mean nothing.

Has been sick, diarrhea. Still, after about two weeks during which he really said little else beside "no more (whatever)" and "toy!" he began to work more on sentences. He combines words to make possessives and makes lists of names plus a verb, or adjective—e.g., "Mommy tired. Nimmy tired, Lydia tired."

He's insistent, e.g., "toy toy toy toy toy," building up to a pitch, "milk, milk, milk." Impossible! At Morris' suggestion, we told him he *must* say: "Mommy, *I want* (whatever) . . . without the frenzied pitch. He does it as a ritual phrase, and he can substitute the nouns as needed, but I don't think he understands the "I want." He also now says, "thank you."

September 1, 1974

Back to the question of training: It seems to be the *only way* to help him adopt the habits he needs to know, because he learns that way. If you try the other approach (respond to his need) he is learning some other message, anyway. He LIKES the "training" of a habit. Because he catches on to the sequence fast, and this gives him the added sense of competence that he gets from knowing one more thing. It doesn't matter what it is. He learns and knows the sequence, not the meaning. The meaning is so far off, but meanwhile, he does have to learn to adapt to reality (even if he does not comprehend the why and wherefore of what he is doing). *"Meaning," for him, is just sequence and predictability. That is all he needs to know and wants to know.*

Comments

For the past four months or so, Benjamin has been developing a sense of himself. Here, he finally puts a verbal label on that. He is "Nimmy." "Nimmy" is someone with a great need for routine. I hypothesize that this is how he processes and makes sense of his world. "Meaning" for Benjamin is sequence and predictability. This kind of understanding substitutes for what he would otherwise know through empathy and intuition. "Understanding," for Benjamin, means learning the sequences and knowing what to expect.

"Yes" equals "I agree," etc. "Yes" therefore signals more self-awareness and communication than "no," which can be just an automatic, reflexive defense or rejection.

CHAPTER FORTY

~

"His 'I' Has Certainly Arrived"

Diary

September 28, 1974
Has become very talkative in the sense that he seems to want to use words to describe experience as well as to express demands. He wants to demonstrate, share, his (just beginning) knowledge and understanding about the world. So, for example: he will try to communicate: here is something, or I found this, that is familiar. It is mainly comparing or matching a present experience with a past one, and communicating this fact: that is, here is a new instance of something that I already know. But also, he is making some attempt to create a brand new description (!!). For example: I had a plant on a magazine he wanted. He said, "Mommy, flower toy" (i.e., the flower is on my toy).

At dinner, he yaps and yells as his way of joining in (though it actually interrupts) the dinner conversation. He cannot comprehend and communicate phrases unless they are parceled down to the words he knows as signals. You still cannot tell him a story. Nor expect him to answer questions about something. For example, if he is going to school, and you ask, "Where are you going? he can't answer correctly. He is likely to say "Hi Rocky" which is his association to "going." "Hi Rocky" is his "name" (word) for shopping at the store across the street where we will see the proprietor, Rocky, and say "Hi" to him. He named it that (i.e., the store, and the entire situation of going to the store), himself. When we leave the house, he will say "Hi Rocky" or, if he doesn't want to go there, "No more 'Hi Rocky.'"

Benjamin completely appreciates that he is expected to eat the "foul before the fair." If he sees the cookie, he knows he must eat the meal. He is possibly on the threshold of trying table food. His school apparently has pushed it and he's responding. He discovered cake, at a birthday party there, and now eats cake.

When Morris and I left to go out, and a baby sitter came, Benjamin pretended to cry—put on a fun show of it!!! Another episode of self-awareness and self-control. He can turn his behavior on and off on command. If I say (as a game), "Benjamin, be Happy!!!," he will "pretend" happiness. This is not just a learned trick (like "stay" "sit" "lie down" etc., to a dog). You can tell from his affect that he knows he is "pretending" himself.

He saw the 4 (for fourth floor) in the hallway. I stressed the F in four. He put his hand to his lips as if to help structure a word and said "or" with some indenting of the upper lip. According to his teacher, the day before he had had a session with the speech therapist, and that must have carried over. He is making some effort to use his mouth differently—can now kiss, with much more use of lips.

He is much better about good-bye rituals in general. Very able now to "conceptualize" my comings and goings. Witness the pretend crying: it was as if to say or demonstrate "this is a good-bye scene where I am supposed to be sad."

Calls the 4, an "A." Must have learned "A" from *Sesame Street.*

He has started to eat more neatly. He opens his mouth W-I-D-E (even this seems to demonstrate more consciousness of his mouth).

I think he has become more able to tolerate being yelled at. He's developing some understanding of anger and punishment, through repetition of and practice with the sequence. He knows that he has to stop crying when I say "No more crying." He is not as devastated by my being angry. He even now gets angry back. (!!) It almost always ends in a laugh, because it's very hard to be angry with him.

He so hopelessly has a "one track mind." It's wanting OUTSIDE and MOMMY, CAR and TV—the highlights of his life. Especially, OUTSIDE—anything out of the house is good.

He quite intentionally won't go on the potty, although he likes to sit there and be read to. But he resists going while on it. There is probably no point in trying. When he wants to, he will.

WHY DOES HE "CLAP" SO MUCH[1]—AND SEEM TO NEED TO— AND WHY DOES HE LIKE SPINNING HIMSELF? He does the clapping with his mouth open. Is it like an "assimilation" activity—like infants whose mouths open when they get excited upon seeing a new toy?

Is now willing, and likes, to play with play-do. This is new. He never was willing to touch it, before. He loves the play-do machine (plastic toy for squeezing out different shapes and strips). Calls it "A-D," as learned from TV. Sings various TV songs and likes certain programs.

Comments

There is a flurry of development, as Benjamin approaches and reaches four years old. He seems so much more a little boy with "a mind of his own." Now, he is using words to "tell" and describe—that is, to communicate from and about that "mind"—not just to signal need and desire. He tries to describe something *new*, something that is *his* own novel, special experience. Here is interest in communication. Here also is some awareness that he is one who thinks, does, experiences, and can talk. He can even "portray" himself. His "I" has certainly arrived (though, still with a difference—see next chapter).

Benjamin names a shopping experience "Hi Rocky," because that is what we say to the proprietor (Rocky), when we enter the store. In so doing, he did not ask or wait to be taught a word for store. Not yet able to parcel out the word "store" from mom's spontaneous comments, he instead made up his own word(s) for the experience. "Hi Rocky" means store.

Why did Benjamin "pretend" to cry when he learned that mommy was leaving? He was not crying simply as an automatic association to the situation. Rather he intentionally initiated the pretence, and did it for "fun," for everyone's enjoyment. Perhaps he was representing and enjoying his ability, now, to cope with the situation; he could master it! Or was he turning passivity (being left by mommy and crying in response) into activity, as a way of coping with it (i.e., "I'll cry when *I* want to, and be in control of it")? In any case, his behavior suggests: "See, this is what I *remember* and know how to do!" Neisser (1993) refers to this as the "temporally extended self."

Note

1. At thirty-six years old, Benjamin is *still* clapping—e.g., if excited while watching movement (on TV). And he has been doing it all these years!! If you saw Benjamin clapping at the waves at the beach, you would think he was a bizarre, regressed, nonverbal youngster. What a surprise you would have if you stopped to talk to him (except that, observing him clapping in his stereotyped way, one *wouldn't* stop to talk to him).

~

CHAPTER FORTY-ONE

Language and Self—Plus or Minus

Diary

September 1974
(Omitted here are thoughts regarding two preschool autistic children [observed at ARC], where I worked at the time.)

October 14, 1974
Benjamin is talking at a slightly higher level. He makes original two word sentences or original adjective noun or noun phrases:

- —oh-oh, light (or uh-oh TV, etc.) = light is off ("Uh-oh" is his word for all "not-right" conditions—e.g., spilled, broken, off when one wants on, etc.);
- —I like you, ice-cream; I like you, Mommy;
- —Light on; TV on;
- —"Nemo toy," for a small animal toy—(Nemo is for Skemo, a dog he knew in Vermont)

These "sentences" are different from "I want" in which the words, I and want, do not seem to be differentiated. Something gives me the impression that the distinction is getting stronger.

More than before, one now has the experience that Benjamin's expressive *ability* lags behind his expressive *intent*. He seems to have something to say but not to know how to say it. Often I can't understand him and that is upsetting because he already seems to sense inability and failure in not knowing how to express himself.

Benjamin has knowledge of his world and seems interested in labeling it. He is beginning to differentiate his inner feelings, as well, and responding to them, as is manifest, for example, in his "pretending" sadness, and fatigue (!) I think he does answer now, with understanding: are you *hungry*?? (Answer: No). That also indicates differentiation of inner experiences.

Benjamin uses "I" with verbs of feeling (want, don't want; like, don't like; love, hate; need, etc.). But he does not yet have words about action, and *plans*. Use of verbs of action and planning would reflect an "I" that is active and *activating* versus only reactive.

Benjamin's insistent, perseverative quality and the relative lack of ORIGI-NAL behavior still gives a sense of something missing in "selfhood" (as reflected in active, self-generated, *creative*, spontaneous behavior). If he were to speak in fully spontaneous language, with full use of "I," I would no longer see him that way (i.e., as still limited in selfhood).

Comments

Stern (1985) writes this about the "verbal self," which comes on the scene between fifteen and eighteen months: "With this new capacity for objectifying the self and coordinating different mental and actional schemas, infants have transcended immediate experience. They now have the psychic mechanisms and operations to share their interpersonal world knowledge and experience, as well as to work on it in imagination or reality" (p. 167). Benjamin, at age four, appears both to be at this level and not. He is, but with a difference.

Hobson (1990b) describes two aspects of self—a self/non-self distinction, and reflective self-awareness. Benjamin surely has the first by now. The second may be present (as manifest, e.g., in imitating oneself), but it is not yet verbally encoded.

CHAPTER FORTY-TWO

~

"M-E-E-E!"

Diary

October 17, 1974

With a candle as the reward, Benjamin ate a solid food, other than a cookie, directly (that is, not on a spoon), for the first time, He bit a banana, and ate half. He still choked eventually because he does not chew. Also, he tried really hard to blow out the candle, but couldn't—but a cough almost worked and he saw that!! Maybe it will carry through.

October 29, 1974

School reports he is eating more solids. Also, they are starting him in training pants. He intentionally won't make BM on potty. He talks *incessantly*, and it is very hard to understand him, because he has so many words that are all made out of two vowels (syllables without the consonants). He is attempting more now to introduce some lip variation (for consonants)—e.g., he'll bring his whole upper lip over teeth, but unfortunately, with little lip contact.

Now tells about recently *past* events—e.g., "man uh-oh"(= man fixed Lydia's broken door). Tells me about things not present, as when he told me to look in my room on my birthday (to find flowers.) Still can't answer questions, though, except with yes and no.

Very affectionate, and still very sensitive if yelled at.

He uses his limited schema to the hilt! Anything that can be assimilated into his concept repertoire is dealt with in that fashion. In this sense, his mind now is very ACTIVE—i.e., he seems always to be trying to fit his experience into an existing schema, to make sense of it. The more his schema can be differentiated, and increased in number, the better he will be. Here are his concepts:

uhoh = broken, not on, not right, etc.
no more = go away, where is it, it went away, take it away
I want
I like
Bye
Where are you (something missing, I'm waiting, etc.)

I have brought his attention to his clapping and whirling as a first step in stopping it. He can control it at will and turns it on mischievously if he knows I want it stopped.

November 7, 1974

Today, Nim played Wind-Wind Little Baby—on me! That is, he took my role and reversed his position. I think this is a first—although he has certainly imitated before and this is probably still close to imitation. Still, he hasn't done this: do back on me what has been done to him. I should try this more now, e.g., tell him to tickle me back, etc.

He is obsessed with triangles. He identifies them all over. He can draw a circle, and differentiates it from a triangle in that he at least, tries to make straight lines for a triangle.

It is very hard to understand him as he talks more and more. One really has to interpret the context because the words all sound the same without the consonants—e.g., Mommy, fix it; mommy, sit down—all sound the same; "er" equals Bert (on Sesame Street!)

Seems now to plan out and visualize and verbalize *before hand*, what he wants to do (e.g., while we are traveling home, he says "puzzle," in anticipation of doing it as soon as he gets home).

It is very clear that when he is able to match his schema with an environmental stimulus or demand, he is "with it" and active, and when not, he seems dazed and off focus. [emphasis added]

Very loveable.

November 16, 1974

He seems to be getting increasingly "alive," active, "normally" related—at least with me, and us (i.e., sisters) and in familiar surroundings. He is so precious now. He seems to have more solidity—a sense of what he can do and what he wants, and of having a control over the world. He is *manipulative with his affection and loving looks*. He knows when he is naughty and hides.

Little experimenter: He "experiments" with closing and opening the refrigerator door, likes watching the slow going away of the inside light as you close it. He watches pages slowly fall down as he slowly turns them. Closes all the doors.

He is actively doing these things, inventing them, as if, it seems to "figure them out."

I am so sure that I have done right by feeding his schema, whatever and wherever they are. And putting in "the aliment" in the right dose. But this makes him very attached to him (error! I meant: to *me*. But it's a Freudian slip, because it goes both ways!!) I truly "understand" him and he feels understood by and with me. It makes him feel comfortable and confident.

(*What is the quality and level in him that I am trying to describe? One of these days, why don't I write up all this stuff?*)

Eats all food (if fed) and peanut butter and jelly sandwich.

Lazy, most passive, re: chewing and eating. He doesn't seem to be hungry enough to want to feed himself, except cookies. He never sits down and hungrily finishes off a bowl of food (I must stop the cookies and milk, and see if that changes it).

Uses "Naughty boy," "Naughty Lydia," "Lydia crying," etc., all appropriately.

You can always stop a tantrum by feeding in some "zappy nutriment"—i.e., say something he really "understands."

When he doesn't understand something, he looks away (e.g., when I ask him to discriminate color and size together). He plays coy: he looks shyly away. He seems somehow aware of himself as an object of interest (!!) and he can control the other person through playing on that interest in him. The locus of control has shifted to himself. He plays Lotto and exuberantly yells "NE-E-E" (= "ME-E-E!") when I say, "who has . . . (whatever)" and he has it.

He seems closer to being able to answer questions. Maybe I'm sort of practicing him on that. He can answer them in the Yes and NO, but something is moving, I think.

It is time to practice use of "I," you and me. [emphasis added]

Comments

We are almost there! So many new leaps that now suggest both a firm "I" and a "me" (James 1890)—that is, a stronger executive function (contributing to the "I") and an awareness of self (the "me"). Here's what Benjamin can do, at just over four years of age:

—Reverse roles in baby games (e.g., Benjamin plays "wind-wind little baby" on me). This is where we began with the "trick," except now, it is Benjamin who sets it up. It's *his* idea. (It is true that he also did reverse roles with the toy on my head—but that was in the context of a game, already initiated by me. Here, Benjamin thinks this up entirely himself, remembers it, initiates it.)

—Anticipate a future event;

—Use words to represent a future event;

   (I had just commented, in the previous diary entry, on the absence of "planning." And now here it is. Indeed, throughout the diaries, I seem to comment on an absence of something, just on the threshold of its appearance.)

—Be aware of *himself* as an *object* of interest, and plays on that interest;

—Create novel sentences even regarding past events (it had looked like it would never be possible);

—Mischievously do forbidden things;

—Experiment with different ways of doing things (e.g., refrigerator door, pages of book);

—Is motivated (and tries) to do things that are difficult for him and beyond his capacity (i.e., motivation, and *coping with challenge* versus perseveration and ritual).

The emerging "I" is seen as well, in the stronger sense of the other—that is, of the other as one who also has an inner world that can be represented. Benjamin appears to have a sense that he is an "I" in your eyes as well as in his own (see Hobson 1993a).

There are still times, however (i.e., at the times of these entries), when Benjamin seems somewhat dazed, off focus, "thick." This is how I described him in the beginning. In these entries, it was generally happening when he was in unfamiliar surroundings, when none of his preferred and familiar objects and activities were available; and when, it seemed, there was no match or similarity between what was available to him at the present, and what he had known about and has done in the past. I must assume that he was dazed and unfocussed back then, as an infant, for the same reason—because there was no way he could make sense of his world, and feel a sense of centeredness and continuity within himself. Clearly, the new developments (at age four) reflect much more advanced cognition, and this has given him more and better tools with which to process his experience.

The book, then, has come full circle. Clearly, there is emerging now, *under the right conditions,* an active "little person," quite unlike the passive baby that we started with. Now, at four, Benjamin is finally like the older infant or young toddler who has a sense of himself, communicates and makes contact, has endearing baby ways, and reaches out to touch, take in and grapple with life. Well—almost. . . .

CHAPTER FORTY-THREE

~

The Difference

Diary

November 18, 1974

Benjamin is on a lower Piagetian level than his functioning suggests. This is either because a) he has different development in different spheres; b) there may be alternate routes to similar effects; or c) certain more *advanced* tasks can be performed simply through elaboration of less complex cognitive skills. Or for any of these reasons. It follows that he can do things and seem more "intelligent" than his actual developmental (Piagetian) level.

But it is just that fact that gives the current stuff that special quality—i.e., that makes it not the same as it appears in a normal child of similar mental age. That's what makes his language still appear to be at the earlier level of "signal" rather than symbol. I must look again at Inhelder's (1968) book. As I imagine she does, I would predict that, in defective children, Piagetian level and "mental age" as determined on a test of cognitive skills, would not match.

Sometimes Benjamin seems at one level and sometimes at another, on the same issue. Why is it that there seems to be a difference between the normal child and the retarded child, even when they are doing the same thing. Because of differences in the advancing development of other things? No . . . it has something to do with decalage phenomena—e.g., their verbal skills capitulate, have the same form as, early sensori-motor functions.

November 30, 1974

He is very active lately, even hyperactive. Can't stop playing, running. As long as he has the toys that he knows and the TV, he is organized and directed. He seems to have an overpowering need to have those things all the time, however—i.e., he is active, but he must have the environmental stimuli to express it and to

require and shape the activity (to the extent that they demand a specific response). He uses one toy after another, and his span is not very long for each because he finishes it, knows it, is bored with it, and needs something else.

In a certain sense, he needs new toys. But he will *always* need "new toys" so
to speak. The *internal* direction for shaping, planning for and "playing with" the
environment is missing (or weak), so he always needs the (external) structure
to "feed" him and keep him appropriate, active and focused. He craves the stimulation; he is happy with it. Without it, he is no longer inactive, but rather, rest-
less, cranky, disorganized, naughty, demanding. *He waits to be played with*, all the
time.

How can you keep supplying the toys (and personal contact), and still try to
encourage independence? Let him learn to play by himself? It is difficult because
he is so dependent upon the materials, to tell the direction, and he is also bored
by them. Bring him some new ones?

Comments

These remaining entries are important, to remind the writer and the reader
that, as always with Benjamin, things are the same (as normal)—but different.
Something is there that makes Benjamin "developmentally delayed" or "retarded." That something is the absence of some type of higher-level capacity
and potential, the absence of which has been manifest and has had implications
at all stages of development, from his earliest moments on.

At this point in the diary, it appeared that Benjamin would always need extra structure and specialized input, because his capacities for generating, organizing, and creating were limited. But those capacities are there to some extent,
and given the right structure and input, the "I" of the previous chapter could
emerge.

CHAPTER FORTY-FOUR

~

"A New Boy"

Diary

January 7, 1975

He has been, for about a month or so, a *"new boy"* [emphasis added]. That's what the teacher called him. His new quality is "playful" but it also means, less manageable. She also described him as doing LESS well in school, meaning his attention to the puzzles, etc., has waned, and he's now interested in big movements, getting around, being mischievous. He is both incredibly loveable (because very affectionate and coy) and a real problem. He has a one-track mind about certain things he wants—mainly, *throwing things into the toilet*—or coming out of bed at night. No amount of instilling fear and trembling in him seems to affect or change it. He is bored with most of his toys and regresses to stereotyped play with them—banging and dropping. Verbally, he is getting better and better. He definitely makes his own two-word sentences—and describes things, in an original way. His articulation remains very poor but he can be told "close your mouth" and he does manage to try a bit with encouragement to change the word.

He uses "ME! ME!" in the right way—and in a way that wasn't really taught to him. It started with that lotto game, "who has . . .?" and he would imitate the other players' "ME-E-E!" Now he uses it on his own—for "my" and "I" and in "I want." He'll say: "me-e! milk" "me-e! toy" with the same song quality of the "ME-E-E!" in lotto.

The other day he wanted me to stop playing the piano. He told me, "No more piano, no more playing." When he finally got me to get up to get him something, he said to the piano, "Bye piano, be right back!"

January 7, 1975

Today, I asked Anny: "What did Mommy buy?" Benjamin answered (!): "a new fish." I didn't think he would understand the question and also, the question was not asked immediately in the buying situation, but about 45 minutes later (i.e., after I had, indeed, bought a "new fish" for the aquarium).

Language comprehension and expressive language improving (see above).

Came and told me (!) "naughty shower" when the sink was overflowing and I didn't know it. This is spontaneous, functional, very communicative language.

He wrote over a picture of a duck that I had made for him, so that it messed up the picture, then said "crayon spilled," where "spilled" equals "mess."

January 28, 1975

I have tried lately to talk to Benjamin in a narrative—i.e., relay a list of events in sequence, describe past events, describe what happened; refer to future events, what will happen, etc. His reaction:

—I think he gets lost after one or two words;
—He associates only in terms of the present, or to the concrete aspect of the communication;
—His answers to questions reveal no comprehension;
—Yet his behavior, or his spontaneous remarks, indicate SOME understanding of what had been told to him.

For example, while waiting for the train, I told him the story: "First we'll take the train home, then go to Nimmy's house; then who is coming? Daddy's coming; then Daddy says 'Hi Nimmy!'"

If I ask him: "Who says 'Hi Nimmy' he answers: 'Hi Rockie.' If I ask, 'Who's coming?,' he responds "train." He doesn't know WHO but he does know "where." I could try to teach him "who," "what," etc.[1]

Comments

If I had another thirty years to write it, the next book about Benjamin would follow his language development. At age four, he has definitely achieved some level of language comprehension, representation, and a capacity to generate original language combinations. He is beginning to use language creatively (e.g., a "new fish"; "bye-bye piano") and to communicate with it about his experiences. The "Benjaminisms" in chapter 55 will give the reader a clear picture of how much further than this he eventually goes.

Benjamin's toilet compulsion is a sequence of behavior that cannot be moderated or stopped. It doesn't seem under control or self-directed. As Benjamin matures, he will develop a capacity to plan his day, follow through on it, solve new problems, use public transportation, find his way home, help a friend, learn to play the harp, vacuum for neighbors, and so on, and in general, he appears to plan, direct, and control his behavior (see part III). Yet he still, on occasion, will stuff the toilets with toilet paper, if unsupervised for too long. This has been, for years, an irresistible compulsion, likely to take over when he is alone, bored, overexcited, or anxious (usually anticipatory anxiety, as, for example, right before Christmas).

At this point, age four and four months, Benjamin knows he's a "ME-E-E!!" And he seems so happy about it. And so it has remained, to this day. Benjamin has great confidence in himself. He thinks he's great (or so it seems). Once, his stepfather said to him, "You know Benjamin, I love you." Benjamin replied, "Yeah . . . I know. . . . Who *wouldn't?*"

Note

1. I never did *teach* Benjamin "who," "what," etc. They came in by themselves. Or for that matter, I, you, and me came in (see chapter 42).

~

Diary Epilogue:
Taking Stock and a
Simple Paradigm

Intersubjectivity is a very robust phenomenon. In the normal child, it emerges and flowers with very little help, if any, in a wide range of "average expectable environments." Virtually all (biologically normal) infants grow into "little people," without anyone trying very hard to make sure that they do. However, in children with atypical development, intersubjectivity may be affected in different ways and to varying degrees, depending upon the nature and severity of the primary disability. Benjamin's story has been an example of the more arduous route to selfhood and intersubjectivity in one such a child.

In this epilogue, I attempt to summarize the material in the diary and highlight general themes that appear to run through it. In particular, I have tried to distill out from the diary account the steps in the progression from the very passive infant, described in the letter to Dr. Knobloch (in the appendix) to the initiating, communicating little boy who emerged by the end of the period covered by the diary.

Before doing so, however, it may be helpful to recap exactly what the phenomenon is that has been the focus of the diary entries—and what it is not. Intersubjectivity is the intention and capacity to "make contact" with the inner world of another person and the ability to understand, in turn, the intention and capacity of the other person to do so with oneself. It refers to spontaneous, self-initiated, reciprocal, two-way social interaction.

In the diary, and in the paradigm below, there is frequent mention of the capacity for perceiving similarities and making use of them in imitation. Matching and imitation are generally viewed as cornerstones of learning, with an important role in the transmission of culture. However, insofar as they appear to reflect and require an appreciation of the likeness between two people, matching and imitation have also been viewed as a cornerstone for "mind-reading," or empathy (i.e., the ability to "read" or grasp the thoughts and feelings of others as they are reflected in nonverbal cues). Specifically, it has been hypothesized that the observer matches the gestures and facial expressions of others with his own, and can then access the emotions and intentions typically associated with these expressions and gestures (see, e.g., Meltzoff 2005 and Iacaboni 2005). In this way, the observer can read, understand, and share the feelings of others. However, although the capacity for both imitation and empathy may be present by the time intersubjectivity is established, intersubjectivity is a step *beyond* imitation and empathy. While they may be necessary building blocks for intersubjectivity, neither imitation nor empathy is the equivalent of, or sufficient for, intersubjectivity. This is because intersubjectivity requires the added component of the *motivation* (or intention) to project this subjective understanding to another person and connect with the subjective experience of the other person, combined and tightly linked with the capacity to do so, through eye contact and a variety of nonverbal gestures and facial expressions. As a two-person, reciprocal phenomenon, it also requires a "receiver" who interprets the message and responds in kind.

Perhaps the point can best be made by imagining a robot that has been programmed to be activated by certain natural gestures or facial expressions that it is then programmed to imitate. The robot might even be programmed to identify or label the feelings associated with facial expressions and natural gestures. One can imagine a person as well who has these capacities, or who has been taught how to imitate actions or "read" facial expressions. I suppose that, conceivably, one could even fashion a robot with moveable facial features that might be programmed to respond in kind. However, the robot cannot *intend* to engage with the other person (or robot!) or *initiate* the exchange on its own (that is, without being programmed to do so) and it cannot desire and enjoy the subjective experience of making a connection with his partner. (Johnny 5 in the movie *Short Circuit* was the exception! He was the robot who became "alive"!) Similarly, I think we can teach individuals "what" to do (e.g., the "make eye contact" that young autistic children are admonished and taught) or what to say (as in the teaching of "social skills") to enable them to appear to be social beings, but the result will have a "wooden" robotic feeling if it is not imbued with a true and natural endowment of intersubjectivity.

Ironically, it has been argued that, unlike the robot, some autistic people do have the motivation and intention to communicate and to engage in reciprocal interaction but lack only the wherewithal to do so. The problem, then, is presumed to be not in social motivation but in the connection between the social intent, on the one hand, and, on the other, the availability or activation of the kinds of actions and expressions that must take place in order for others to be able to recognize it. Intersubjectivity, then, involves a strongly wired, ready connection between the motivation to project and share subjective experiences with another sentient being *and* the capacity to engage in the nonverbal cues required to do so.

In reviewing the diary material, I found four strong themes. These will be discussed in the chapters that follow in part II. The first theme is the important role that "effectance" played in the development of Benjamin's sense of self and self-awareness. The second is that Benjamin's deficits with respect to the recognition, matching, and imitation of affective expression and gesture posed a serious obstacle to the emergence of intersubjectivity. The third is the critical role that simplification, repetition, sequence, and routine played in getting the most out of the effectance/selfhood connection and in circumventing the obstacles to intersubjectivity. The fourth, in the title of the book, is about what needs to happen in the interaction of caregiver and child in the two-person job of fostering self and intersubjectivity.

In addition to these themes, it seemed to me that there were certain signposts firmly rooted throughout the story—developments that seemed critical for the emergence of self and intersubjectivity in Benjamin. They seemed to be the basic frame about which the house was eventually built, albeit with somewhat unusual materials, and over quite a long time. As a transition from the diary to the more theoretical chapters to follow, I made a list of them. As will be seen in part II, they are all familiar developments, identified by developmental theorists as important achievements in the first two years of life. The normal child effortlessly negotiates them. Benjamin had no trouble negotiating some of them; for others, he seemed to need our help. Eventually, however, they all had to be in place, whenever and by whatever means they could be brought into the picture.

The following "simple paradigm" summarizes and recapitulates these steps on the road towards intersubjectivity.

The Simple Paradigm

Step 1. Matching/Sharing
In the beginning, in normal development, the infant demonstrates shared affect and cross-modal responsivity. This suggests an innate mechanism by virtue of which the infant's expressivity is somehow "matched" to the expressiveness of another. This matching underlies a mutual affective attunement.[1] It is *not yet imbued with intentionality*.

Step 2. Intentionality (The Infant as "Doer")
Soon the infant begins to display agency (with objects) and efforts at mastery with his body. Random or instinctual movements give way to intentional actions. In intentionally "doing," the infant experiences "effectance"—the ability to make a difference by what he does and on that upon which he acts.

Step 3a. Joy in Effectance
Simultaneously, the infant "takes pleasure" in effectance. In normal infants, there appears to be an innate predisposition *to take great joy in the exercise of*

agency—that is, in making things happen, whether with their own bodies or with objects.

Step 3b. Sharing the Joy
Infants early on seek to *share their joy* with another. This is one of the first indicators of primary intersubjectivity.

Step 3c. Joy in Others' Enjoyment
Whether or not the tendency to enjoy effectance is innate, it certainly seems true that typical babies appear to be innately programmed to *thoroughly enjoy the enjoyment that others then take in them*. They will perform to get that response.

Step 4. Imitation
Now a "doer," the infant also observes others "doing." The perception of their "doing" is matched with his own movements and the intentions associated with them.[2] This provides a basis for imitation and also allows for understanding the intentions of the actions of others.

Step 5. Effecting a Change in the Other
Normal infants extend the *wonderful, enjoyable* exercise of effectance with objects and with their own bodies to *making things happen in and by another person*. They relish the experience of effecting action in others (e.g., throwing something down over and over again, to have parents pick it up). They also experiment with and learn how to affect the facial expression and affect of the other (e.g., they may tease or act coy.) They are *making things happen in the relationship* and experience themselves as controlling the show. It is when, in this way, the baby appears to be *intending to change the state of the other* that he or she really begins to take on a quality of *personhood*.

Step 6. The Baby as "Knower"
At this point, the baby appears to act in ways that suggest that he "knows" he can do things—*he knows he's a doer*. He seems to have ideas about what will happen if he does this or that, and about what he wants to happen. These are not verbally encoded thoughts, but a sense of a "self" as one who is able to anticipate events and initiate and choose what to do. The "knower" at this point is, at the very least, one who "knows" or acts as if he knows that he is an "intender."

Step 7. The Other as "Knower," Too
Next, the infant experiments with something that goes beyond the fun of doing something that makes the other change his or her actions or affect in a predictable way. In experiencing himself as a "knower," the stage is set for *the leap* involved in approaching the "other" as if he were a "knower," too. The other also has a "mind" that the infant has to work in different ways to affect. Now

the child will have to *appeal* to the "knower" (or "intender") within the other, to get the desired changes. He may also *show or point* to get her attention. This appears to be intentional communication, as if from one (independent) soul to another. This is true secondary intersubjectivity.[3]

In step 7, the child is again matching self to other (as was done first with affect, then with action potential). The match this time seems to be between "knowing" or intending minds. Typically, an object (or a third person, as object) is involved, as in behaviors such as requesting, giving, showing, or pointing. The behaviors still have some quality of imitation (e.g., giving is the same as getting in reverse, showing and pointing have been performed for the baby). However, in their coordination with eye contact, it appears that it is not so much the *object* that is shared as the *thoughts, feelings, and intentions* around it. This match is also more advanced, in that it involves not only recognition of similarity but recognition of a difference as well. Thus, *the other's inner world may not necessarily be the same as the baby's*. Just as he had before effected changes on objects, then on the other's observable affect and behavior, now the child has to effect a change on the other's *mind*—through requesting, showing, pointing, etc.

Step 8. "I Have Something to Tell You"
This is part and parcel of step 7. It is listed as separate to emphasize the coordination of steps 6 and 7 into *communication*. At this point, secondary intersubjectivity often involves verbally encoding that which the child wishes to show or *tell* to the other (see, e.g., the Laundry Basket, chapter 35).

The ways that the above steps did or did not appear in Benjamin, and what had to be done when they did not, will be reviewed in part II, in the context of discussions about the general development of self, intersubjectivity, and theory of mind. There will also be discussion about how different conditions could affect whether or not or how an infant or child negotiates each step. This, in turn, may allow one to tailor interventions to respond to the step that appears to be stifled and the conditions that may have put obstacles in its way. For example, if problems begin in step 1, because a child appears to have limited range of affective expression, one might become *vigilant for any subtle signs of changing affect* and attempt dramatically to *respond to or mirror it*. Or one might try to stimulate affect and change in affect, and then seize the moment to share it, by an exaggerated response. If the problem appeared to be in step 2, it may be appropriate to pattern certain actions, hand over hand. If the problem lies in step 3, one might join the child in the mastery behaviors, imitate them, model expressions of pleasure, and/or continually reward the child's mastery with an exaggerated response, all while also remaining vigilant to any signs at all of spontaneous expression of pleasure to which then to respond fully and happily. If the problem is in step 4—that is, in matching his agency with that of other—then work might be done in perceiving similarities in actions, and in learning or shaping imitation. (It is interesting in this regard that one of the very first steps in Lovaas' discrete trial approach [see chapter 7] is training the child to *match and imitate*.) And so on.

Notes

1. *Cradle of Thought* (Hobson 2002) is a vivid account of the emergence of intersubjectivity, language, and thought in the young child, which describes the transformation of this early affective mutuality in the parent–infant relationship into the capacity for thinking and communication.

2. This is hypothetical, an "as-if" model for some of the processes involved in imitation and, in any case, is not meant to imply that the infant consciously and intentionally engages in these processes. There is some neurophysiological support for the model (see Iacoboni 2005 for review).

3. These are the "protoimperative" (requests) and "protodeclarative" (showing) behaviors described by Bates (1971). Gomez, Sarria, and Tamarit (1993) argue that the first are more strictly instrumental in intent, while the second reflects an intrinsic motivation to gain the other's interest and attention, in and of themselves.

PART TWO

THEORY AND PRACTICE

~

CHAPTER FORTY-FIVE

Triple Your Pleasure

In the normal infant–caretaker relationship, mutual enjoyment can be seen as early as in the second and third months of life. Babies coo and crow, for example, and give rewarding smiles in response to mother's enthusiastic and adoring "mother-ese." In normal development, the infant appears to have an innate propensity to experience and interpret the caregiver's pleasure in him as something good and pleasurable; at the very least, the caregiver's expressions of pleasure perpetuate his responsiveness. Whatever the baby's subjective experience, it appears to the observer that the baby *enjoys being enjoyed.* Within the synchrony and attunement of the infant–caretaker interaction, the parent, for her part, has a readiness to enjoy this response from the child and demonstrate her pleasure in it.

At first, this mutual adoration does not appear to involve intentionality (on the part of the infant). However, the baby may soon differentiate his or her role in starting or perpetuating it. With intentionality comes what appears to be an innate inclination to feel pleasure in being *effective* (White, Kaban, and Attanucci 1979). One can imagine, therefore, that it must be especially pleasurable for the baby to experience himself as having done something himself to bring about the pleasurable experience of being enjoyed by another. At that moment, his pleasure in effectance is combined and magnified by his enjoyment in being enjoyed. At the same time, the intentionality involved in initiating these interactions bestows upon the child a quality of "personhood." This quality of personhood in the baby appears to be highly rewarding to the caregiver and may stimulate even greater affective responsiveness from her. In Benjamin's case, for example, the "trick" (of offering me his food; see chapter 3) bestowed upon him an aura of selfhood not seen before, and this resulted in my intense and positive emotional reaction in him. This in turn established a new connection, a relationship between us. Benjamin's ability "to make mommy smile," in fact, became a leitmotif in his development, from the time the "trick" was first learned, through to today.

The direction of the relationships amongst these "three pleasures"—in experiencing the pleasure that another takes in oneself; in mastery; and in feeling able to "effect" (bring about) the pleasure that another takes in oneself—may not always be clear. It did seem clear in Benjamin's case, however, that the first and third were experienced only for the first time, in the "trick" situation, when he was sixteen months old. The "trick" was the first time Benjamin was capable, by his own actions, of bringing about pleasure in another. His ensuing happy excitement suggested that he took pleasure in this; the fact that he subsequently, and repeatedly, initiated this action indicated that, in some sense, he had experienced himself as active and effective in the interaction. The "trick" thus revealed, for the first time, to mother and, it appeared, to Benjamin, too, that he had the capacity to *make a difference* in an interpersonal context; that he *enjoyed making a difference* in an interpersonal context; and that he enjoyed *being enjoyed* by another. It appeared to be a special "moment" in his life (Pine, 1985).[1] Once performed, the "trick" also seemed to establish for him a modus operandi that he used over and over again, to re-create a positive emotional experience—that is, to "make mommy smile."

Children with autistic disorders seem to be compromised from the start in all aspects of the above formulation. Although these children undoubtedly achieve mastery in relation to their bodies (they may, for example, have excellent balance and athletic ability), their affect typically does not reveal or suggest that they enjoy the experience. They either do not feel and/or are not able to express (communicate) their pleasure in it. As well, even if it were true that these children do experience pleasure in "effectance," they typically do not seek out an audience with whom to share it. Moreover, it appears that they often do not appreciate or at least do not respond to the pleasure of others in their accomplishments. Thus, for example, the affect or behavior of the young autistic child typically does not appear to be affected by praise. In short, the autistic child does not appear to have an intrinsic love for and feeling of pleasure in the other's pleasure in him (though there are exceptions). Or, if he does appreciate such responses, he does not appear to seek or anticipate them, and he is not able and/or likely to demonstrate or communicate his appreciation to those who are responding to him (Grossman, Carter, and Volkmar 1997; Sigman et al. 1986; Kasari, Sigman, and Baumgartner 1993).[2]

Even a pleasurable experience of mastery with things appears to be delayed or side-tracked in children with autism. Some autistic children appear to suffer from apraxias that limit their ability to engage in and experience mastery when asked to do something on command. And, at least from the perspective of the nonautistic person, the autistic child's engagement in repetitive, stereotypic, ritualistic, and/or nonfunctional use of materials (e.g., spinning wheels) appears to be devoid of any pleasure in mastery, although the child might seem to enjoy the sensory aspects of what is he doing.[3]

Benjamin's apparent pleasure in being the object of another person's pleasure and his subsequent efforts to bring this about might, in and of itself, rule out the diagnosis of autism (Grossman, Carter, and Volkmar 1997). On the other hand, it is also true that he had never demonstrated this interpersonal capacity before the occasion of the "trick," at sixteen months of age. Before then, Benjamin had appeared to be missing a repertoire of self-initiated behaviors, such as are typically exercised by normal infants in the second half of the first year of life, with the purpose of bringing about a desired response from another. In the "trick" situation, at least, the conditions and opportunity for one such behavior were created for him.

In the preceding paragraph, it is important to note the reference to self-initiation. Prior to learning the "hand-to-the-mouth-of-the-other" movement, Benjamin's spontaneous behavioral repertoire did not include *initiation* in a social context. Once having learned "the trick," however, he soon intentionally put it into play, to signal an interest in social interaction. This, then, was the first time Benjamin engaged in intentional communication. For some time thereafter, the "hand-to-the-mouth" movement, later abbreviated to a hand raised into the air, was Benjamin's sole means of bringing about, through self-initiated actions, a social response that was pleasing to him. It also seemed to provide him an opportunity, for the first time, to experience pleasure in being able to do so.

How does one understand the normal child's seemingly innate propensity to enjoy another's enjoyment of himself or herself? Where does this come from? The sharing of affect (i.e., the ability to read and respond in kind to affective expressions) has been described as innate and as the earliest form of communication (e.g., Hobson, Ouston, and Lee 1988; Hobson 1993b). The normal infant appears to be preprogrammed to mirror back affect. The normal baby also appears innately to "understand" the valence of emotional expressions (positive or negative). Therefore, the normal tendency to *enjoy* positive feedback may be, at least initially, an extension of the ability to share or empathize with affect. That is, at least at first, the child may only be mirroring and sharing in the pleasure displayed by the other.[4]

Dimberg, Thunberg, and Elmehend (2000) have found "mirror neurons" activated in the observer when the observer observes facial expressions by another. If "mirror neurons" are present in infants (this has not yet been determined), they would provide a plausible mechanism for the possibility and appearance of "shared affect" between baby and caregiver. In this case, by virtue of the apparently universal association of certain facial expressions with certain affects, the neuronal activity activated in the baby would connect up with the same emotions as were being expressed by the caregiver. How this develops into pleasure in being the object of the other's pleasure, however, is more of a mystery. Somehow, the infant goes beyond merely participating in and "empathizing" with the loving affect of "the other" and begins to appreciate and "empathize with" its direction and object as well. Somehow, as he matures, he seems to take pleasure in "knowing" that mommy is happy *about him*, and in being the one who is making her happy. This seems to be a step forward in intersubjectivity, one which involves awareness of the perspective of the other and a fitting of that perspective onto oneself (see Hobson 1990b and further discussion in chapter 3).

However it comes about, the baby does come to *enjoy being the subject of the pleasure of others*. This is matched by the caregiver's spontaneous inclination to feel good when her child seems happy in response to her and, perhaps even more so, to be warmed and excited when he *actively* seeks this reaction from her. Parents of atypically developing children, however, may be deprived of this experience of responding to their child in a way that pleases him and of having their child seek such a response. The baby does not seem "hard-wired" to be interested in and/or to know what to do with positive social interaction. The caregivers then must create situations in which there is opportunity for the child not only to experience the other as pleased (as created in the "trick" situation) but to learn to like and to want that positive response from the parent, in the first place—and then, to do things and feel pleasure in doing things that are effective in bringing it about.

This may seem a formidable or impossible task. Insofar as the absence of this element may be a core feature of autism, for example, it may be as impossible to train it into the autistic child as it is to take it away from a normal child. Still, several interventions have sought to "teach," build in, or stimulate the reinforcing value of a social response by pairing it with something that is intrinsically rewarding to the child (see Greenspan and Weider 1998 and Heflin and Simpson 1998 for a review). For example, in discrete trial interventions, tangible reinforcers are eventually replaced with verbal praise ("good job!") or "high fives" which the child appears to be conditioned to accept as a positive reward. On the other hand, there is growing evidence that children diagnosed autistic, earlier thought to be protectively armored against human contact, *do* have attachment needs which, in certain situations and with certain individuals, they will demonstrate quite reliably (Sigman et al. 1986). Certainly, clinically, we often observe some young autistic children able to respond positively and affectionately to the parent. Whether this can be extended (and if so, how) to the child's feeling pleasure in his attachment figure's pleasure in him, and to his doing things to earn that pleasure, is a question that deserves further exploration.

That prior to "the trick" Benjamin was not observed to initiate and engage in behaviors just because others took pleasure in him doing them may have been, in part, because, to begin with, he was so passive and did so little, actively, in which others *could* take pleasure! He had a responsive social smile, and in this sense he did "share affect," for he smiled when approached in a warm and positive way. However, there was virtually nothing that he did on his own initiative that seemed aimed at perpetuating that interaction, nothing that he did on his own initiative to "cross the interpersonal divide." In the "trick," this kind of behavior was modeled for him. Thereafter, however, he used a variation of the "the trick" on his own, as an invitation to another person to reinstate an experience of mutual pleasure. Though it was not a natural or conventional gesture, I was able, through knowing its history, to see in it the first inklings of intersubjectivity.

What would happen, however, if the individual did not seem to desire a positive emotional response, did not recognize a positive social response, and/or did not experience it as rewarding? What if he or she were unable to read, appreciate, and/or feel warmed by a positive social response? The possibility must be considered that these various reactions might not all be one and the same. That is, some individuals:

May be limited in the expressive behaviors (e.g., gestures, facial expressions, etc.) conventionally associated with emotions, yet still experience them (see chapter 21; also Travis and Sigman 1998, as described below);

May be able to "read" emotions in others, yet not appear to be "warmed" by them (Capps, Sigman, and Yirmiya 1995)—that is, not respond emotionally to them. In another scenario, an atypical child;

May be unable to read expressions of emotions in others, perhaps because he does not have similar emotions in his own repertoire with which to match them (see chapters 17, 25, and 27, and consider Benjamin's failure to understand the meaning and purpose of negative social responses).

With respect to the first possibility, consider individuals with Moebius syndrome (congenital facial diplegia). These individuals may not be able to smile or express the full range of emotions through facial expression. However, most still have and can convey feelings (e.g., through the eyes) and/or are able to interpret and respond appropriately to affective communication in others (Szajnberg 1994). As mentioned in the diary notes, however, autistic symptoms may be disproportionately represented amongst individuals with Moebius syndrome (Gillberg and Steffenburg 1989; Gillberg 1992). Besides suggesting possible neurobiological links between the two conditions, the finding raises the possibility of a relationship, in some instances, between the ability to express or communicate an affect, on the one hand, and the apparent ability to read and/or respond to it in others. Giannini et al. (1984) have this hypothesis regarding a Moebius patient found to be unable to perform on a task of interpretation of facial cues. One is reminded again of the "mirror neurons" and of how they are presumed to be implicated in shared emotion. The neuronal pattern for the expressive acts by oneself might be needed to mediate understanding of the expressive acts of others.

In Moebius syndrome, the emotions may exist but not the facial expressions with which to express them, and this may impair the ability to read facial expressions in others. Not actually having an emotion in one's own repertoire may also prevent one from perceiving it in another. This appeared to happen with Benjamin, as will be discussed in chapter 47. Calder et al. (2000) describe a similar situation in a stroke patient who lost the ability to feel disgust as well as to detect expressions of disgust in others. Conversely, Travis and Sigman (1998) found that autistic children may have an emotional reaction (as indicated by behavioral and heart rate changes), even though they do not respond to them in others. Their findings suggest that "neither lack of awareness nor aversion to emotional displays mediates the(ir) lack of emotional responsiveness" (p. 69). They conclude: "Thus, factors underlying lack of emotional responsiveness in children with autism remain to be discovered" (p. 69). Goldman (2005) wonders whether irregularities of the mirror neuron system may be implicated. Recently, a research team at the University of California, San Diego, under the direction of V. S. Ramachandran, has reported EEG findings suggestive of a dysfunctional mirror neuron system in individuals with autism (personal communication and in press, *Cognitive Brain Research*).

It summary, then, it may be necessary to consider all of the following possible explanations of an individual's apparent inability to appreciate or care about the positive reactions of others. He or she may:

Have the capacity to experience pleasure in this situation but not the wherewithal to express it;
Have the capacity to feel pleasure himself but be unable to read it in the behavior of others;
Not experience pleasure and therefore not be able to read it in the other;
Not experience pleasure and therefore not express it; and finally,
Not be "programmed" to feel pleasure in social interaction, in particular, and have no inclination to seek out and be motivated and reinforced by the pleasure of another.

Perhaps there are different subtypes of developmental disorders and/or different situations, or different points in development, for which different explanations or combinations of explanations may apply. In addition, the possibility should be considered that we may not be able to read the particular way in which an atypical child expresses his emotions. We might therefore interpret his emotion as absent just because we do not recognize it when it presents in an atypical way. We also may not know how to express ourselves in ways the atypical child will comprehend. Some autistic children, for example, do respond to praise. Perhaps so too would others if we found the way to express it that they could understand.

Notes

1. As mentioned in the diary comments, "moments," as described by Pine (1990), are emotionally charged events, involving the child's actions and the interactions with "the other" which they engender. Pine views "moments" as important in shaping the infant's emotional and cognitive development. The first time the infant engages in a self-directed, intentional act for the sole purpose of bringing about some change in the caregiver may create such a "moment." The "moment" will then have a positive or negative valence, depending upon the feelings evoked in the "other" and her manner of sharing them with the baby.

2. The failure to respond to the affective display of others is not limited, of course, to praise. Thus, it may not be that the child is impervious to praise, in particular, but rather that, in general, he tends not to acknowledge and/or interpret emotional responses in the other (see Travis and Sigman 1998, for review).

3. Some, however, may argue that they *do* involve mastery, if interpreted as the child's attempt to create and maintain an optimal level of stimulation (e.g., Gillingham 1995) or to master anxiety by creating order and predictability in the face of overwhelming or disorganizing experience (Park 1982, 2001).

4. At least in our Western culture, parents seem naturally to give, and are expected to give, an excited pleasure-filled response when the child has mastered something—a motor milestone, a particular play skill. It might be difficult, therefore, at first, to separate the child's apparently god-given pleasure in mastery from what appears to be his equally innate propensity to share in the pleasure experienced by those observing it.

~

CHAPTER FORTY-SIX

Development of Self

It was a challenge to decide the order in which to present chapters on self, intersubjectivity, and "theory of mind." In attempting to write about these three developments, each separately, the chapters kept stepping on each other's toes! As described in various theories, the developmental phenomena of self, intersubjectivity, and "theory of mind" are not sequential but rather overlap and draw from each other. As we shall see, many view "primary intersubjectivity" as the breeding ground for the development of self and for the sense of self in others. The "shared humanity" experienced in "primary intersubjectivity" is viewed as the "identification with the other" from which the sense of self evolves. Yet "secondary intersubjectivity," which pertains to comprehension and communication between two persons, seems to require, a priori, some sense of the separateness and selfhood in each. A chapter on selfhood then would rightly precede one on intersubjectivity. Theorists writing about "theory of mind" (i.e., understanding other minds) tend to view secondary intersubjectivity as "theory of mind" in its infancy (both literally and figuratively). But the child's ability to imagine the mental perspectives of others (about oneself) is then viewed as contributing to the sense of self!

I have chosen an order that essentially separates primary intersubjectivity from secondary and places selfhood somewhere in between. "Theory of mind" is viewed as a cognitive development that may require a sense of self and self in others, but not necessarily the communication that is the hallmark of secondary intersubjectivity. It will be discussed last.

In these three chapters, I will also discuss these concepts as they relate to each other, in normal development and in Benjamin's development, and raise questions about their presence and relationships in autism and other developmental disabilities.

⌣

The term "self" is freely used in everyday parlance, with apparent conviction that it refers to some very "real" phenomenon. The speaker presumes a shared understanding of its meaning, and feels no need to explain it. "I did it myself," self-confidence, self-esteem, "sense of self," self-directed, self-centered, self-awareness—are established parts of our everyday lexicon. Many children begin to say "I" and talk of "me" and "mine" by age two. They are not generally taught what the words mean. It does not seem that they sit back and reflect upon an experience that they then designate and refer to as "I" or "me."

Despite the ease with which we refer to it, and our apparent trust that it is meaningful and valid, the concept of "self" is elusive and difficult to define. The construct has been studied and debated by philosophers for centuries and many different points of view may be found amongst theorists, clinicians, and researchers regarding its meaning, phenomenology and ontogenesis (see Cicchetti and Beeghly 1990 and Hobson 1990b for reviews and Stechler and Kaplan 1980 for psychoanalytic conceptions of self). The Oxford dictionary has nearly six pages of definitions for "self." Moreover, while the concept of "self" is familiar, the experience of it is far less so. "Self" lies beneath the surface; we do not pay attention to it or become aware of something about it, except when the waters are disturbed. Indeed, it may be that we are most aware of "self" or "sense of self," in either ourselves or others, when it is absent (or appears to be so, as in some autistic children), when pathology affects it, or when we or others are feeling or appear to be "not ourselves."

Theoretical contributions regarding self almost invariably refer to the two aspects of selfhood described by James (1890)—the subjective, knowing, reflective "I" and the empirical or objective "me." The subjective "I" appears to have functions such as intending, perceiving, recognizing, knowing, experiencing, and comprehending. It is invisible. The "me" has attributes, which can be visible, and palpable. Perhaps "self" or "sense of self" lies somewhere between "I" and "me." In speaking about the emergence of a sense of self or "personhood" in a baby, for example, we refer to something over and above the baby's physical attributes that includes qualities that suggest to us that the baby is *intending* and *initiating*, *knowing* and *comprehending*. We perceive the baby as a little "person," executing such functions, with "a mind of his own." This self-motivated little being also soon behaves as if he "knows" he is a "person" in the eyes of others. He will, for example, "show off" and seek and appreciate praise.

Many writers point to the ubiquitous tendency of human beings to interpret the infant's gestures and facial expressions (including expressions in the eyes) in terms of the meanings associated with them in their own experience. This is the "flip-side" of the explanation given for the baby's sharing affect with the caregiver.

That is, in this instance, the parent "reads" the baby's affect, by virtue, once again, of the apparently universal and innate association of different emotions with certain behaviors and expressions (see Baldwin 1902; Eibl-Eibesfeldt 1979; Ekman 1973).[1] In this view, babies begin with the potential for the same emotions and feelings as those around them, and these are correctly interpreted as such by the observer. The baby enters the world as "one of us."

Others, however, view the inclination to read "personhood" into the infant's gestures and expressions as "anthropomorphizing" the infant. Newson (1978), for example, writes, "The desire to establish a degree of shared understanding with her baby is normally a powerful motive for the mother. She treats him from birth as a person who can be credited with feelings, desires, intentions, etc., and looks for confirmation that he will relate to her in a person-like way" (p. 37). Newson describes the mother as "automatically interpret(ing) (the baby's) facial expressions as reflections of inner states." The infant then learns to become "one of us" by virtue of the meanings that caretakers attribute to his or her random behavior and expressions, and the responses that these meanings then elicit from the caretaker (see Baldwin 1902; Cooley 1992; Mead 1935; Vygotsky 1978; Shotter 1978; Newson 1978; also see Cicchetti and Beeghly 1990 for review). This "sociogenic" point of view, then, at its extreme, places "selfhood" in the eye of the beholder, before and in order for it to become a part of the child.[2]

In truth, of course, the infant's subjective experience is not ours to know. One can only say that the behavior of the infant and preverbal child suggests this or that about his subjective experience. However, regardless of where the apparent "personhood" of the year-old child is believed to originate or reside, it is incontestable that, in the case of the normal infant, we observe in his behaviors and expressions something which is familiar to us, which we have no difficulty seeing and reading as similar to our own.

The situation with the atypical child may be very different. Given likely differences between the neuroanatomy and neurobiology of atypical children and our own, they may not be able to "read" our program and we may not be able to "read" theirs. The cues from the atypical child may be unfamiliar and difficult to interpret or empathize with (see Cicchetti and Schneider-Rosen 1984 for extended discussion; also Cicchetti and Sroufe 1976, 1978; Emde and Brown 1978). The expected cues may not be present. Upon observing atypical behaviors in the infant, and/or the absence of typical behaviors, we may not know whether the infant is having the kinds of inner experiences that would be signified by normal behavior. In any case, the stimulus for our own response repertoire does not exist, and we are left confused and unsure of what to do. In so doing, we may be withholding the feedback that may contribute to the emergence of selfhood. The early entries of the diary describe this experience.

Given that mutual recognition and interpretation of affect may have such a central role in self-development, one may wonder about children who cannot see the affective expression of others, or children who have limitations in their own ability to display affect. That is, what effect would congenital blindness in the infant have on the parent–infant interaction and the development of self? What affect would Moebius syndrome have on the ability of the parent to empathize with the "personhood" in her infant?

As described in my notes in the diary, Fraiberg (1977b) describes the faces of blind infants as less expressive than those of normal infants but attributed this to the fact that they did not have the faces of others to stimulate their own expressions. However, their faces were expressive when spoken to or touched by their mothers. With considerable effort, caretakers of blind infants could circumvent the limitations on visually based attunement, through intense contact with the baby through other sensory modalities. In Fraiberg's selected research sample, in which parents received a great deal of help, infant–parent dyads appeared to find ways to compensate for the barriers to empathy and intimate communication and make "the vital human connections" (p. 273). (See also Hobson, Lee, and Brown [1999], discussed below.)

Little has been written about the effects of the absent smile in Moebius syndrome on the infant–parent interaction, possibly because, in many cases, the syndrome severely affects other vital aspects of the child's functioning (e.g., swallowing, breathing, etc.) as well. As a result, it would be difficult to isolate the effects that reduced or absent facial expression may have on the parent–infant interaction, from those resulting from these other very serious complications (see, e.g., Horne and Horne 1999). However, Szajnberg (1994) refers to the "resilience and adaptability" of one six-month-old infant with Moebius and her parents in achieving "affective communication" and attachment, despite the extraordinary challenges: "alternate pathways may exist or be found that result in social-emotional competence" (p. 461). As mentioned earlier, there is some evidence that autism may be overrepresented amongst individuals with Moebius (Gillberg and Steffenburg 1989; Gillberg 1992). This leads one to wonder whether, in certain cases, a condition resembling autism may result because the Moebius condition affected personal relatedness in ways that could not be overcome. (This having been said, the majority of individuals with Moebius syndrome do develop normal capacities for relating, attesting again to the robust nature of intersubjectivity.)

Regardless of one's preferred theory of the development of self, there is likely to be agreement that the self does have to "develop"—that the infant is not born with it. Theories of the normal development of a sense of self tend to focus attention on the following interrelated topics:

differentiation (e.g., self from the external world, self from one's own actions, self from "the other");
internalization of affective and regulatory interactions in the caregiver-infant dyad;

selfhood and agency;

the interdependence of the development of a sense of the "self" and of "the other";

self and intersubjectivity; and

representation (of "self" and of "the other") as reflected in self-awareness and in awareness of the mental states of others.

Differentiation

Mahler's (1968) theory of (normal) self-development worked backwards from her observations of atypical children (Stern [1985] terms it a "pathomorphic" theory). The emphasis is on differentiation. Mahler believed that the so-called psychotic child had not emerged from an early matrix in which self and other were merged. This fusion was presumed to be present (in normal children), as well, in the first two months of life. Within it, Mahler ascribed feelings of "omnipotence" to the very young infant, by which was meant that the infant, unable to distinguish self from other, experiences his or her wishes or needs to be sufficient to make things happen.[3] There is therefore no appeal to the other and communication, as these would not be necessary and, in any case, given the fusion, would be, so to speak, mechanically impossible. Mahler presumed this experience of omnipotence to be typical in normal development in the early weeks during which the infant does not appear to engage in active, intentional behavior. The severely autistic child, she believed, lacked the ability to move on, or regressed back to, such a state.

In theories presuming an undifferentiated matrix, the newborn is viewed as not having a sense of his or her own boundaries—that is, an awareness of "the other" as a separate entity. Infant research, however, has revealed that even the newborn infant is able to differentiate between self and the rest of the world, by virtue (it is hypothesized) of innate properties of the perceptual and proprioceptive systems (e.g., Butterworth 1990; Neisser 1993; see also Hobson 1990b for review). Others describe a rudimentary self-system, which is developed beginning very early in life through experiences in the world. In this case, the "self" is that core of invariant internal sensations that is differentiated, distilled, and consolidated in the course of the infant's earliest interactions (both passive and active), with both animate and inanimate features of the external world (e.g., Escalona 1963; Werner and Kaplan 1963; Stern 1985). Thus, in addition to interpretation of affect and expression, development of a sense of self rests upon the (normal) infant's innate processing capacities (such as differentiation and synthesis) to allow for this "distillation" of a "core self."

Internalization of Affective and Regulatory Interactions in the Caretaker–Infant Dyad

At the same time as invariant internal sensations are distilled from and within the infant's interactions with the external world, comprising a "core" sense of self, the infant derives an internal set of expectations about interactions within the infant–caregiver dyad from the repeated, regular, and regulating responses of the caregiver to his feelings, needs, and behaviors. Several writers view these internalized expectations and patterns as an important part of the bedrock of the sense of self (see Sroufe 1990; Stern 1985; Sander 1975; Bowlby 1969).

Selfhood and Agency

Beyond the distillation of a "core" physical self that is both a constant and continuous, there lies development of a sense of oneself as an intentional agent, as a causal power (Stern 1985; Sroufe 1990). Selfhood has long been associated with agency and intentionality (e.g., Cooley 1992; James 1890; and "folk psychology"). It certainly appeared to be in Benjamin, as described in the previous chapter. Agency appears to contribute to the sense of an "I"—as one who does things. As we saw with Benjamin, agency also adds to the sense of the baby's "personhood" in the eyes of the beholder.

In Mahler's view, it is agency that contrasts with omnipotence and signals the emergence of self from the undifferentiated matrix of self and other. A sense of self appears when the infant "discovers" that he or she is capable of initiating and executing actions. (But this implies a "self" that makes the discovery! That is, "who" is the "he or she" who makes it? In describing the ontogenesis of "self," it seems hard to escape this infinite regress of homunculi!) As described by Sroufe (1990), with the emergence of agency, the infant plays a more active role in initiating, seeking, and maintaining infant–caregiver interactions that had earlier been laid down in his more passive participation in the dyadic relationship.

Several theorists believe that intentionality, too, evolves through a process of differentiation. Thus, for example, in Piaget's (1952) account of development, the sense of the self as a causal agent emerges gradually through differentiation from an earlier experience termed "efficacy." According to Piaget, "efficacy" is experienced only in the earliest weeks in life and involves lack of differentiation of the self from the consequences of one's actions. In efficacy (as compared to the later effectance or sense of agency) the very young infant appears to feel that his or her intentions alone cause the effects that occur as a result of the movements to which they give rise. (The concept therefore shares features in common with Mahler's notion of omnipotence.) Presumably, this occurs because the infant has not yet differentiated internal sensations associated with his or her wishes and intentions from the kinesthetic and proprioceptive feedback from the motor acts they have put into effect, and from perceptual experiences (visual, auditory, tactile) related to the consequences of these acts. In time, however, the infant will differentiate actions from consequences and intentions from actions, ushering in the "dawn of intentionality" between four and six months of age (Hunt 1961). A sense of self as an agent is an epiphenomenon of this differentiation.

(Parenthetically, it does not seem reasonable to talk about "wishes and intentions" during the presumed early period of undifferentiated efficacy, since the existence of wishes and intentions seems already to imply or require a "self" that has them [the homunculus, again]. It would appear that efficacy would be more closely aligned with random movements or instinctual behavior or drives [e.g., rooting or crying when hungry] during the first days and weeks of life.)

Intentionality is seen in the older infant's exploration and experimentation with objects. But it also extends into the relationship with others. As described in the previous chapter, the infant intentionally "does things" to produce a change in his caregiver. He also "knows how" to make it happen.

The Interdependence of the Development of Self and of Other

Several theorists write of the synchrony, parallels, and/or interdependence of the development of self and of "other." Hobson (1990b), for example, points out that one cannot perceive oneself as a person unless there is a concept of what a person is, and that, in turn, would be based upon the infant's observation of "the other." "For what does 'human' mean," writes Hobson, "if not defined by the perception of, and sharing in the 'humanness' in others?"

If one accepts the differentiation explanation of self-development, then development of a concept of "the other" would have to be contemporaneous with the emergence of a sense of self, since, by definition, differentiation leaves aside something "other" from which the experience in question has been separated. Along similar lines, Neisser (1993), based on Gibson's perceptual theory, writes that, in perceiving the "other," one "co-perceives" one's self.

While these hypotheses presume simultaneous development of the concept of self and other, less synchrony appears to be proposed with respect to the infant's capacity to experience his own agency and intentionality, on the one hand, and on the other, his or her appreciation of causal power in the other. Thus, for example, Piaget places agency in the infant at stage 4 (eight to twelve months) but awareness of causality in the other only much later, at stage 6 (eighteen to twenty-four months). Similarly, Wolf (1982), based upon his observations of a child between one and two years of age, describes the one-year-old as already appreciating her own ability to initiate action but as tending to use others as instruments, presumably because she did not yet perceive a shared "human-ness" between herself and "the other" (this seems doubtful!). Months later, according to Wolf, she perceived the other as an agent and actor equivalent to herself but not capable of planning and generating behavior independently. Only as the child approached two years, Wolf claims, was she able to appreciate that the other was an independent agent, with a mind of her own, who may or may not share the perspectives, perceptions, and motivations of the child. (Many, I think, would dispute the relatively late ages at which according to Wolf these developments take place.)[4]

Wolf's interpretation mirrors Mahler's inferences regarding the behavior of the psychotic children whom she classified as symbiotic. In contrast to the autistic children (who were presumed to have remained at or regressed to the zero-to-two-month level), these children presumably had begun the process of differentiating self and other but were resisting it and attempting to restore reunion. Mahler viewed these children as having intentions of their own but as still not able to experience "the other" as a separate agent, hence their use of the limbs of others as tools, and as an extension of themselves, to accomplish their own goals (as also reported by Kanner [1943]).

Little toddlers also occasionally move around the other to accomplish their own wishes and intentions (although Benjamin never did). In so doing they clearly have intentions of their own. Moving others around is an active, "self"-generated behavior that belies a sense of purpose and agency. That the child, in addition, is now aware that his intentions do not operate and are not shared by the other is apparent in his need and inclination to take the initiative to move the other about in the first place. Clearly, the person is an "other" for the child, and one that he trusts will do his bidding. What is not clear is whether, at this point, the child is also able to recognize that the other has mental states (including intentions) similar to his own. In contrast to Mahler's theory, however, Carpenter, Pennington, and Rogers (2003) recently demonstrated that even autistic children (mean age four years old) are able to recognize intentions in the minds of others.

Self and Intersubjectivity

To review, primary intersubjectivity refers to the affective, social "connectedness" seen in the early infant–caretaker relationship, a sharing of emotion and ability to respond to it in kind. The ability, on the part of both infant and caregiver, to understand the meaning of affect in each other is the first instance of a "shared humanity" and provides a "window" to each other's inner world (Hobson, 2002). Hobson views this affective relatedness as the first step in building a sense of self, since in it, the child matches himself to another person and experiences himself as like another person.

This rudimentary sense of self is further developed when the child shows signs of "secondary intersubjectivity." The baby appeals and communicates with another who is perceived as "one of his kind" as he is of theirs. In normal development, the rudimentary "match" between self and other is required for secondary intersubjectivity. Secondary intersubjectivity then goes beyond the "match" in that it involves an interest, motivation, and intention to connect with the other. Thus, at this stage of "connectedness," intentionality is also required.

In the case of autism, "selfhood" if often described as "decoupled" from communication or intersubjectivity. Hobson (1990b), for example, distinguishes between I–it relationships and I–thou relationships (see also Gopnik and Meltzoff

1997). In normal children, both exist, always appropriate to the nature of the object in the relationship (animate or inanimate). Hobson proposes that, even in the atypical development of autistic children, there has been differentiation of "I" and "it" and a capacity for I–it relationships. There is also recognition of the self as separate from other persons. The child may also be able to recognize himself in the mirror (Spiker and Ricks 1984). What appear to be missing, however, are *active efforts to communicate and engage with the personhood of the other* (i.e., indications of secondary intersubjectivity). Thus, these children may have a sense of themselves as separate agents, and possibly a sense of the other as agent as well, but have *no interest in, understanding of, and/or the requisite ability for communication between the two.*

In contrast, in normal development, self (as agent, as a causal center) and intersubjectivity, as communication, appear to emblazon one another and together yield a sense of "personhood" in the child. Stern (1985) sees agency as a component of the "core self," developed between two and five months, and intersubjectivity—manifest in the sharing of intentions, affective orientations, and meanings—as reflecting the emergence of the "subjective self" at seven to nine months. If, indeed, in the autistic child, "self" is experienced as a causal agent quite apart from action to engage with the personhood of the other, then, within Stern's model, in their self-development, autistic children would indeed be stuck, as Mahler had argued, in the earlier stages of infancy—that is, at the "core self" phase, before the emergence of (secondary) intersubjectivity.

To summarize, it would appear that a) a sense of the separateness of the self and of "the other" may emerge early in infancy, even in atypical children; and b) agency may contribute to selfhood in certain atypical children. However, in autism, despite having a sense of self and awareness of the separateness and agency of the other, the concomitant developments in intersubjectivity seen in the normal child (both primary and secondary) may not appear. The young autistic child may or may not display shared affect, and will likely not display secondary intersubjectivity.

Self-Awareness and Awareness of the Mental States of Others

Bruner and Feldman (1993) write: "There are good primatological, evolutionary and even better human ontogenetic grounds for accepting (Zajonc's 1980) view of an initial, pre-programmed primitive readiness for attributing mental states, and particularly, *agentivity*, to conspecifics" (p. 271, emphasis added). As mentioned above, Carpenter, Pennington, and Rogers (2003) recently demonstrated awareness of the intentions of others, in young children with autism as well. However, Kanner (1943) had described autistic children as "treating people as furniture" and as apparently oblivious to the humanity of others. Some theorists interpret such behavior as evidence that autistic individuals lack an understanding that others have an inner world of thoughts, beliefs, and wishes. The capacity for this understanding is referred as a "theory of mind" (TOM).

TOM theorists postulate that, in normal development, a child's awareness of the mental contents of other people's minds parallels his awareness of the contents of his own. Following the logic of this theory, then, the autistic child who lacks a theory of mind would perceive himself in like manner as he appears to perceive others—that is, as not intending, feeling, and aware, as perhaps inanimate and mechanical (as, e.g., in Bettleheim's [1967] description of "Joey"). Alternatively, it might be argued that, in autism, the expected parallels in representations of self and of other simply do not apply. In the latter case, the autistic child would have awareness of his own intentions and motivations but be "mind-blind" (Baron-Cohen 1985) with respect to the intentions and motivations in others. Several high-functioning autistic individuals appear to describe themselves in this way (e.g., Grandin 1995b). Citing recent theory of mind research, Povinelli (1993) also concludes that "autistic children provide an interesting test case to the idea that self-recognition can be *decoupled* from some but not all forms of mental attribution" (emphasis added)—that is, the attribution of intentions and beliefs to others as well as to the self.

According to Hobson (1990b), what is apparently missing in autistic children, is *"a sense of 'themselves' as potential objects of other people's evaluations."* This, in turn, according to Hobson (1990b) and others, impedes the development of self-awareness. This is because self-awareness is presumed to develop through first having a sense that *others* have a perspective on oneself—that is, that one is represented in the minds of others. Autistic children are viewed as unable to "reflect on themselves from the viewpoints of others." According to Hobson, this is in contrast to normal development in which, as described by Stern (1985), the "subjective self develops *pari passu* with—in effect, is defined by—the infant's evident regard for the subjective life of others."

Hobson (1993c) describes certain psychological handicaps in a young blind child (e.g., confusion in the comprehension and use of personal pronouns, and relative lack of reflective self-awareness) that are similar to those seen in many autistic children. He raised the possibility that congenital blindness may contribute, as does "autistic disturbance of affective contact," to atypical patterns of personal relatedness. These in turn would slow the development in the child of an understanding of the different perspectives of "the other." Some congenitally blind children, in fact, do present with an autistic-like syndrome. However, as mentioned earlier, in a more recent study, Hobson, Lee, and Brown (1999) found that the presentation of these children was somewhat different from those of sighted autistic children, specifically in retaining greater social-emotional responsiveness. Moreover, not all congenitally blind children present with autistic features.

As will be discussed in chapter 48, it would appear that theory of mind requires certain cognitive and language capacities, but that these are not necessarily required for communication, the capacity for which has already come to the fore well before these more advanced mental abilities.

Self-Development in Benjamin

How does Benjamin's development of self measure up against these presumed steps in his development of selfhood? Benjamin clearly was delayed in developing the "little person" quality of the year-old child. He was close to two when he first called attention to himself, close to three when he moved that chair in his grandmother's house (his first "own idea"), and nearly three when the "laundry basket" vignette took place, in which he appeared to have "a mind of his own" and to know it! However, in addition to delay, we will also see in descriptions of Benjamin in his later years (in part III) that his development of self was "same but different." Not necessarily autistic, but different.

The diary entries repeatedly refer to an apparent delay in Benjamin's ability to identify himself as "one of us" through a matching of affect and facial expression. His own range of affect and facial expression was limited, as was imitation. A turning point in his "selfhood" appeared to come on the heels of his developing an ability to match his face with others.

Thus, at the time that Benjamin first learned that he could do things to make others bestow upon him the affection and positive feelings that he so much enjoyed, he was not yet able to perform imitations which involved parts of his own body that he could not see (i.e., his face), an ability usually seen more than a year earlier in normal infants. However, he had learned that he could use his smile to be "cute." Close on the heels of "being cute" (for others to see), he developed the ability to imitate others' facial expressions. This seemed to be facilitated by efforts to help him imitate mouth movements, in the hope of promoting speech. At about two, Benjamin was finally able to match his mouth movements to mine, through their association to sounds he had been trying to make (see chapter 16). Once there, his newfound ability to imitate facial expression had the very interesting consequence that his own face became more expressive, with facial expressions that were more like those of a "typical" baby. As a result, I began to see more of the typical "little person" baby in him. He also then "becomes (even) more endearing." With his newfound ability to imitate my facial expressions, as in "sneaky eyes" (chapter 18), Benjamin now seemed to be "one of us."[5]

As described in chapters 13 and 14, using hand-over-hand techniques in baby games may have also played an important part in Benjamin's learning to see himself as "one of us" (see also Bruner 1974). The games were played repeatedly (over and over again, month after month after month, and year after year!). They became a part of his concept and experience of "the other." Hand-over-hand may have then led to the development within him of a proprioceptive template to match that experience of "the other."

Two vignettes in the diary, three weeks apart, nicely illustrate how inextricably the development of Benjamin's "selfhood" and "self-awareness" was tied up with "effectance" in an interpersonal context.

At twenty months, Benjamin "is practicing standing without holding on. He is completely turned on by his own greatness! (i.e., in standing alone). . . . He's ecstatic! He also crawls over to share (his success) with me. His sisters scream with excitement (that is happy pleasure) so now he's learned a special scream to go with the standing, a combination of calling attention to himself and expressing the glee." At this point, in the diary, Benjamin seems to be experiencing pleasure in mastery (in what he can do with his body) and pleasure in the happy response he receives from his sisters and from me (to whom he comes to share his success and get the positive reward of my pleasure in it, too). He intuitively appears to appreciate that his sisters' screams are something wonderful and a mirror of his own excitement at his triumph. He imitates these screams—and, according to my notes, I was quite convinced that this had the quality of "calling attention to himself" (or at least, of making sure he could bring about again, through his actions, something from us that pleased him). In this vignette, what seems important is Benjamin's extreme pleasure and excitement in mastery, and in *his doing something* that makes a change in us that he desires.

Just three weeks later, however, there is a further development in his sense of selfhood, wherein his sense of his "self" is now more independent of the response of others. The emphasis now is on the "he" who is making things happen. Here is the quote. "There is something new and good happening. . . . Benjamin is showing that HE wants something of ME . . . (in his appeal) he watches to see if what *he does will affect me*. . . . What is really different today is the look in his eyes that seems to me to express 'WOW!' I am aware of me, I am someone who does something, I am one who *waits to* see where it goes." In the diary, I added that the emphasis should be on the WOW!—that is, on Benjamin's pleasure in experiencing himself in this way. "I would swear he seemed to want me to know that he was onto something new and really digging it." In the first entry, Benjamin's pleasure is in the *doing* and in the response he gets from others; in the second, it is in the experience of himself as "the one who *does*."

It is interesting, then, that in this same chapter in the diary (i.e., at the same time), Benjamin is described, for the first time, as seeming to experience his limitations as a restriction (chapter 15). If a valid interpretation of his behavior, it would imply an "intelligence" somewhere that wished or intended more than it could achieve. This, again, would imply some sense of self and beginning self-awareness.

As we will see in part III, Benjamin, today, clearly is aware of himself (has a sense of himself) and is happy (very) with who he is. When we tease him, by imitating him to himself, he recognizes that it is him that we are imitating. He gets a kick out of that. He would not be able to imitate anyone, however. It would never occur to him to try to imitate someone. He has absolutely no acting ability. He cannot pretend he is someone else. If instructed to do so, he would say, "But I am *Benjamin!!!*"

Benjamin also seems to have little awareness or involvement in what others think about him. He is not "self-conscious." He does not do things out of concern about, or with an eye towards, what others will think. He has no sense of modesty (we have to teach him to care about nudity); he does not experience shame or embarrassment. (Once, when he came out from a bath with no clothes on, at his sister's house, she screamed "Benjamin! Put a towel on you!" He did— on his head!) He does, however, try to please others—that is, to *please* others, *not* change the way *they think about him.* That would not be necessary, anyway, because he simply *does not think about people thinking about him*, and if he did, he would certainly expect it to be positive. He has a very good concept of himself, and a concept of himself as good. Though he seems content with who he is, he is not vain, not "conceited." He recognizes the "bad guys" in movies and stories and knows that he is not like them. He harbors ill will toward no one, and does not appear to expect it from others. And indeed, he has always been viewed as a good person and treated that way. On the other hand, part of what makes people see him as a good person, and treat him so well, in the first place, may be his "selflessness"(!)—that is, his lack of competitiveness, envy, vanity, and self-aggrandizement (as more fully described in part III).

In the above description of Benjamin, it appears that now and in fact throughout his life, Benjamin has not "reflect(ed) on (himself) from the viewpoints of others." As described above, Hobson (2002) views this as a very important component of developing a sense of self, and as absent in individuals with autism, who do not seem to see themselves in the (other's) "mind's eye." However, one might salvage Hobson's thoughts on this matter—at least, somewhat—by considering what went into the initial development of a self in Benjamin that is both so positive and so "self-less." Those who have spent time with Benjamin, throughout his life, have mirrored back to him his own sweetness and gentleness. He has been treated with full acceptance—really really well!— throughout his life. People (continually) see him as a sunny soul who brightens their day. Many years ago, when Benjamin was a young child with a halo of blond curls, and years before he actually did take up the harp, a friend of ours, having met him for the first time, wrote back to us, after his visit: " Little Harpo still glows in my mind." That well sums up the effect he has always had on people. *Benjamin's nature has determined how others see him.* So perhaps he has integrated (back) into his own sense of himself, the image of him that is in their mind's eye.

Self and Autism

Benjamin was incredibly "loveable" in the years covered in the diary, in his sunny disposition and innocence. In his early infancy, however, the active "grasping" at the world which appears to be innate in the normal child appeared to be very weak, if there at all. It continued to be so throughout his first year and into the second. It was his relative absence of initiative and of active, self-directed "grasping" at the world that gave the impression that Benjamin lacked "personhood." As he got older, his lack of speech and language also contributed to the sense of a "missing person," as did the fact (even more so) that "words did not get through" to him. Delays in the capacity for imitation certainly slowed down the appearance of "personhood" well into his second year. In chapter 5 of the diary, I query whether Benjamin's oral-motor dyspraxias had contributed to his communication delays (see Prizant 1996). They may have. There were some advances in speech and language after his surgery.

A relative lack of spontaneity, initiative, self-direction, and pointed intentionality is not uncommon amongst children with mental retardation when compared to normal children with the same (test-based) "mental age" (see, e.g., Kopp 1990). Still, neither these children nor Benjamin appear to be blocked in communicating a sense of self. It just seems weak or very slow in developing.

Some of the issues discussed in this chapter suggest that this may not be the case with children with autism. That is, in autistic children, in contrast to typical children or children like Benjamin with delayed development, the ability to communicate and/or an interest in or understanding of the communication process does not appear to develop or emerge hand-in-hand with "selfhood" (this is the "decoupling" referred to earlier). The child may have a sense of self and other, which, however, he either is unable to communicate or lacks an interest or appreciation of the need to do so.

In this regard, it is interesting to consider the "hand-over-hand" technique typically used with autistic children. This may be conceived of as similar to, although in reverse, the autistic child's tendency to move the hand of the other to do what *he* (the child) wants. The autistic child, in moving the hand of the other, is presumed (e.g., by Wolf, Mahler) to have no understanding that the other has a concept of what he or she wants to do. That is, according to these authors, the child who uses the other as a "tool" does not appreciate that causality and choice exist in the other. Some persons using the hand-over-hand approach with the autistic child appear to make a similar inference regarding the inner world of the child. That is, they assume that the child's behavior has to be patterned in this way because he has no independent awareness of its purpose and no motivation and intention to pursue it.

Is this necessarily the case, however? Just the contrary is claimed by proponents of facilitated communication (FC). Use of the hand-over-hand technique in FC is based on the premise that the lack of an inner world in the autistic child, and the manifest absence of any interest in communication, is more apparent than real. It is a motor limitation, alone, that interferes with self-expression. In their view, autistic children have awareness, knowledge, and intentions that, because of motor-planning and initiation difficulties, they are unable to reveal. According to the FC formulation, hand-over-hand interventions assist the child in overcoming these difficulties.

Whether or not one feels comfortable with the way advocates of FC portray the inner world of autistic children, it is possible that, in some children, their apparent limitations in selfhood may be, at least in part, an artifact of their severe impairments in communication. That is, the possibility cannot be ruled out that in some atypical children, there may exist subjective experiences, including self-awareness, which cannot be made apparent to others (see also Cicchetti and Schneider-Rosen 1984). In very autistic individuals, one might then inquire, what would become of an "inner self" and, perhaps, the desire and intention to communicate about it to another, after years of being unable to reveal its existence (see also Lord 1993)?

Notes

1. This is so, apparently, in animals too (see Plooij 1978). Animals are also able to interpret the facial expressions, behaviors, vocalizations, and so on of their offspring. Once again, the recently discovered "mirror neurons" (in monkeys and humans) may provide the mechanism by virtue of which perception of emotional expression is immediately understood in terms of one's own emotions.

2. A similar point has been made with respect to the study of selfhood (and intersubjectivity) in animals (e.g., Moses 1994). We tend to look for, in animals, the indicators that, in humans, appear to reflect a sense of self and comprehension of the selfhood of the other. An amusing example of this was reported in a recent *L.A. Times* interview with Jean-Jacques Arnaud, the director of a film about two tiger cubs. Thirty tigers were used in making his film. Arnaud states that he detected a (different) personality in all the tigers. "I wasn't expecting the complexity in the tiger's expressions." He described the tiger cub stars of his film as "dignified and charming." One large male, however, was nicknamed Sean Connery. "He was a very good actor but his style was, OK, I've done my scene well, so I am not going to do it again. Too bad! Too late! Be as professional as I am!" But what if, in animals, there *are* differences either in their "selfhood" or in the manner in which it is revealed? (see also Cicchetti and Schneider-Rosen 1984 for similar point).

3. Stern (1985) challenges this formulation by pointing to the inevitable frustration that meets the infant's wishes and needs, so that the independence and substantiality of the "other" is very early imposed upon him. One may then wish to ask why, in Mahler's view, this does not happen in the autistic child. What explains the child's apparent inability to "learn from experience"?

4. Clearly, there are differences amongst observers of infants with respect to when they believe agency is experienced by the child and/or perceived by him to exist in others.

5. It should be mentioned, however, that Benjamin's range of facial expressions never fully matched that of a normal child. Moreover, if "sneaky eyes" did involve an *intentional use* of facial expression to have an affect on others, it was an isolated example of such behavior. To this day, Benjamin does not intentionally use facial expressions to communicate. That is not to say that one cannot read his feelings from his facial expressions. One can. Rather, he does not *intentionally use* facial expressions (e.g., raised eyebrows, or looking askance to express doubt) as nonverbal "gestures" to convey a particular point or attitude to another person. Also, to this day, he would not be particularly good at imitating facial expressions, although he does, of course, know where the features of his face are, and he would be able to *try* to imitate a facial expression, if asked to do so.

~

CHAPTER FORTY-SEVEN

Intersubjectivity

In the introduction to this book, intersubjectivity was described as an invisible bridging of the space between two people. This phenomenon first makes its appearance in fledgling form, as primary intersubjectivity, or what Stern (1985) refers to as "affective attunement." Primary intersubjectivity may be mediated by an apparently inborn understanding of the (universal) manifestations of affect, including, amongst others, facial expression, eye expression, voice quality, and gesture (Eibl-Eibesfeldt 1979; Ekman 1973). It then emerges or develops into full form (secondary intersubjectivity) in late infancy, at which point it is manifest in *intentional communication*, even without words, from one "mind" to another. Several theorists assign as a third stage, the development of "theory of mind," at about three or four years of age, which in turn evolves to even more sophisticated versions over the next few years. Various theories of autism place the core deficit in autism at different points in this developmental continuum, either in the primary and/or secondary phases of intersubjectivity or in the later developing "theory of mind."

Theory of mind (as, e.g., Baron-Cohen, Leslie, and Frith 1985), its relation to autism, and its "same but different" manifestations in Benjamin will be discussed in chapter 48. In this chapter, I will expand upon primary and secondary intersubjectivity (as described by Trevarthen 1979) in normal development. I'll then describe Benjamin's slow and somewhat atypical development in these realms, during his first four years. The chapter concludes with a discussion of the role of impairments in intersubjectivity in autism and other developmental disabilities.

Intersubjectivity in Normally Developing Infants

As described earlier, primary intersubjectivity involves an innate orientation and responsiveness, on the part of the infant, to multiple manifestations of affect and feeling, across a range of sensory modalities (Trevarthen and Hubley 1978; Hobson 1989; see also Stern 1985, Meltzoff and Moore 1977). Infant and caregiver respond, reciprocally, and in kind, to these cues from each other. As we have seen, Hobson, like Kanner (1943), views the capacity for this "affective relatedness" as the area of primary deficit in autism. In this view, its absence in autism compromises development of a sense of having a "self" that is like the "self" of others. This, in turn, precludes an understanding of and communication with other minds (as well as other cognitive achievements, as discussed further below). Thus, in Hobson's view, primary intersubjectivity is a necessary building block for both a sense of self and an understanding of other minds.[1]

As defined by Trevarthen and Hubley (1978), secondary intersubjectivity is "a *deliberately sought* sharing of experiences" (emphasis added), the focus of which is an object, event, or person outside of the dyad (although it can include, as well, a focus on a member of the dyad itself—e.g., something that he or she is doing). Secondary intersubjectivity begins in late infancy. The infant appears to seek out, appeal to, and address the "self" in the other. To the extent that the infant deliberately communicates and appears to have a sense of shared understanding with the other, he or she appears in some fashion to "know," or in any case behaves as if he or she knows, that within the other person there exists another soul, capable of understanding the meaning and intent of his or her behavior. A sense of selfhood in others, therefore, would be required for secondary intersubjectivity.

As also described earlier, secondary intersubjectivity is seen in the older infant's attempt to direct the other's attention to something through eye contact, combined with pointing, showing, vocalizing, or bringing; the baby's wish to perform with an eye on the audience (e.g., the initiating of coy or silly behavior to make others laugh); the infant's ability to share a point of reference with another (joint attention); and his or her beginning to engage in "social referencing" (e.g., checking on the other's reactions before acting). In a somewhat older child, secondary intersubjectivity is in evidence when the child appears to be "telling about something" to someone else.

Intersubjectivity must be differentiated from merely anticipating the behavior of another on the basis of learned associations. Thus, if a child is behaving in a certain way, simply because he has learned that the behavior in question will always elicit a certain desired response, his behavior would not involve intersubjectivity. Although the behavior pattern may *look* the same as one involving intersubjectivity, it would differ insofar as it was not based upon (and did not require) a presumption on the part of the child that the adult shared with him an understanding of the *meaning and intent* of his behavior (see Newson 1978). Certain animal behaviors which appear to take into account the intentions of others may, in fact, be based upon or reflect only a correct anticipation of the other's behavior, based on learned association (Savage-Rumbaugh 1986; Povinelli 1987).

Intersubjectivity is also quite different from attempting to influence the other simply by physically moving her to the place or in the manner desired. Although such action may communicate intent, it does not appear to involve an appreciation that the other person would understand that intent, if direct physical contact were not involved (see, e.g., Attwood, Frith, and Hermelin, 1988).

It must be emphasized that, although intersubjectivity tends to be defined in terms of observable behaviors, it actually refers to that which one *infers* from these behaviors, or that which one assumes must be there, to make the behaviors possible. That is why it is argued that instrumental animal behaviors must be differentiated from similar behaviors in babies. What is inferred is the invisible communication between the intending, thinking, perceiving minds of two people. It is also important to recognize the two components of intersubjectivity—on the one hand, the appreciation, in some way, that there *is* another "mind" with which to communicate, and, on the other, the interest and intention to communicate with that mind.

Most observers will agree that the (classically) autistic child appears to have no interest in this kind of communication, and/or *does not appear to understand that such communication is possible or necessary* (i.e., that it is something that could or should be done). As a consequence, efforts in both early diagnosis and early intervention for autistic disorders have focused on the developmental milestones in infancy (such as pointing, joint attention, and joint referencing) that indicate secondary intersubjectivity. The absence of these markers in infancy is considered diagnostic; in early intervention, the teaching of these behaviors is considered imperative.

It has been hypothesized that intersubjectivity is the breeding ground for symbolic thought (or meta-representation) in normal development (see, e.g., Werner and Kaplan, 1963; Hobson 1990a, 1993b, 2002). In this formulation, the experience of sharing attention to the same object or event involves or creates a rudimentary understanding that there is something in the mind of the other that stands for the object of attention. In this way, it sets the stage for or reflects representation—the ability to distinguish "thought" from "thing" (Hobson 1990a, 1993b, 2002).

Intersubjectivity in Benjamin's Development

The observations in the diary which pertain most directly to intersubjectivity as described above can be grouped in the following four categories:

1. innate understanding of affect;
2. innate capacity for communication;
3. intersubjectivity and imitation;
4. intersubjectivity and representation.

Various entries in the diary suggest that, in Benjamin's atypical development, there were significant limitations in his recognition of affect and sharing of affect. As well, there were atypical patterns in relation to his expression of affect, and in his use of natural gestures and ability to interpret them. There was also a significant delay in his identification of himself as "one of us," and consequently, it appeared, in imitation and communication. And there was an atypical sequence of intersubjectivity and representation. The result appears to have been, once again, the "same but different" quality to his intersubjectivity.

Innate Understanding of Affect.
1. If being *able to resonate with and respond in kind* to affect in others is innate, it surely lays the groundwork for understanding the other, since in so doing, one *matches* something in oneself with something in the other. Benjamin's repertoire of innate emotions appeared limited, however, and this may have contributed to his apparent limitations in perceiving and/or empathizing with a full range of affects in others. Thus, anger was a feeling which did not appear to be in his repertoire of emotions; in turn, he did not seem able to appreciate the meaning of negative emotions—specifically, anger—in others (see chapter 18; see also Calder et al. 2000). In contrast, Benjamin did understand and respond to positive feeling. He appeared able to respond in kind with the affect, albeit not with gestures. Thus,
2. Benjamin did not spontaneously generate the affect-related behaviors and gestures typically associated with certain feelings, behaviors (such as a kiss or hug) which seem universally to communicate those feelings. He eventually learned what to do, when it was "taught" as an association to the feeling. These actions seemed awkward, however. They did not appear to be a spontaneous and integral part of the feeling. Did Benjamin not have the emotion to begin with? Did he have the emotion but not the acts and facial expressions that reflect them? Or did he not have the ability to make the connection between the two? Cicchetti and Schneider-Rosen (1984) raise similar questions regarding the expression of affect in other children with developmental disabilities. Observations recorded in chapters 16 and 18 suggest that Benjamin most definitely did have the feelings, and the facial expressions that accompany them (although not a full range of expressiveness), but not the conventional gestures for them. He had to learn these behaviors and how to connect them to the feelings.

   The relevance of this issue to intersubjectivity is this: If natural gestures are not in one's own repertoire, can one interpret them in others? In Benjamin's case, the answer may have been yes, in terms of facial expressions and gestures related to positive emotion, but no, to gestures and facial expression of negative emotion.

3. Benjamin appeared unable to appreciate the relationship between the af-fect-related behaviors on the part of another person, and the actions on his part that had given rise to them, when the other person's affect-related be-haviors were reflections of emotions that seemed foreign to him. He could learn the temporal association of one with the other but not the meaning of the relationship of one to the other. Thus, he did not appear to under-stand that one was angry at him because of something that he did. At first blush, this would appear to require an ability to appreciate that one is the object of another's intentions, thoughts, and feelings, and to have some sense of what those intentions, thoughts, and feelings were—in other words, some "theory of mind." However, in Benjamin's case, the problem may have been more primary, in his not having a concept or template of "angry" of his own, to which to match and thereby understand that feeling in others. Without having had experience with that affect, he would also not have experienced the notion of its having an "object."

Innate Capacity for Communication.
4. Benjamin did not appear to understand the natural communication ges-tures of others (e.g., pointing).
5. In his first two years, Benjamin never pointed while sharing a focus of at-tention with another person, and pointing on his part was an extremely rare occurrence, even after age two. He first approached it, but it was not fully achieved, when, at age twenty months, he looked first at me, then positioned his arm in the direction of the ball he wanted me to retrieve. At twenty-eight months, he pointed for the first time, *and just that once,* in the context of a request. He did not, thereafter, point or have other natural communicative gestures in his repertoire. What gestures he used (and even those he uses today) were awkward approximations of natural gestures that he imitated, learned by association, or was taught. (This would include the idiosyncratic arm signal that he developed himself from the "trick.")

Neurophysiological factors (e.g., oral motor dyspraxia) appeared to compromise the progress of verbal communication. These may have been involved as well in Benjamin's limited use of gesture (see chapter 31).
6. Benjamin never did use others as an "extension of himself" (i.e., as de-scribed by Mahler [1968] in atypical children and by Wolf [1982] in nor-mal toddlers before the age of two), to communicate his wishes and in-tentions to others.

Intersubjectivity and Imitation.
7. As discussed in the previous chapter, a big boost to the development of self and intersubjectivity in Benjamin seemed to come from the very late

emergence of his ability to imitate, using parts of his body which he could not see. When, at age twenty-eight months, he could finally imitate the eye and facial expressions of others, it was easier for others to see him as a person "like themselves." This made it easier for others to relate to him, to connect with the "soul" within. At the same time, his own sense of himself seemed to be strengthened by our imitating him for himself to see. In turn, a stronger sense of self in Benjamin may have provided a stronger stimulus for others to try to engage with him.[2]

Intersubjectivity and Representation.

8. Typical babies intentionally communicate well before they begin to use words. As described in the diary, Benjamin did not demonstrate "appeal" until he was almost two and a half years old. ("Appeal" refers to a request specifically directed towards and communicated to another person, as opposed, for example, to just crying or complaining "into the air" as a signal for the other to respond.) At the time that "appeal" first tentatively emerged, he still had no imaginative play, did not interpret another's pointing, and was just beginning to have an understanding of words. Then, after a "static" month with illness, much repetitious rigid behavior, and no advances in language, examples of representation and symbolic function suddenly appeared. These included being able to "imitate" himself in pretend play. Thus, in Benjamin's case, manifestations of the representation came before or, at best, at the same time as, manifestation of secondary intersubjectivity (such as appeal), rather than after, as in typical development.

In summary, if there is an innate preprogrammed ability for affective relatedness (Kanner 1943; Trevarthen and Hubley 1978; Hobson 1990b) in normal development, it was at best weak and uneven in Benjamin, from the start. An innate propensity for imitation and communication also appeared absent, at first, and then weak and much delayed. He also did not demonstrate or appear to understand natural gestures, and he did not appear to have the repertoire of behaviors innately associated with specific affects. Benjamin had difficulty understanding emotions in the other that he himself did not experience, although he could perceive the other as an agent and (presumably) could match that to agency in himself.

Evidence of secondary intersubjectivity did not appear until Benjamin was two to three years old. It is also true, however, that certain tools for communication were significantly impaired (speech) or absent (natural gestures). It appeared that certain cognitive advances had to take place before communication would appear (see also Kopp 1990). In particular, a very tardy appearance of imitation and some development of representation appeared to be necessary to "scaffold" (Bruner and Sherwood 1983) the development of the weak or absent indicators of secondary intersubjectivity.

Benjamin, today, is very interested in telling and communicating (it is hard to keep him quiet). He is fully communicative, although he still has a speech defect and tends to leave out consonants. He will correct this if reminded. He understands the concept of imitation, and can try to imitate a motor act, but the result is generally incorrect with problems in directionality, *unless it is specifically embedded in a meaningful act that he can see himself doing*. For example, he still cannot comb his hair in the right direction, when the correct direction of the combing is modeled for him.[3] He can imitate words, and to some extent intonation, but, as mentioned earlier, he really cannot imitate (that is, mimic) the persona of another person. It is also interesting that, in a sense, to this day, Benjamin doesn't point. His verbal communication also lacks a quality of "pointing." Thus, he may start in the middle of a story, having no sense of the need, first, to introduce and orient the listener to the characters and events to which he refers.

Some Implications Regarding the
Primary Deficit in Autism

Autistic children are often described as having severe limitations in the ability to make sense of social cues. However, it is also frequently reported that an autistic child had developed normally until the age of eighteen months to two years. If so, these children would have displayed primary and perhaps secondary intersubjectivity at one time (see, e.g., Catherine Maurice's description of her infant in *Let Me Hear Your Voice*, 1993). The findings of studies that have attempted to verify these accounts (i.e., of normal development) through home movies have been inconsistent or inconclusive. Some differences in the behavior of children later diagnosed as autistic do appear to be present from the start (Adrien et al. 1991; Baranek 1999). However, eye contact and sharing of pleasure may be seen in the infancy of children who will no longer display these characteristics when they are later diagnosed autistic. This quality of affective connectedness in the first year may be what gives parents the impression that their child had been developing normally in early infancy. These observations would appear to conflict, however, with the supposition that an inability to read affect or to engage in affective interaction is the area of primary deficit in autism. At least in some children, this could only be the case if the autism were not present at all (or was remaining dormant) until the age at which it was noticed, at which point these capacities were then lost.

Some children appear to retain eye contact and some degree of shared affect even after the point at which they were diagnosed with autism (Goldfarb 1998). In my clinical work with young children with autism, however, it is my impression that, even when these children *do* engage in eye contact or appear to be sharing their pleasure, they are not (or at least do not appear to be) responding to the emotional communications (verbal or nonverbal, and including facial expression) *of the other person*. That is, while their (primary intersubjectivity) behaviors may reveal a rudimentary intent to share their own affective experience, they still appear to be "blind" to, uninterested in, and/or unable to respond to the meaning of communicative acts originating in "the other" (see also Attwood, Frith, and Hermelin 1988). It may be important then to separate the wish or ability to express oneself *to* others, from interest in or ability to read communications *from* others.

This distinction is perhaps seen in some of the writings about facilitated communication. As mentioned earlier, advocates of facilitated communication argue that autistic individuals do have an interest and desire to communicate, but they are unable to initiate and program the motor components of communication (Biklen 1990; Sellin 1995; also Prizant 1996). This is the impression conveyed in the purported writings of Birger Sellin, for example, a nonspeaking autistic young man who reportedly expressed himself in poetry, using facilitated communication. Asked how he felt about having a movie made about himself, Birger allegedly replied, through facilitated communication,

> The idea of quoting my so-called comments is something I think is very good, that way I could finally talk to people I so much want to be able to tell everyone how I feel inside my autistic walls. (p. 131)

In his poetry, this young man describes himself as suffering terribly from an inability to access, initiate, and/or carry out behaviors that would allow him to convey his thoughts to another person. Behind the absence of behaviors that indicate that "this is from me, directed to you" is an individual who would communicate conventionally if he could.

Purportedly, Mr. Sellin also wrote:

> For important reasons I think
> Total madness is easier than living boxed up in the mistaken
> isolation already mentioned I cant find out how come I have to
> live
> walled in like this
> I can think clearly inside my head and I can feel too
> But when I want to put the so-called simplest action into
> Breath-taking practice in these surroundings outside the
> crate
> I can't do it. (p. 138)

These two quotes, then, clearly reflect a wish to communicate *to* others, and anguish in not being able to do so. Mr. Sellin's poetry is replete with references to the torture and loneliness of not being able to communicate with and interact with the world. Given his situation, it is perhaps understandable that this should be the focus of much of his writing, rather than curiosity about what others may wish to communicate to him, or information about how he understands communications from others. Understandably, too, advocates of facilitative communication would stress that silent individuals with autism *do* have an inner world *and* that they *do* wish to share it with others, while speaking less about whether the silent individual is also able to know and/or is interested in knowing about the inner world of others. Perhaps, however (and this I imagine is what FC advocates would claim), this is because these individuals are not presumed to have any problems in comprehension—that is, in understanding others—rather, only in communicating their understanding to them.

The accounts of so-called "higher functioning," verbal individuals with autism also suggest that, in at least some autistic individuals, there may be a desire or intent to communicate and an understanding about the communication process. What appears to be missing is the knowledge of how to relate to others and the ability to interpret the social cues that are providing them with feedback about the appropriateness and relevance of what they are saying and doing. Individuals with "high functioning autism" have also reported feeling lonely and longing for friendship (e.g., Bauminger, Shulman, and Agam 2003). It appears that they understand, at least intellectually (how else?), the meaning of friendship and recognize that two people can share ideas and emotions. Reportedly, they may also *feel* the loneliness and the desire for social relationships. They may, however, have difficulty grasping the complexity and subtleties of social interactions and not have the "know how" to develop the satisfying social interactions they crave. As mentioned above, there may be, as well, an imbalance between interest in communicating their own thoughts and feelings, on the one hand, and interest in knowing about the thoughts and feelings of others, on the other. Hence the frequent reference to one-sided communication in higher functioning individuals with autistic disorders.

Especially given the rapidly expanding definition of autistic spectrum disorders, we may have to consider many different subtypes, each with deficits affecting different points in the developmental progression towards intersubjectivity and communication. An individual may have deficits affecting the interpretation of affect and natural gestures, interfering with primary intersubjectivity, the experience of "shared humanity," and the development of a sense of self and selfhood in others. Other individuals may have developed a sense of self and be able to understand the selfhood in others, yet have no *interest* in others, no wish to *share* experience with others, and/or no interest in that which *others may wish to share* with them. In still others, the ability to express oneself (rather than the motivation to communicate) may be impaired, or there may be impairments in the cognitive capacities required to make inferences and juggle perspectives. Based on a recent study with higher functioning children (mean age nine years old) with autism, Rieffe, Terwogt, and Stockmann (2000) claim children such as these do, in fact, have intact mind-reading capacities but that these capacities remain latent and unused in everyday social circumstances. The authors hypothesize that this is due to the stress inherent in dealing with their everyday lives. Reiffe et al. claim that the "mind-reading" abilities of higher functioning children with autism may be revealed under more "optimal" conditions (e.g., reduced stress and anxiety, and appropriate prompts).

In children without autism but with other developmental disabilities, neurodevelopmental quirks may also affect any step along the way to selfhood and intersubjectivity and affect the ways these phenomena are expressed, in dramatic or in subtle ways. For example, although somewhat deficient in understanding other minds (see part III), Benjamin experiences no loneliness at all. Because of his outgoing nature, he has, in his mind, many "friends." Many of these are not true friendships, because they are with chronological-age peers who are much "older" than he is in their interests and much more advanced in their cognitive level. These "friends," however, totally accommodate his wishes and needs and at the same time, appear to enjoy joining him in his childlike, stress-free (or so he perceives it) world, discussing or sharing in his various passions and obsessions (Herbie the Love Bug, bowling, vacuum cleaners, theme parks, to name a few). It is important to note that in these interactions, Benjamin is clearly communicating, initiating, and engaging in an intentional, enjoyable meeting of minds despite his apparent problems in taking the other's perspective (see part II) or, for that matter, expressing any interest in it. On the other hand, if he hears about someone in distress—for example, a friend or relative in the hospital—he will have genuine concern, and with incredible responsibility and independence call them daily to find out how they are and to offer his sympathy.

Conclusions

There is wide variability among atypically developing children. Children with diagnoses of autism vary widely, as do children with other developmental disabilities. Some theories of autism posit sequential, functional links between various psychological capacities (see chapter 48). Within such a framework, one may try to determine when, where, and why a problem took place in one system that has resulted in a later problem in another. However, development may not proceed in such a clear and logical fashion in atypical individuals. While deficits in one system may affect functioning in another, the developmental course of different systems may be off-track, independently of the malfunction in others. Or, as Goodman (1989) suggests, deficits may not be functionally related to one another but, rather, only appear together, due to some other primary cause—for example, because of an organic insult or systemic problem that has affected several different capacities simultaneously. Finally, while in normal development the emergence of one capacity may build upon, emerge from, and require another capacity, atypical neurodevelopmental structures and processes may have an impact on isolated capacities or on two or more unrelated capacities. The final outcome may be different in each case and include different types of problems in social relatedness.

Notes

1. See also Gallese (2002, 2005). A "shared space" develops through the mechanism of the "mirror neurons," insofar as these motor representations are innately and intimately linked to the same feelings and intentions in the observer as are being expressed through the gestures and expressions of the other person. Gallese also views the ensuing "like me" experience as the prerequisite for the apparent "mind-reading" in secondary intersubjectivity.

2. How do babies come to match parts of their bodies that they cannot see (e.g., facial features) with these same features in others? Heyes (2005) refers to facial expressions as "perceptually opaque acts." As stated earlier, Meltzoff claims that there is an innate "cross-modal" capacity to make this match, as seen as the purported ability of very young neonates to imitate tongue thrusts and other facial movements. If mirror neurons associated with facial features were found in neonates, they would provide a mechanism consistent with this proposal. However, this kind of imitation seems more or less "reflexive" and does not have earmarks of true imitation, which involves *selection* of the actions to be copied and the *intention* to copy them. In any case, automatic activation of imitation, such as might be predicted by the "motor neurons," would need to be inhibited, if one is to get on with one's life! Heyes, like Piaget, believes that, in true imitation, later in the first year of life, the understanding of the location of facial experiences is learned through experience, mediated by associations with other sensory experiences. For example, Benjamin might have been able to imitate the lip formation for an "m" sound, through mediation by the sound of the "m." He would have had to make the "m" sound spontaneously at some point. Then, hearing (and seeing) the "m" sound by another would activate the neural patterns associated with the actions (with his mouth) associated with that sound.

The question needs to be asked: Why does early imitation drop out and why does true imitation only come in towards the end of the first year of life? What inhibits imitation when it is not adaptive? Why do monkeys who do have "mirror neurons" engage in so little imitation, of either kind, or do so only with difficulty (see Jones 2005)?

3. See Iacaboni (2005) for neurophysiological studies related to *specular* (as in a mirror) imitation (e.g., moving the right hand to imitate the left) and anatomical imitation (e.g., moving the right hand to imitate a right hand); and Decety and Chaminade (2005) for the neurophysiology of imitation that incorporates appreciation of the *intention* of the act, versus imitation without integration of the intention. The important point here is that, despite his (continuing) limitations in imitation, Benjamin is capable of intersubjectivity—albeit with some differences (see part III). If matching and imitation play a role in mind-reading and intersubjectivity, Benjamin and other neuroatypical individuals likely use other means to the same or similar ends.

~

CHAPTER FORTY-EIGHT

"Theory of Mind"

"Theory of mind" pertains to the ability to appreciate that other people have motives, feelings, beliefs, and points of view and to recognize that this "inner world" in others is similar or equal to one's own. At the same time, it also refers to the recognition that the contents of the "inner world" (e.g., the perspectives) of others may be different from one's own. Appreciating this difference is a developmental step forward from sharing like affects and sharing the same focus of attention. Mitchell (1997) proposed that, in an evolutionary context, what came first was the ability to plan and then, for survival in a social unit, came the ability to recognize the existence of plans in others. "Theory of mind," then, involves the recognition that you and I have "thoughts" that influence the way we perceive and act upon the world and that these thoughts may differ from one person to another.

During the past two decades there has been ongoing friendly debate between those who proposed a primary cognitive basis and those who proposed a primary affective basis for the social and communication deficits in autism (see, e.g., Baron-Cohen 1988; Hobson 1989). As was described in the previous chapter, intersubjectivity—the connection and commerce between the "inner worlds'" of two people—appeared to emerge from, begin with, and require an innate comprehension of affect. Autism, it would be argued, is rooted in deficits in that capacity. The "cognitive" theory of autism attributes the autistic individual's problems in relating to an absent or profoundly impaired "theory of mind" (e.g., Baron-Cohen, Leslie, and Frith 1985; Baron-Cohen 1988). Individuals with autism are seen as not able to experience others as having motivations, feelings, and thoughts and/or as not able to infer or interpret the "inner world" of others from their words, actions, gestures, and facial expression. Baron-Cohen coined the term "mind-blind" to capture the nature of this deficit. Without the presumption that the other has a mind similar to one's own, it is argued, it would not occur to one to try to communicate; one would have no reason for or possibility of doing so. Hence, according to this conception of autism, the *communication* deficit in autistic individuals can be accounted for and is *secondary to* a deficit in *"theory of mind."*

"Theory of mind" (TOM) is typically demonstrated in the laboratory by setting up situations in which the subject must understand another's objectives and perspectives in order to respond correctly to the questions about the situation. One method is the "false belief" paradigm (Wimmer and Perner 1983; Baron-Cohen, Leslie, and Frith 1985). Situations are contrived (typically, with children as subjects) in which one child may be led to have a different (false) belief than another about an objective event. One child knows the correct version of reality because he has been privy to the manipulations which brought it about, while the other child would not have observed the manipulations and would therefore have no reason to alter his expectations about the situation. To demonstrate TOM, the child who had seen the manipulations must be able to attribute to the other child a belief about the situation that is different from his own. As defined in such laboratory tests, this "first order" TOM (false belief) capability appears to be established in normal children at around the age of four. "Second order" TOM (requiring the participant to infer one individual's thoughts about another individual's thoughts) usually emerges at six to seven years (Baron-Cohen 1988).

The diary entries included in this book end when Benjamin is age four, the age at which in a normal child, "theory of mind" (as assessed in the laboratory) is claimed to first emerge (although some studies place its appearance earlier, at age three). Benjamin, however, is developmentally delayed or "mentally retarded," so that one would not expect him to be able to demonstrate "theory of mind" at that point. Yet he did appear, by age four, to have achieved *secondary intersubjectivity*. That is, he seemed capable of communication, as if between like souls. Doesn't this call into question the presumed connection between "theory of mind" and communication?

One does not need these discrepancies between the theory and the nature of Benjamin's development to question the "theory of mind" theory of autism. There appear to be several problems with it. For one, communication and relatedness are clearly present in the normal child before the age of four, well before the meta-cognitive capabilities have developed which, as described in and defined by the laboratory tests, are required for TOM (see Grossman, Carter, and Volkmar [1997] for a fuller discussion of this issue; also Bruner and Feldman 1993; Lord 1993). Communication and relatedness, after all, are synonymous with the intersubjectivity that begins to appear as early as during the second part of the first year of life, if not before, and accomplished, as Newson (1978) describes, "without the help of formal language and without even a passive understanding of words as such" (p. 32). Communication appears to rest, not upon the cognitive developments required to pass the "theory of mind" tests, but upon some preverbal and nonverbal comprehension of the "minds" and emotions in others.

Proponents of the TOM theory of autism came to recognize that certain behaviors in infancy reflect an intersubjectivity that comes well before the meta-cognition exemplified in successful solving of the TOM problems in the laboratory. To maintain the thesis that TOM is the *primary* deficit in autism, they argued that indicators of intersubjectivity in infancy (e.g., joint attention, pointing, social referencing) reflect precursors of meta-cognition and TOM. Intersubjectivity and TOM, in effect, would be one and the same, or two points on the same continuum. Intersubjectivity, as observed in infants, would be part and parcel of an early manifestation of TOM (see, e.g., Mundy and Sigman 1989b).

This proposition, however, may beg the question. Intersubjectivity includes more than and goes beyond awareness or appreciation of the existence of mind in self and others, regardless of the source of that awareness (i.e., an affective connection or meta-cognition). We know about intersubjectivity through observable behaviors, and in particular, actions that demonstrate an interest in others and in communicating with them. In turn, communication between two "minds" involves initiating and/or maintaining the (invisible) connection between them. Thus, as stressed in the previous chapter, intersubjectivity involves and requires a *motivation* to share experiences and an appreciation of and *interest in* the *purpose* of communication. Although intentionality is not necessarily involved in the earliest expressions of shared affect or imitation, even in primary intersubjectivity, one experiences the infant as orientated towards maintaining the pleasurable connection, and his ability (e.g., through eye contact and repetition of sounds) to do so.

Clearly, some rudimentary appreciation of the mind of the others must be involved in acts of communication in infancy, since one does not see joint attention or social referencing in relation to inanimate objects. However, while this appreciation may be necessary for communication (and sets the stage for it), it is not sufficient. Individuals may still differ in whether they are drawn to communicate at all. Individuals with autism, then, while they may (or may not) have a problem in appreciating the perspectives of others and/or taking them into account, might also (or instead) have a more primary problem in relation to an innate interest in and/or intrinsic motivation for relating to and connecting with others. A deficit in either component would result in a failure to communicate. Individuals with autism may fail TOM tests because of impairments in the language and/or cognitive capacities required to understand and respond appropriately to them (Bowler and Briskman 2000). In turn, these cognitive and linguistic capabilities appear to be independent of and not a prerequisite for communication and relatedness (see Mitchell [1997], pp. 82–86, for discussion of this issue; also Bauminger and Kasari 1999; Mitchell and Isaacs 1994; Happe 1995b).

That difficulty in passing theory of mind tests is not specific to autism (Yirmiya et al. 1998, 1999) appears to support a "separate and not necessarily equal" notion of the cognitive, affective, and motivational components in communication. Thus, in contrast to individuals with autism, some developmentally delayed individuals might fail TOM tests but *still be related and communicative*. As you will see, it is possible to have a reciprocal conversation with Benjamin, with turn-taking and shared affect, in which he is able to talk about (what he assumes to be) the feelings and motives of others (see, e.g., the "getting the point" story in chapter 55, "Benjaminisms"); at the same time, he may be quite unable to answer questions about or articulate the perspective of another person (see, e.g., the Sears story in chapter 55) or take that other person's role (see the job interview story in chapter 55). He "knows" that people have minds, and therefore, that they are potential communication partners. However—and this varies quite a bit—he is (often, but not always) not nearly as good at knowing what they are thinking about and/or taking it into account.

That communication and interpersonal relating may require elements that are independent of the skills required to pass TOM tests is seen, as well, in the disappointing results of studies in which an attempt was made to improve the autistic child's communication skills, conversational ability, and sensitivity to others by teaching the child how to succeed in laboratory-based theory of minds tasks (Hadwin et al. 1997; also Ozonoff and Miller 1995). Along the same lines, Chin and Bernard-Opitz (2000) failed to find that efforts to improve conversation had an effect on TOM.

None of this is to argue that young autistic children are not deficient or delayed in the understanding and/or use or demonstration of conventional indicators of intersubjectivity (e.g., joint attention, pointing, social referencing, imitating). They clearly are, just as they may be in their performance on TOM laboratory tests (see Kasari et al. 1990; Mundy, Sigman, and Kasari 1993; Stone et al. 1997; Attwood, Frith, and Hermelin 1988). However, some atypical children do eventually develop these "indices," yet still do poorly on the more cognitively-based theory of mind tests. This in turn suggests that, whether or not intersubjectivity indicators in infancy are actually forerunners of theory of mind, they are not sufficient for passing tests of TOM in the laboratory. That some individuals with PDD who have atypical patterns of relatedness may nevertheless be able to *pass* at least some TOM tests (Hadwin et al. 1997; also Ozonoff and Miller 1995), suggests that relatedness may not be necessary, either.

TOM tests, in the laboratory, appear to have a cognitive/linguistic component involving the capacity to integrate and mentally manipulate information from several sources and perspectives, and to encode and articulate such integration verbally (see, e.g., Bowler and Briskman 2000). Understanding the language of the questions (an ability to get beyond a concrete understanding of the meaning of words and phrases) is also involved (Happe 1995b). Atypical children may be weak or deficient in basic *integrative capacities*, sophisticated versions of which are required for success on TOM tasks. In normal individuals, these cognitive abilities may initially develop concomitantly with, and in interaction with an understanding of emotion and social cues (Buitelaar and van der Wees 1997; Cicchetti and Schneider-Rosen 1984; also Hobson 2002). In autistic individuals, however, there may be less or no integration of the two domains, so that TOM tests may be passed, or failed, on cognitive/linguistic grounds alone.

To summarize, the TOM theory of autism attempts to explain the language, relatedness, and communication deficits of autism as a consequence of limitations in the meta-cognition required for awareness of one's mental states and for understanding and taking into account the mental perspectives of others. However, phenomena associated with relatedness and communication appear much earlier than the age of 4, the age at which TOM theorists claim that children develop this "metac-ognition." They also take place earlier than the end of the sensori-motor period (18 months to 2 years), the time at which representation is presumed to be first achieved. Intersubjectivity is observed in normal infants by the second half of the first year of life and often much before. That infants and young children clearly communicate with others, as one soul to another, and even develop language, well before the age of 4 would appear to pose a significant problem for the TOM (meta-cognition) theory of autism (see also Lord 1993 for critique of the TOM theory of autism).

The intangible, pre-verbal connections of primary and secondary intersubjectivity cross and bridge the (psychological) space between two people well *before* the infant has any "cognitive" or verbal recognition of the perspectives of others. The phenomenon of "crossing the interpersonal divide" may be unique to humans (though some will argue it is present to some extent in higher apes [see Povinelli 1996]). It appears to require an innately determined "hard-wired" ability to understand the meaning of the actions and/or affects of others, combined with an innate propensity to *make good use* of that understanding. Autistic individuals, whether or not they have the ability to interpret the affects and behaviors of others, appear either not able or not oriented to making good use of that understanding in relating with others. Higher functioning individuals with autism, however, may use cognitive powers to interpret social cues that are effortlessly understood by others without cognitive mediation (Happe 2001).

Benjamin's Theory of Mind

Benjamin, today, often starts a conversation in the middle of a narrative, not providing adequate information to provide the listener with the context for his remarks, and uses pronouns to refer to characters in his story who have not yet been introduced to the listener. He often interrupts, or introduces a topic into a conversation that is *a non sequitur* (although just as often, he tries very hard to find something to say that *does* relate to the matter at hand). He generally does not think ahead to take into account what others might think. This means I often am worrying about what he is doing or where he is because it would not occur to him to let me know. However, through practice, insistence, and training, he now knows that he is supposed to call. Though he is *highly* social, related, and communicative, he is weak in his capacities for abstraction, symbolism, and imaginative play, capacities that tend to be weak as well in individuals with autism. As mentioned earlier, he literally *never* initiates imaginative play and even would have trouble playing a part if told what to say. This is because he is so literal, that he will simply find it impossible to "be" someone that he isn't. He only half understands teasing and joking, so that he is never quite sure whether or not to believe someone who is teasing him, and even when he is sure they are, it is difficult for him to disregard what they are saying. Every Christmas, e.g., we tease him with phone calls to Santa Claus—he pleads with us not to tell Santa about this or that transgression, even as he laughs at our antics. Yet, correctly anticipating how you will react, he may carefully word his request to get the answer he wants, or lie to protect himself. *And he often will surprise you with an incredibly keen understanding of what others may be thinking or feeling.*

In part III, you will find a host of examples of Benjamin's real difficulty grappling with situations in which he is asked to imagine or take into account *the perspective of the other*. All of these examples, however, are revealed *in the context of a conversation with him* in which he clearly is willing and able to "tell" his listener about something—and even insists upon it. These examples suggest that, in developmental disabilities other than autism, thinking may be concrete, and the cognitive capacities required for pragmatic skills and for passing theory of mind tests may be weak or lacking, just as they are in autism. But the non-cognitive aspects of intersubjectivity and relatedness, while they may be delayed and atypical, may still be alive, either less profoundly impaired or affected differently than in autistic disorders. The source or cause of the more profound and different social impairments in autism, and of different variations of them, remain to be determined. Deficit functioning in "theory of mind" may be an outgrowth and reflection of these same causes, but is not likely, itself, to be the primary source of failures of intersubjectivity and communication. The core of the ability to communicate seems to lie deeper within.

What, Then, Is the Primary Deficit in Autistic Disorders?

As mentioned in the introduction to this book, there are *many* different theories about the primary deficit in autism. They include, *amongst others*, the meta-cognitive deficit proposed by Baron-Cohen, Leslie, and Frith (1985); failures in "executive function" (e.g., Ozonoff 1995), "central coherence" (Frith 1989), or motor planning (Biklen 1990); cerebellar abnormalities that affect the capacity to shift attention (Courchesne, Townsend, Akshoomoff et al. 1994); failure of "psychological birth" or "defensive encapsulation" to protect against awareness of a precocious separation from a maternal figure (e.g., Tustin 1981); and processing problems leading to withdrawal in the face of overwhelming sensory bombardment from stimulation which cannot be adequately screened, filtered, or understood (Bemporad, Ratey, and O'Driscoll 1987; Gillingham 1995, 2000). If differentiation of self from other is a prerequisite for intersubjectivity, and if self-development, in turn, requires, or emerges as a result of integration of information from multiple sources (see chapter 2), then limitations in the capacity to integrate information from multiple sources might be the "primary" area of deficit in autism.

In the theory of mind theory of autism, a deficit in meta-cognition results in absent or impaired communication. In Hobson's (2002) theory, affective connectedness precedes and makes possible the development of self and self-other distinction, which in turn allows for infant-caregiver interactions from which evolve symbolic functioning, language, and thought. These then are theories that propose *sequential* causal relationships between various psychological functions.[1] In contrast, Goodman (1989) proposes that there may be multiple "primary" deficits in autistic disorders that are *independent*, rather than causally related to each other (that is, the existence of one does not necessarily explain the appearance of the other). Thus far, in our inquiry, we can identify as the areas of primary deficit: affective relatedness; communication; and integrative or processing capabilities. While these may interact, and contribute to or exacerbate one another, they may have independent sources. These three, of course, match well the triad of deficits, first formulated by Wing and Gould in 1979, and incorporated in the DSM diagnostic criteria. (Integration and processing deficits would relate to impairments in abstract thinking, symbolic function, breadth of interests, etc.)

Autistic disorders may occur when there is a failure of *integration* of psychological systems, whether or not there is, in addition, some impairment within one or another of the systems. In this scenario, phenomena such as "theory of mind" which, in normal individuals, may occur in the context of a smooth integration of cognition and intersubjectivity, may either not occur in individuals with autistic disorders, or do so, in a somewhat different fashion, because of the deficits in or barriers to the integration and co-ordination of different systems. The "same but different" quality in cognitive and relatedness phenomena in developmental disorders (including autistic spectrum disorders) would arise because one or another system must operate, in relative isolation of the other, and in an effort to compensate for the absence of the other. Along these lines, Baron-Cohen has recently proposed that "empathy" can involve both a cognitive ("theory of mind") and an affective component. While in some instances of empathy, one or the other will suffice, in others, the two processes must be concomitant or overlap, in varying degrees. This model allows that, in certain situations, understanding between people will need to draw simultaneously upon both a cognitive ("theory of mind") and affective component (Baron-Cohen and Wheelwright 2004).

Note

1. Hobson (1990b) acknowledges that one cannot prove the causal links, although he strongly suspects them. In his most recent book, *Cradle of Thought* (Hobson 2002), however, he passionately maintains this position and gives a vivid account of how mental representation and symbolism may herald back to parent–infant affective attunement in infancy.

∽

CHAPTER FORTY-NINE

Increments and Leaps

Theories of development are of interest to educators and rehabilitation workers because they provide a framework within which to devise strategies to facilitate and to consolidate development or to "set it right" when it has gone awry. Strategies of education or remediation tend to reflect a theory regarding the way in which the individual is presumed to learn. For example, the behavioral approach to improving a child's adaptation appears consistent with Skinnerian learning theory. The child will learn through the consistent associations and consequences given to his words and actions by the external world. In a Piagetian scheme, on the other hand, the child's skills and understanding of the world will develop only through experiences which match and can be integrated by the child's own particular type of internal "structure" at that time. This means one must teach in a particular way at a particular time, and that no amount of teaching will work if the child's mind is not ready (i.e., at the right level) to receive it (see Cowan 1978).

Theories of development tend to fall at or somewhere between the two poles of nativism (i.e., development follows an innately programmed sequence), on the one hand, and sociogenesis (environmental and social factors influence and are required for the emergence of developmental phenomena), on the other (see Cowan 1978). However, while theories may lean more or less in either direction, most theorists today acknowledge, either implicitly or explicitly, the interaction and cofunctioning of innate and environmental influences in determining the course of development (Richards 1978). This is the case even in the more extreme positions. Thus, for example, in Vygotsky's sociogenetic view, social experiences give meaning to what initially may be meaningless actions or utterances on the part of the infant (Vygotsky 1978). The infant internalizes the meanings implied by the way significant others respond to her and ultimately develops into a more active, organized individual, with a sense of herself as able to initiate and control interactions with others. However, that babies do learn from social experiences in a "sociogenetic way" would have to be part of their "hard wiring." That language and a subjective "I" can be forged through social experience (Vygotsky 1986) would indicate that there is some programming, intrinsic to human babies, that allows these particular effects to take place. They do not appear to happen in other species. Primates, for example, do not attain the human child's level of linguistic, symbolic, and cognitive competence, even when raised as children in human families.

Although Piaget postulates universal, inevitable stages of development, his theory is quintessentially an interactionist model that weighs in both the nativist and empirical points of view. On the one hand, the Piagetian infant is innately organized to accomplish adaptation, through the processes of assimilation and accommodation. On the other hand, new and successive cognitive and behavioral systems develop when these processes act upon appropriate "aliment" from the environment. Aliment is appropriate when it matches the child's existing capacity for processing and integrating information.

Any developmental theory must address the relative uniformity of (normal) development, in terms of the rate and sequence of changes, throughout the life cycle. This is somewhat easier for those on the nature versus nurture side of the argument. That is, if development were merely a function of experience, or deeply dependent upon it, how would one account for the relative universality of the nature and order of developmental progress, and the vigorous survival of that order under a wide range of environmental conditions? On the other hand, development in at least some domains may be facilitated or impeded, as a function of the nature of environmental input (Skoyles 1999; Buss et al. 1998). And extremely adverse or extremely facilitative environments may affect the appearance, timing, rate, and degree of developments assumed to be maturational in nature and even, some claim, the neurological structures underlying them (Carrey et al. 1995; O'Leary, Schlagger, and Tuttle, 1994).

Developmental theories on both sides of the fence must also grapple with the relatively sudden appearance of *qualitatively different* modes of processing experience. Does one acknowledge qualitative "leaps" as well as increments in development, and if so, how does one explain their emergence? To a certain extent, although not entirely, a focus on increments may be associated with social learning theory (one just keeps learning more and more, and generalizes and applies one's learning to more and more situations), while "leaps" or stages may be associated with a more nativist position (i.e., new developmental phenomena "kick in" at genetically preprogrammed points in a maturational sequence, when the proper neurological/biological conditions take place).

In Piaget's theory, the qualitative leaps signal universal developmental stages. The evolution of these new structures is the inevitable product of the interaction of the inborn invariants of organization and adaptation, on the one hand, and appropriate aliment, on the other. New structures, once formed, introduce new and different ways of processing experience, leading once again to new structures (i.e., qualitatively different ways of making sense of experience). Piaget does not refer to maturation per se as contributing to this development. But neo-Piagetians recognize that maturational changes affecting neuronal development and appearing according to a prewired timetable must have a significant effect on how the child processes and integrates experience and thus may contribute to the emergence of qualitative leaps (Case 1996a and b; Pascal-Leone, 1988). These maturational changes may, for example, increase the speed of processing and the number of sources of information that can be attended to and integrated at any one time. Similarly, Gopnick and Meltzoff (1997) refer to the "leaps" as new "theories" of how the world works, held by the child who is viewed as a mini-scientist. The likelihood of coming to a new theory rests on exposure to what are presumed to be fairly uniform experiences in life, interacting with maturational advances in memory, attention span, and so on.

The infant's capacity to imitate that which he cannot see on himself seems to be one of the remarkable, inexplicable "leaps" in infant development. It does not appear to emerge as a linear function of practice and repetition. According to Meltzoff, infants have this ability virtually at birth, in relation to a limited range of facial expressions (see review of this research in Meltzoff 2005). This presumably reflects what Harris (2005) terms "an innate dictionary" of equivalencies between facial gestures in self and others. However, this neonatal "imitation" soon disappears. Imitation of parts of the body that cannot be seen does not then appear until late in the first year of life. How does one explain its sudden emergence, and at about the same time in the development of most babies?

Meltzoff explains neonatal imitation in terms of an innate cross-modal resonance but seems to assume some contribution, as well, of inference and intentionality on the part of the infant. This view is disputed by others (see Anisfeld 2005; Heyes 2005). Piaget also did not consider the earlier imitation a true imitation in that it did not involve intentionality. He attributed early imitation to "primary circular reactions" mediated by experience-based associations. However, when it reappears, there is no question that imitation of parts that cannot be seen involves intentionality. Is it now based on *experientially based* associations? Or is the early "innate dictionary" still involved?

Perhaps, in normal development, the earlier cross-modal matching does not so much drop out as remain silent (or inhibited) until it becomes somehow connected and integrated later on with the child's intentionality and agency. The earlier, more reflexive vision-to-motor loop might prove nonadaptive and "in the way," as the baby matures and is increasingly involved in intentional behavior. True imitation, however, may still require the early, innate matching capacity, except that at this later point, it must connect with intentionality. Either without the other will not work to produce a true imitation. Thus, all the intention in the world will not produce an imitation, if there is no system capable of registering the stimulus (visual) and matching it an action potential in the observer. On the other hand, the cross-modal matching without intention will not produce true imitation.

In the diary, we saw how difficult it was for Benjamin, at twenty-one months, to "imitate" my placing a toy on my head, even with many opportunities to observe it. Imitation of eye movements (in "sneaky eyes") suddenly emerged and seemed to develop at twenty-three months of age, without any obvious attempt on our parts to teach it to him. However, in Benjamin's case, I interpreted this as possibly based more on experiential factors than on an innate matching capacity, since the latter still seemed quite limited, if not absent, in him (see comments at end of chapter 18). If so, this would illustrate my impression that different theories of development (in this case, a Piagetian one) may better explain the *compensatory* ways that the atypical child learns than the spontaneous developmental progress of a normal child.

I am awed by the leaps, as anyone might be who watches a baby acquire, from one day to the next, more and more mature characteristics in the first months and years of life. Even with Benjamin's slow motion development, I could not see them coming. I have come across no adequate way to explain them. Perhaps leaps come about through increments, as a result of maturation, in the capacity for integration, where integration refers to the taking into account and cross-referencing of information from varied and multiple sources. In children with cognitive disabilities, these innate processing capacities may be weak. If, on the other hand, developmental leaps are fully preprogrammed, after all, the program may be entirely missing or dysfunctional in children with developmental disabilities. In either case, are there strategies that will help to compensate for the weakness, promote integration, or create the missing structures?

Instead of intrinsic motivation, activity, and curiosity in his infancy, there was passivity in Benjamin's early months. Instead of the steady and fast slope in the first year of the infant's life, development in Benjamin's case was slow and characterized by lengthy plateaus. Leaps were few and far between. The plateaus, it seemed, might never have changed course, were it not for efforts at different times either 1) to feed just the right-size chunk of experience as needed to stimulate existing "schema," and allow assimilation/accommodation and development to take place (see Hunt 1961 re: "optimal mismatch") or 2) to impart meaning, and to teach and train in certain developmental milestones. Both notions of how the normal infant develops seemed useful in helping Benjamin move along. Whether or not either or both is correct in explaining development in typical children, the way that Benjamin developed in his first four years suggested that both models may apply well to development in children whose innate equipment for development is atypical or impaired.

In the next three chapters, we will take a closer look at interventions for fostering the development of intersubjectivity.

~

CHAPTER FIFTY

Interventions: Fostering the Emergence of Self and Intersubjectivity in the Atypical Child

There is growing evidence, from laboratory studies and special treatment programs, that intensive early intervention with autistic children in the preschool years may be effective in improving the children's cognitive and adaptive functioning (Rogers 2000; Mundy and Crowson 1997; National Research Council 2001). Largely through wide media coverage, however, the message has been given to parents that interventions for children with autistic spectrum disorders must start as early as possible and that the earlier the intervention, the greater likelihood of a "cure." An array of interventions (but few scientifically proven to be effective) promising dramatic improvement if not cure in the child's communication, cognition, and social development are now available. Parents are desperate to find in their communities the programs that have promised to turn their child around, workers to help implement them, and funds to pay for them. The race to get the intervention in time is emotionally draining, and tremendous amounts of time and energy may be expended in efforts to advocate for resources and funding. It seems reasonable to assume that, once the panic button has been pressed, these efforts may often be at the expense of the time and focus required to observe and think about what one's particular child might need and, as important, why.

In this respect, Benjamin and I may have been fortunate in having lived through his early years at a time when there was not that much to choose from in the way of organized programs and not much pressure to choose amongst or enroll in them. I had not identified Benjamin as "autistic" and, in any case, there were no programs and promised "cures," back then, for either autism or retardation. I was not warned to get to such treatments, *fast*. In those days, after giving birth to a "retarded" infant, one was told either to take him home and love him or put him away. So I was left to my own devices to get to know and understand my child. Benjamin's slow-motion development had the advantage

221

of providing relatively long periods of time in which to observe and ponder about a given behavior. I had time to think about what was going on with him, and to think though each roadblock.

In this chapter, I discuss the theory and practice of different interventions strategies. More specifically, I ask how different theories of development play out, in developing strategies to deal with the marked deficits in social interaction that characterize certain developmental disorders. I then discuss the interventions described in Benjamin's chronicle. Inevitably, reference is made to the model that was derived from the material in the diary (see Diary Epilogue). Inevitably, too, questions are raised about the role of parent–child interaction in the treatment of disorders in early childhood that affect self and self–other relationships. This is further discussed in the following chapter.

Current Intervention Strategies—Theory and Practice

Kanner (1943) identified impairments in the biologically based readiness for affective contact as the core deficit in autism. Trevarthen and Hubley (1978) describe in the normal infant a "strong innate readiness for relations with other people." These "nativist" conceptions of intersubjectivity assume innate, evolution-based propensities for successful adaptation that are hard-wired in the infant and developing child. In this case, the question for treatment would be: Can this "readiness" be schooled and created anew when it does not appear to be "innate," and if so, how? What can or should one do to foster adaptation when that hard-wiring is absent or impaired?

In contrast to the nativist view, the *social learning* theory of development gives experience the central role in creating concepts and shaping behaviors. Nevertheless, it too must presume some god-given equipment—in this case, that which allows one to *learn* from social experience. From the social learning prospective, then, one must answer the question, How can one learn from social experience when the equipment or ability to process or make use of social experience is absent or impaired?

Although both models refer back to the innate capacities of the child, both presume what psychoanalyst Heinz Hartmann (1939/58) termed "an average expectable environment" in order for development to follow its prescribed course. The infant and young child must be exposed to sufficient amounts of the right kind of stimulation and responsiveness from the environment to evolve along normal lines. This point had been made clearly by Piaget, in relation to intellectual development. In the Piagetian child, knowledge is a construction, resulting from interaction and "balanced synthesis" of the child's internal motivational and cognitive structures and (proper) external materials and stimulation. Psychoanalyst Peter Hobson (2002) goes further, in viewing cognitive, language, and social development as emerging from and entirely dependent upon early infant–parent interactions and, in particular, the stimulation and response by the primary caregiver to the child's innate propensity for reading and responding to affective cues.

These theories pertain to normal development and presume normal equipment within the child for processing and responding to the world. "Good enough" parenting (Winnicott 1965) and a "good enough" environment allow the child with this "equipment" to actualize its potential and develop along normal lines. Cognitive and emotional problems may arise in children who have more or less intact equipment when parenting and environmental factors have not met their developmental needs. Interventions in these cases will involve manipulations to reverse or compensate for these inadequacies. In the case of the child with absent or profoundly impaired innate equipment, however, the questions must be raised: Can environmental manipulations actually *create* the missing inner structures or correct those that are impaired? And if so, on the basis of what capacities in the infant, and with what tools, does one try to create and shape the missing behaviors? Or should it be the goal of treatment to find ways to approximate or compensate for structures that are absent or deficient?

The above considerations have been drawn from theories about cognitive development. With respect to mental retardation, when the neurological or biological structures or processes required for cognition are severely impaired, interventions are not typically aimed at changing those underlying biological givens. Rather, efforts are made to make adaptations in the environment to accommodate the individual's handicaps and provide educational curriculum with appropriate modifications in content and expectations to make use of existing faculties. But what about social interaction phenomena? The "atypical" infants to whom the title of this book refers may demonstrate abnormal development either in the early infant–parent interaction or, at a later date, in the kinds of social behaviors that typically emerge in the first year of life in the context of that interaction. Their social deficits are also the consequence of a primary neuro-developmental disorder, not a faulty environment. These children would appear to be structurally incapable of normal patterns of interaction. How does one intervene, and with what goal? Is the goal to "undo" (cure) the primary deficit, or to find ways to compensate for it? And if so, how?

A Quick Review

Since the demise of the psychogenic theory of autism, there has been, until recently, surprisingly little attention given to treatment of the social interaction impairment in autism. The recent work that has been done in this area falls into three categories:

1. Attempts to teach young autistic children early nonverbal social communications skills, such as pointing, eye contact, or joint attention, the presumed precursors of "theory of mind" (e.g., Lewy and Dawson 1992;

Buffington et al. 1998; see Mundy and Crowson [1997] and Hwang and Hughes [2000] for review and discussion of these early intervention techniques).

2. Attempts by researchers and/or clinicians to improve social interaction in older (usually verbal) autistic children, by teaching "theory of mind" (e.g., Hadwin et al. 1997; Ozonoff and Miller 1995) or language skills (e.g., Koegel, O'Dell, and Koegel 1987; McGee et al. 1983), by attempting to stimulate motivation and initiation in social situations (e.g., Koegel and Koegel 1995; Krantz and McClannahan 1993; Laushley and Heflin 2000), or by teaching specific social skills (Barry et al. 2003). This has been tried in both laboratory settings and naturalistic settings (see also Hwang and Hughes [2000] and Rogers [2000] for recent reviews).

3. Attempts to work directly on parent interactions with infants and very young children with pervasive developmental disorders, with the goal of building a foundation of "basic learning relationships" from which more normal ways of relating, communicating, and thinking can emerge (Greenspan 1992a,b; Greenspan et al. 1997; Greenspan and Weider 1998).

Interventions within the first two categories may use the discrete trial behavioral techniques, originally applied to autism by Lovaas (1987, 2003), or the pivotal response methods, pioneered by Koegel and Koegel (1985, 1995). In the former, social and communication skills are viewed as behaviors that can be taught, using techniques such as selective rewarding of preferred behaviors, extinction of unwanted behaviors, and the creation of desired behaviors through techniques of shaping, chaining, and repetition, based on a Skinnerian model of learning. A desired behavior is broken down into small components. The child is then rewarded for learning each component in a series of trials. Through such step-by-step teaching, the child may be taught (conditioned) to communicate in ways that will be instrumental and effective in achieving his or her goals. In the discrete trial approach, the child plays a relatively passive, and responsive (versus active and initiating) role vis-à-vis the learning experience. (Some of the efforts to train social communication skills, described above, may borrow from this approach. See Hwang and Hughes [2000] for review.)

In the pivotal response method, the interventionist attempts to stimulate and reinforce motivation, initiative, and choice while working with the child in more naturalistic activities and with materials that are highly attractive to them. This approach credits the child with *intrinsic* motivation and makes use of his or her own preferences.

In Greenspan's "developmental, individual-difference relationship-based" (DIR) approach, amongst other techniques, the child who does not spontaneously initiate and engage in normal interaction patterns may be virtually "forced" into doing so, first by having the parent join the child in the activities of his own creation, and then, within that activity, altering conditions so that the child will have to acknowledge, use, and communicate with the parent in pursuing his own aims.

All these approaches hope eventually to develop a true capacity for reciprocal interpersonal interaction. The theory of mind approach is based on the assumption that, once developing a theory of mind, the individual would have the basis and incentive for communication. Greenspan and Weider's DIR approach hopes to arouse, stimulate, and nourish dormant relational patterns. And, although Lovaas's approach appears to be an attempt to work around, conceal, or compensate for an impairment in intersubjectivity which is recognized to be immutable, even this intervention promises more in-depth changes in the child's capacities. For example, it is acknowledged that an innate gift for imitation might be missing in these children, so that behaviors that normal children will spontaneously learn through imitation must instead be taught. The behaviorist, however, may also attempt to "shape" imitative behavior, itself, with the goal that it will eventually become part of the child's repertoire of spontaneous behaviors.

The behavioral approach also promises increased capacities in the child, by virtue of the increased social opportunities and feedback made available to him, as a result of the behavior patterns he or she has learned (Maurice, Green, and Luce 1996). That is, it is assumed that the child's defective patterns of interacting with the world have cut him or her off from social experiences necessary for developing more advanced levels of interaction and language. Correcting the maladaptive patterns would open up opportunities for more normal development. A good example of this expansion of opportunity and feedback is the vicissitudes of "the trick" when Benjamin was sixteen months old. From the moment he performed it the first time, it changed our perception of him and led us to react and interact with him in new ways. By lending an aura of "selfhood" to Benjamin, the "trick" encouraged more person-to-person communication, on my part, with him. Meanwhile, his success in "causing" such a tremendous reaction in me appeared to "kick-start" an interest, on his part, in communication.

Finally, several behavior theories now propose that, with early intervention, their methods of training the child may result in the development or activation of new neuro-developmental pathways due to the plasticity of the young brain. This will result in the creation or emergence of new, more adaptive ways of learning and processing experience. The behavioral, developmental/relational, and psychoanalytic schools (e.g., Bergman 1998; Tustin 1981) all claim some success with their methods, although whether or not, and if so why and how the reported positive outcomes were achieved, remain in question. Lovaas's (1987) claim that 47 percent of autistic children treated with his methods became indistinguishable from others in regular classes has been questioned, specifically with respect to the initial diagnosis of the children who appear to make the dramatic improvements (Gresham and Macmillan 1998) and their subsequent development. Recently, Greenspan (2004) reported that, in a chart review of two hundred children receiving a DIR-based assessment and intervention program, "the vast majority . . . learned to relate and engage with warmth, trust, and intimacy" and "the vast majority learned to interact and read and respond to social signals" (p. 13). Reportedly, Greenspan and his colleagues are currently conducting studies comparing Lovaas's discrete-trial technique with their DIR approach to treatment of autistic children (reported by McIntosh 1999).

Fonagy and Target (1996), in a study of more than 750 cases of child psychoanalysis, report that autistic children did least well in psychoanalytic psychotherapy as compared to children in other diagnostic categories. The authors speculate that, in these cases, deficit functioning, most likely of organic origin, limited the likelihood of change. However, the therapy (both "insight oriented" and "developmental help") appears to have been offered in individual sessions with preschool and school-age children and did not appear to have involved direct work with the infant–child or parent–child interaction, such as might then be continued throughout the child's week.

Researchers working with younger autistic children report that the children can be taught certain nonverbal communication techniques (e.g., pointing) and may even then generalize them to novel situations (Buffington et al. 1998; also Mundy and Crowson 1997). However, whether the techniques are learned by rote or are accompanied by a "true" appreciation of their meaning is still at issue. Attwood, Frith, and Hermelin (1988) mention that certain nonverbal communication techniques may be learned because of their instrumental value, but do not reflect a true social reciprocity. Hwang and Hughes (2000) found limited generalization or maintenance of target behaviors in sixteen programs for increasing early social communicative skills. Similarly, Barry et al. (2003) found that four older children in a clinic-based social skills group did not generalize learned social skills (conversation, and play skills) to peer interactions outside of the clinic group. Rogers (2000), however, claims better results with a variety of different interventions to facilitate socialization in older autistic children, but initiation of social contact remained difficult for them.

As described earlier, attempts to improve social interaction through instruction regarding theory of mind (e.g., Hadwin et al. 1997) have also had disappointing results. The students learned to pass the theory of mind tests, but this did not improve their interpersonal skills. In interpreting their findings, Hadwin et al. rejected the conclusion that a failure to understand the mental states of others may not, after all, underlie the specific communication deficits in autistic children. Instead, they conclude that, because the intensive teaching used in their study was short term, the children's understanding of theory of mind was too superficial (i.e., the children did not "understand the conceptual ideas underlying these tasks"). They call for future research to address the possibility that improvements in communication would be seen with a longer-term teaching method.

Some of the conclusions reached in earlier chapters of this book suggest another way of looking at the disappointing results in attempts to teach communication. "Affective connectedness" or primary intersubjectivity (including the ability to perceive and interpret social cues) may be a necessary (though not a sufficient) component of communication. As Hobson (2002) has cogently argued, the early parent–child affective connection may be a necessary substrate and prototype for all later language and communication. Therefore, attempts to teach the behaviors associated with intentional communication (secondary intersubjectivity) in the absence of this layer of *affective* exchange would result only in rote performance. As well, as discussed earlier, the capacity to appreciate the other's perspective (TOM) may be independent of a motivation, and need for communication. Therefore teaching how to know the other's perspective should not be expected, necessarily, to enhance communication (i.e., it will not do so, in the absence of an understanding or investment in communication, and especially, once again, in the absence of the ability to read affective and social cues).

Behavioral Versus Developmental/Relationship Models

Cowan (1978) describes the "clean slate" model of (normal) cognitive development as one in which external sources impose and transcribe "knowledge." However, the child cannot be just "a clean slate" but, rather, one that is *predisposed to be written on*, and in a particular way. That is, one must still postulate a modus operandi by which that child receives what he or she is taught. The teaching method would need to match that style of learning. Lovaas (1987, 2003) makes the assumption that the laws of learning (i.e., those that apply to typical individuals and animals) can be successfully applied to an individual with autism, despite his having "deviant organic structures." To enable the child to learn according to these laws, however, the stimuli must be modified and presented in a special way and in a special learning environment.

The developmental/relational therapeutic interventions work within the parent–child interaction, with the goal of stimulating or activating more normal social interaction patterns. This draws upon the approach that was originally proposed by psychoanalysts such as Margaret Mahler, when autism was still considered to be caused by faulty parenting (Mahler 1968; Mahler, Pine, and Bergman 1975). Mahler (amongst other analysts and developmental psychologists with similar views) viewed the parent–infant interaction as the "crucible" in which all subsequent developments in cognition, language, and social interaction are forged. Her approach was aimed at unlocking the child from the "autistic phase" by directly changing the dynamics of the parent–child interaction so that the child could get onto a normal developmental trajectory. The emphasis on early patterns of parent–child relationships has now been integrated into current treatment interventions (such as Greenspan 1992a,b), thankfully without the premise that it was faulty parenting that had caused the interaction deficits in the first place.

Many therapists and teachers work with autistic children in a "hand-over-hand" manner, in which the child's hands or limbs are passively put through the desired motions, in the hope that the movements will eventually become part of his or her own spontaneous repertoire of behaviors. With this exception, however, in virtually all the approaches referred to above, the parent, therapist, or instructor must work with something that is spontaneous or spontaneously responsive in the child. There must be some rudiment of a desired skill or behavior, some component of the desired behavior, or something similar to it, which the parent or therapist can then expand upon and develop. Just how it is expanded upon, however, must then take into account the particular formal properties and limits of the child's learning machinery at the time (see Cowan 1978; also Case 1992 regarding general and modular-specific input).

In clinical practice, I have often met with parents who are opposed to behavioral techniques, on the grounds that the approach does not respect the child's nature and individuality. Yet, in some instances, it may be that it is the behavioral approach that best matches the child's way of thinking and learning. For example, my notes in the diary, referring to a Piagetian framework, cite the importance of providing "aliment" that is in accord with existing schema, to stimulate the child's innately given processing capacities and allow them to be effective (see, e.g., entries and comments in chapter 23). Benjamin's particular style of learning was more concrete, less integrative than in a normal child.

Using Piagetian concepts, once again, there appeared to be an only weak propensity for "assimilation," and a relative inflexibility in Benjamin's "accommodation." Therefore, to respect his form of learning, to follow his lead, it was necessary to "build up schema" through creating, exaggerating, and reinforcing associations—between events, and between his actions and the responses of the environment to them (see "Interventions with Benjamin" below).

The issue, then, appears to be not so much whether behavioral techniques at times may be needed when teaching or raising a neuro-developmentally atypical child (they are), but rather, who should be doing them, in what context, and with a focus on what types of behaviors. Should the intervention follow a "two-person model," with the goal of achieving interaction and mutual participation in learning? Or should it involve a more one-way instruction, in which the child's behavior is trained and shaped by the adult? Should the child be taught discrete cognitive skills, such as discriminating, sorting, or matching at a table-top? Or should the emphasis be on social milestones, interaction patterns, and attachment behaviors in a more naturalistic context? An added question might be, When in the course of development should you intervene, and with what techniques at different points in time or for different developmental challenges? It is worth noting that, despite the intense interest in earlier and earlier diagnoses of autism, with the expectation that this will allow for better treatment outcome, existing treatments have been designed for children who are at least two years of age, if not older. If autism can be identified in infancy, and before age two, what techniques will be proposed for intervention then?

Interventions with Benjamin

Although not entirely absent, Benjamin's "innate readiness for relations with other people" definitely appeared weak and restricted, in early infancy. Nevertheless, it did emerge, over time, albeit in a somewhat different guise than that of normal children. Were there specific interventions that contributed to this development?

As reflected in the diary, Benjamin's development in self and intersubjectivity appeared, at the time, to emerge as "leaps." It was not clear to me what had preceded or "caused" these changes. Moreover, it was an odd but quite consistent phenomenon that developments in Benjamin's sense of self and capacity for intersubjectivity often emerged just at the point at which I was feeling despair about whether they would ever appear at all! I had no explanation for this, except perhaps that, during the seeming plateaus in development, some neurodevelopmental work was being done that prepared and nourished the ground for the change that occurred after sufficient repetition or when some necessary trigger had taken place. In retrospect, however, certain factors appeared to have facilitated those changes and perhaps, to some extent, can help to explain or predict them.

The "paradigm" in the Diary Epilogue describes a progression that begins with matching, followed by agency and effectance (first with respect to objects and self, then to the caregiver). What had to be done with Benjamin to move him through this progression?

a) *Strengthening assimilation/accommodation.* I had formulated Benjamin's problems, from the start, as related to an inadequacy in assimilation/accommodation (i.e., the integrating mechanism by which, in Piaget's theory, learning and adaptation and the development of new structures takes place in normal development). This would be the modus operandi that I had presumed for Benjamin's learning. Although Piaget did not deal with self and intersubjectivity directly, I assumed that, as in the cognitive domain, developments in these realms would also be affected by the assimilation/accommodation impairment. If so, the development of selfhood and intersubjectivity in Benjamin should benefit from any steps taken to aid and support his weak processing mechanisms.

Describing the invariant processes of assimilation and accommodation, and the coordination of these two processes, as weaker from the start had important implications for the nature of the "optimal environment" or "good enough environment" required to sustain and nourish them. It had implications, as well, for the nature of Benjamin's learning style and, therefore, for what the environment had to do to capitalize upon that style, to promote learning.

Assimilation (I assumed) required a match between a stimulus and a neurological structure (innate or developed through experience).[1] Or it would require recognition (at a neurological and unconscious level) of similarity between the new event to which the infant or child was exposed and events previously experienced, for which there was a neurological trace or schema. Failing to find a match, or failing to recognize (abstract) similarity, the infant would be unresponsive (i.e., not respond at all), because there would be no apparent recognition of the input, no schema with which to grasp onto and interpret it. (When Benjamin appeared "flat," "foggy," or passive, I assumed that there was nothing around that he could make sense of, in this way.)

Accommodation, in contrast, seemed to require registering the differences. Failing to recognize differences, the infant or young child would respond only to that part of the event that was identical to an existing schema. This response would be inappropriate to the situation, because the differences were not acknowledged and taken into account. Benjamin's use of the "mmmmmmm" sound for *every* attempt to say or imitate a word might be an example of a failure in accommodation.

In normal development, the relative match between the brain's way of organizing and processing experience and the kinds of experiences the child is likely to have in the "average expectable environment" is taken for granted. In providing an enriched environment, the caregiver hopes to enhance the richness, content, and texture of the schema, increasing the normal child's knowledge base and skills. In contrast, the present formulation suggests that teaching of the atypical child *must be geared towards developing and strengthening the sluggish integration process itself*. The diary entries suggest a number of ways in which we tried to compensate for Benjamin's perceived weakness in this process, in order to promote learning and adaptation.

For one, Benjamin's environment was constant, routinized, and repetitive (as discussed further below). Any new events to which Benjamin was exposed had to be limited and simplified so that he was required to cope only with those that were the same as or very close to ones for which an approximate response was already in his repertoire. The "optimal dis-crepancy" (i.e., to permit "assimilation and accommodation") had to be very slight indeed. Novelty had to involve only miniscule, subtle differ-ences, small enough that the similarity could still be perceived, even with a relatively weak assimilation capability. The environment (his care-givers) then had to promote and encourage integration (i.e., assimilation *and* accommodation) by energetically emphasizing (demonstrating, bringing attention to, dramatizing) the similarities and also, dramatically, demonstrating and teaching the accommodation that was necessary.

The above paragraphs are about learning and cognitive development. Will supporting "assimilation/accommodation" also foster developments in self and intersubjectivity? In chapter 46, we heard arguments that in-tegrative processes are involved in distilling a sense of self from experi-ence, and in differentiating self and other. I would argue that, in addition, in fostering learning and helping to create effective, adaptive patterns, feelings of mastery and agency are fueled, and that this, in turn, con-tributes to a sense of self, with ramifications within the relationship with others. At the same time, there was no explicit, focused attempt at "teaching" Benjamin communication and connectedness. Whatever Benjamin did do, spontaneously, that could be nourished and elaborated upon, was met with warmth and enthusiasm (see "e" below). The rest was a waiting game. Meanwhile, keeping demands and expectations firmly tied to the child that he was must have conveyed acceptance and secu-rity, and as such, would, at the very least, pose no barrier to developments in relatedness, if and when they were to appear.

b) *Repetition and ritual involving passive movements of the infant and young child.* Throughout the months and years covered in the diary, Benjamin was engaged repeatedly in "baby games" in which he became a partici-pant by virtue of direct stimulation and manipulation of his body. Baby games are part of any baby's infancy. In normal infants, the ability to im-itate and participate actively in baby games such as peek-a-boo emerges early and "effortlessly," to the joy and wonder of his caregivers. Babies are quick to imitate and learn the gestures and sounds in the games. In Ben-jamin's case, however, the use of baby games went on and on over months and years, and he had to be "patterned" through the movements.

Since it has been argued that "mirror neurons" underlie the baby's abil-ity to imitate movements, spontaneously, they would also be involved in active, intentional participation in these games. Perhaps, in Benjamin's case, this innate basis for instant imitation (namely , an innate neuronal correspondence between action perceived and action potential) was weak or missing. The many months of passively putting him through the same games may have set up the proprioceptive and kinesthetic templates which could serve to compensate for this missing program for imitation. Eventually, he could associate and match them to the movements of the persons playing with him. Like the repeated caretaking rituals in infancy, the repeated baby games may also have established multi-modal patterns of expectations, from which, eventually, the common factors that become the sense of self, and the corresponding sense of the other, could be distilled. Consolidated and more deeply engraved over numerous repetitions, these interpersonal games, then, may have contributed to a sense of both connection and identity with the other.

c) *Ritual and repetition (to create sequences of behavior).* It is well known that the atypical child seems to have a great need for repetition and tends to flourish in highly structured and predictable environments (Schopler, Mesibov, and Hearsey 1995). Such children demand familiarity. For reasons described below, they seem less stressed by and better able to respond to a familiar world. Perseveration and ritual reflect their attachment to sameness.

As described in chapter 46, it has been hypothesized that the repetition of everyday infant–caregiver interactions contributes, in normal infants, to the development of a " core self." Given a delay and/or impairment in integrative capacities, the atypical child may require a prolonged, if not perpetual, repetition of these familiar sequences to distill a "core self" and to maintain the organization of, and to experience, the cohesiveness and continuity that appears to be essential to a sense of self. The diary entries suggest that repetition and predictability of events, as arranged by his caregiver, also helped Benjamin to learn, and eventually to engage in, *meaningful sequences of behavior.* They thus contributed to his becoming more *active* as an *agent* affecting his environment, and this, in turn, fostered an appearance of "personhood" in him. He could also demonstrate *anticipation,* and an ability to "fill in the gaps" when the sequences were begun but left to him to complete. His caretakers would respond positively and enthusiastically to these developments. This, in turn, would consolidate the behavior and, most likely, "pump up" his fledgling sense of himself. In addition, being effective in this way, in an interaction with others, appeared to strengthen a sense of a connection between himself and "the other."

d) *Establishing connections between emotion and behavior.* In the normal child, a particular motivation or emotion would likely spontaneously trigger certain conventional expressive or adaptive behaviors, intrinsically linked to it. In Benjamin, these intrinsic associations initially did not appear to exist (see chapter 18). In chapters 21 and 25, however, we saw that he was able to learn what to do, through associating an emotion with a behavioral sequence performed by others. It would appear that, by exposing him to the same emotion-behavior sequences on the part of "the other," over and over again, the caregiver had provided ready-made chunks of meaningful, directed behavior which he could imitate when he experienced a particular emotion or motivation himself.

For Benjamin to do this, however, he would have had, first, to match his own motivation and emotion with that of the other. And exactly how would he be able to do this, to begin with, if he did not have those same behaviors associated with the emotion in his repertoire? It seems that Benjamin must have been able, at some level, to recognize and match the emotional experiences, themselves. Having done that, he was able to borrow from "the other" the appropriate behavioral sequence. Once again, the more Benjamin behaved in a familiar "human" way, the more he was perceived by others, and by himself, as "one of us."

e) *Resisting withdrawal.* The child must move ever closer to perceiving similarity between self and other. The parent must resist the pull away from the atypical child. When the usual cues for attachment and interaction are not there, this is very hard to do (see, e.g., the initial diary entries). But parents and caregivers can stay involved by becoming vigilant observers, on the look-out for any behavior on the part of the infant which can take on significance and power in their interaction with him, because of its ability to reliably elicit a genuine affective response from them. This will need to be a positive affective response, an experience for the parent that makes the parent want to continue to be with and enjoy, rather than withdraw from, the baby. That is how the "trick" was born. When the child is capable, through his own actions, of "grabbing" the other's attention, engaging the other, eliciting an emotional response in the other that leads the other to prolong social contact, this is a huge step in crossing the interpersonal divide, and in laying the groundwork for communication.

It is important to note that our work with Benjamin began in his infancy, with the aim of stimulating behaviors that should have occurred right at that time, but had not. In contrast, most early intervention programs for autistic disorders begin much later (because the disorders are not diagnosed in infancy), albeit with an emphasis on similar behaviors. It is also important to note that, insofar as we were Benjamin's family, with him all the time, and insofar as we were not engaged in executing a specific program, our "interventions" were essentially round the clock. They were also not experienced as interventions but rather as just whatever seemed right and fair, in the context of parenting and loving him.

Earlier in the book I ask, Would Benjamin's "same but different" sense of self and intersubjectivity have emerged, anyway, with a different style of parenting?

Or would they have emerged sooner and/or in a better and more familiar form? Would these be the proper strategies for a different type of child? Would they be the proper strategies for a different type of parent? Do variations in parenting style beginning in infancy significantly affect the course of development in the atypical child? Does the emotional tone of the interaction affect what is learned and whether or how the learning takes place?

These are empirical questions, the answers to which seem both perfectly obvious and yet difficult to prove. We have yet to fully determine how emotional factors may interact with and influence whether and exactly how the stimulation of cognitive and social development takes place, although clinical experience and clinical theory surely suggest that they do. Gray (1978) attempted to demonstrate this by showing that two (normal) babies differed, even in the way they took an object from their mothers, as a function of differences in the ways their mothers had interacted with them while they were learning this skill. As we have seen, Hobson (2002) argues that individual differences in the language and thought of adults may be traced back to differences in the emotional tone and parental availability and empathy experienced by the individual in the parent–infant relationship. He cites two studies suggesting "specific and long lasting effects" of maternal postpartum depression on the cognitive skills of the children as observed at four and five years of age (Murray et al. [1996] and Sharp et al. [1995] in Hobson [2002], pp. 136–137).

I will discuss parent–child factors in intervention in the next two chapters. In this chapter, however, it seemed important to call attention to the obvious: that, regardless of the approach given to the parent (e.g., behavioral versus developmental-interactive, etc.), it most certainly will affect the emotional exchange in the parent–child interaction, if for no other reason than that the parent may become less anxious, and more confident in her interactions with a challenging and confusing child, or more accepting because of greater understanding and support. The affective tone and quality of the communication between parent and child will also improve, to the extent that challenging behaviors are better managed (see Greenfield 1972). This may be a therapeutic factor that cuts across different interventions and different strategies From this point of view, an important element in determining intervention would be to match the intervention to the parent's style of learning, and to the style of parenting with which he or she is comfortable. This will increase the chances of compliance and success with the intervention plan.

Note

1. A concept of how the body is put together was also very late in developing for Benjamin. For example, he could not represent the relationships of body parts in a stick figure until well into the elementary school years. Perhaps he was helped along with a puz-

zle that was created for him, when he was about five years old. It was a life-size puzzle of himself that I made out of a sheet of foam rubber. Benjamin lay down on it so that I could outline his form, then I cut it out and colored it in to look like him, then cut up the figure into large puzzle pieces—head, legs, arms, torso. Needless to say, this made quite a hit, and over several months Benjamin finally got the idea of how to do it, and then, of course, did it again and again and again. I don't know for certain if it helped his body image, but it probably helped him develop some idea of how to do a puzzle! It may have worked well with any puzzle portraying something in which he had already shown an interest, although I suspect there was something special about the closeness of the puzzle to the experience of himself, laying down to have it made.

~

CHAPTER FIFTY-ONE

Parent–Child Interaction with Children with Disorders Affecting Self and Self–Other Relationships

The psychoanalytic approach to the treatment of autistic and autistic-like children is associated with a dark period in the history of our understanding of autism, during which the disorder (despite some lip service to constitutional factors) was attributed to psychogenic factors, and in particular, to deficiencies in maternal functioning. "Refrigerator mothers" and otherwise inadequate or "bad" parents were presumed responsible for the deviations in their child's development. Bettleheim (1967), for example, claimed that autistic children "withdrew" to shield themselves against the devastating noxious influence of insensitive parents; he therefore advocated separating the children from their parents and exposing them to therapeutic relationships with understanding staff.

In contrast to Bettleheim's approach, Mahler (Mahler, Pine, and Bergman 1975) devised the "tripartite" therapy session in which the parent learned how to understand and respond to her child's behavior through "participant-observation" in the therapist–child interactions. The parent, for example, might learn with and from the therapist how to interpret the child's atypical communications. Mahler's approach fell in disfavor as research began clearly to demonstrate the organic basis of the children's pathology. With the perception of autistic children as intrinsically defective, treatment options shifted away from psychotherapy and the parent–child relationship to an emphasis on education, skill training, and the management and modification of behavior through behavioral techniques. Thus, the notion that the parent–child relationship might have something to do with treatment disappeared along with the psychogenic theory of the etiology of this disorder.

But, in rightfully discarding the "bad mother" theory of autism, was the baby thrown out with the bathwater? Selfhood and intersubjectivity are generally acknowledged to be of central importance in autistic spectrum phenomena. As we have seen, in normal development, the mother–infant interaction has long been regarded as the "crucible" in which these milestones are forged and developed (Winnicott 1965; Mahler, Pine, and Bergman 1975; Stern 1985; Pipp 1990; see Cicchetti and Beeghley [1990] and Emde [1999] for reviews). While innate, biological underpinnings to the developments of selfhood and object relations may be acknowledged, the literature regarding normal infancy clearly stresses the role of the mother–infant interaction in releasing, facilitating, and supporting these developments (see, e.g., Pipp 1990; Winnicott 1965; Hobson 2002).

Cicchetti and his colleagues, for example, studied children who had been maltreated as infants, in order to determine how the deprivation of "average expectable" or "good enough" mothering affects the development of a sense of self and the child's capacity for relationships with others. It should come as no surprise that the interventions they recommend for disturbances in self and object relationships in these (biologically normal) children include opportunity to experience more positive child–caretaker relationships and efforts to change the child's "working model" of the parent–child interaction (Cicchetti et al. 1989).

In contrast, developmental research and theory concerning infants and children with autistic spectrum developmental disorders make little mention of early parent–child interaction when discussing deviations in the children's self-development and relatedness. And for some time, following the near-demise of the psychoanalytic approach to autism (at least in North America; it persists, e.g., in the work of Frances Tustin [1981] and other analysts in England [see Alvarez 1992; Mitrani and Mitrani 1997]), treatments for children with autistic disorders reflected little or no appreciation of the fact that the autistic child, like any other child, is necessarily involved in, and contributing and reacting to, a parent–child relationship, beginning at birth. Thus, with respect to autistic disorders, it appears that only when "nurture" was considered at fault did treatment specify and address the parent–child interaction in particular, with respect to developments in selfhood and interpersonal relating. With the realization that it was "nature" (neurobiology) that had failed the child, "nurture" was more or less limited to issues of behavior management and education. Indeed, parents were even given a reduced role in the parenting of their children as teachers and therapists took over the task of teaching the child when he or she was still very young, in "early intervention" programs often located away from the home and family.[1]

The pendulum is beginning to swing, however. Theorists and clinicians are again asking that the parent–child interaction be considered, in efforts to help the atypical child to develop, this time, however, without the presumption that the parent had been guilty of causing the child's problems in the first place (see, e.g., Bromwich 1976; Gravida-Payne and Stoneman 1997; Berger 1990;

Greenspan 1992a and b; Greenspan et al. 1997; Greenspan and Weider 1998; Weider 1992 ; Marfo 1992). As we have seen, Greenspan and his colleagues, in particular, attempt to affect the core difficulties in children with pervasive developmental disorders directly through the parent–child relationship. Attachment theory and research have also brought attention back to parent–infant interactions, in recognizing the potential for disruption in attachment caused by reactions to the birth of a child with disabilities and the absence or distortion of normal attachment cues from the child (see Howe 2006; Goldberg 1977; Fraiberg 1977b; Dawson et al. 1990; Marfo 1984, 1992). Finally, as theories of autism and assessment tools (e.g., the Autistic Diagnostic Observation Schedule, Lord et al. 2000) return to a more developmental model of autism, clinical interventions have begun to focus on ways to stimulate the manifestations of communication and reciprocity which are found early on, in the normal parent–infant interaction.

It should be obvious, of course, that the characteristics of babies with biologically based developmental disorders will play no less a role in determining the nature of the parent–child relationship than those of any other baby, and that babies with disabilities, no less than normal babies, will be sensitive to and responsive to variations in parenting (see Cicchetti and Schneider-Rosen 1984; Capps, Sigman, and Mundy 1994). Nevertheless, these truisms are often overlooked when the focus is on diagnosis and on arranging for the structured environment and behavioral and educational programs to which the disorder has been shown to respond (see, e.g., Schopler, Mesibov, and Hearsey 1995). In my experience, it is not uncommon, today, to find clinicians and educators diagnosing an autistic spectrum disorder if the child shows any differences at all in social relating, and to any degree. Once the diagnosis is in place, the parents are then directed to one or another agency dispensing a particular intervention for the child. Therapists then work with the child according to a more or less fixed curriculum applied to all their young clients. Very little if any time or attention is given to individual differences amongst these children and their families. Individual differences amongst children with disabilities are mentioned only with respect to the type (diagnosis) and/or severity of the primary disability itself, not the environmental factors that may also be contributing to them.

Yet, were more attention paid to individual differences in the personalities of atypical children, the possibility would most certainly have to be considered that these individual differences are a function, not only of the type and severity of the children's disabilities, but also, to some extent, of differences in their life experiences, including their interactions with their parents and families. These experiences, in turn, will reflect or involve the child's disabilities and parental reactions to them, but also, other inborn qualities (not necessarily pathological) of the child and parents, and interactions amongst them.

Of course, all theories of development have to address the parent–child interaction, as no baby is raised in an interpersonal vacuum (see, e.g., Winnicott 1965). And there is every reason to believe that the relationship between a baby with disabilities and his or her parents may have an important influence on the extent to which and particular ways in which the baby's strengths and deficits may manifest themselves (see Pipp 1990). In the previous chapter, however, we asked whether the parent–infant interaction could affect, as well, the primary, biologically based impairments, in the capacities for selfhood and interpersonal relating. A related issue is the extent to which the inborn impairments cause interruption and deviance in the kinds of caregiver responses (e.g., attunement, attachment) which are believed to contribute to, or be necessary for, healthy development of self and object relations (e.g., Beebe and Lachmann 1992; Clark and Seifer 1983) and language and thought (Hobson 2002).

While there certainly are other factors which will influence the course of development, there is evidence that early parent–child interaction can foster or impede development, even with respect to the course and outcome of biologically based functioning (Eagle and Struening 1987; Kopp 1990; Berger 1990; Capps, Sigman, and Mundy 1994; Schanberg 1994; Meaney et al. 1990). As mentioned earlier, the possibility of neurobiological plasticity in the early years, though still controversial, is infusing new life into early intervention programs which hope to affect positive changes in conditions of delay or disorder, even when the etiology of these conditions is biological (Chugani, Muller, and Chugani 1996; O'Leary, Schlagger, and Tuttle 1994; Skoyles 1999). It has also been argued that extensive and intensive positive stimulation (as, e.g., in intensive musical training) may create changes in neurological substrate in the early years (e.g., Sloboda 1994).

In working with parents, I find that there are two difficulties that arise in counseling parents that how they interact with their child may play a role in effecting a change in a primary (biologically based) interactional disorder. For one, some parents may perceive the proposal as suggesting that they are to blame for their child's problems (i.e., that if they had only done it right in the first place, the child would not have the disorder). In this case, parents must be helped to understand that the child's relationship problem is primary, and constitutional, and that, even were significant remediation possible, the conclusion cannot be drawn that the parenting style had caused the problem in the first place.[2] Furthermore, in most cases, efforts to change the parent–child relationship are aimed at optimizing the child's development, by reducing the possibility of secondary problems or the exaggeration of primary ones. The child's primary problem, however, will likely remain.

(Parenthetically, in this regard, I do take issue with Hobson's [2002] theory that the various symptoms of autism itself are caused by the disruption in the parent–child interaction that occurs because of a primary deficit in affective connectedness. On the other hand, Hobson's theory leaves room for the argument that I am making here—namely, that the way the parent then deals with this disruption may make a difference in subsequent [other] characteristics of the child, such as self-esteem, level of anxiety, and mood—which in turn will effect his learning capabilities and motivation for learning, as well as his social and emotional adjustment. This is perhaps the main message of this book, and of Benjamin's story.)

The reassurance that they are not to blame for the primary disability and that it will likely persist in some fashion despite changes in their parenting leads to the second difficulty. Some parents may find this assurance (i.e., that their parenting had not caused a problem that is essentially "incurable") difficult to hear, because they are desperately seeking a "cure." They may therefore turn to a lengthy roster of interventions promising a cure and grasp onto many or all of them (auditory, visual, biochemical, dietary, sensori-motor, etc.) whether or not they have been validated, and whether or not it has been determined that the intervention chosen is likely to be what their particular child may need (Freeman 1997; Heflin and Simpson 1998).

Although one can understand and sympathize with a parent's intense desire to help her child, to find a "cure," and to that end, to "leave no stone unturned," the desperate rush to do so may, in and of itself, affect the quality and quantity of parent–child interactions. As stated earlier, there is little time to "wait, watch and wonder" (Muir 1992; Wesner, Dowling, and Johnson 1982) with the clearly atypical child, when parents feel desperate to do and try anything—immediately!—to change him. It is worth repeating that, even if early intervention is extremely important, it must include time to listen and learn about each particular child, in an effort to select and individualize interventions. Parents must also pay attention to, and sufficiently value, the importance of their own interaction with the child.

Teachers and therapists, working with all kinds of children, including normal children, have long recognized the importance of the right moment—that special time, place, level of arousal and emotional experience that focuses the child's attention and enhances learning (see, e.g., de Hirsch, Jansky, and Langford 1966; Simons and Oshi 1985; Pine 1987, 1990). Respect for the right moment is even intrinsic to a good behavior management program, wherein attempts are made to reinforce spontaneous behaviors that are "good" and extinguish no less spontaneous, but nonadaptive behavior. These moments must be grabbed as unique opportunities to bring about some new development. Bringing attention to the parent–child interaction raises the likelihood that the parent will be available at the right moment to capitalize on new or unusual spontaneous actions or a special increase in the child's motivation. This point tends to get lost when parents, teachers, therapists, and researchers attempt to instruct and impose learning according to a rigid schedule and agenda (Goodman, 1992).

Concluding Remarks

Children with inborn disabilities in relatedness are not equipped to understand our world; it is therefore necessary for us to learn theirs. The primary caretakers are in the best position to know the infant's or child's capabilities, and to find out the child's particular way of communicating. With that understanding, they can arrange experiences for their children that respect their difficulties and protect them against experiences that will overwhelm them. In this way, parents both afford their children an experience of mastery and communicate to them acceptance and respect. At the same time, as Goldberg (1977) points out, learning to understand her child is also important for the parent's sense of self-confidence because she may see encouraging results flow from a correct interpretation of his behavior. There is mutual regulation in a parent–child interaction which, if properly tuned, will benefit both parties in the dyad, even with a child with disabilities.

In my diaries, I can read a step-by-step account of Benjamin's developing capacity to achieve a sense of self, a sense of the other, and to establish a connection between the two. However, these did not develop and could not be observed in him, alone. By their very nature, intersubjectivity and communication between self and other are two-person events that emerge, are influenced by, and can be observed, only in an interaction. There cannot be a "pure" natural history of the development of intersubjectivity and communication that follows only the child, in isolation. The qualities of the parent and her or his interaction with the child will necessarily be part of the subject matter in any study of intersubjectivity. I recorded Benjamin's progress because of my tremendous involvement with him. The intensity and nature of my involvement no doubt significantly affected the developments I describe. But any involvement, including noninvolvement, would have done so.

Notes

1. It is interesting in this regard that Kanner's 1971 follow-up study of his twenty cases of autistic children and Szatmari et al.'s (1989) follow-up of high-functioning autistic children both found that whether or not a child was institutionalized versus remained with his family appeared to correlate with positive outcome. The problem here, of course, is the existence of selection factors (in both child and family) by virtue of which the better functioning children may have been more likely to have been kept at home.

2. Except, of course, in those instances (e.g., of extreme neglect or abuse) where it had. Here we are talking about the autistic spectrum disorder itself or other congenital

developmental disabilities, which in no way can be attributed to faulty parenting. Reactive attachment disorders, on the other hand, which are attributed to inadequate parenting, are considered to be relatively responsive to changes in parenting (see American Psychiatric Association 1994); and even the "atypical autism" of certain Romanian orphans from profoundly inadequate orphanages may improve after adoption (Rutter and the English and Romanian Adoptees study team 1996).

CHAPTER FIFTY-TWO

∼

Help Him Make You Smile

In Introduction 2, I asked whether one can draw from the story of one atypical child any conclusions about other atypical children regarding deficits in intersubjectivity and selfhood, and how to address them. Of course, the responsible answer is "no." Atypical children comprise a widely heterogeneous group. Nor do I know whether Benjamin might not have developed differently with different caregivers. Still, our experiences with Benjamin suggest certain conclusions that are general enough that they likely can be applied to many children, including children with typical development. These are considerations that certainly would not prevent, and more likely would foster and maximize, selfhood and the capacity to relate to others, even in children who appear to have primary deficits in their biological capacity for these developments.

The key to Benjamin's success in these realms appears to have been the very simple paradigm set down in his first "trick," which was a joint parent–child event that set the tone for a style of intervention that appeared to have encouraged and consolidated the impressive developments that followed. In it, the child's actions had the power to elicit a genuine favorable affective reaction to him by his caregiver. In the lives of typically developing children, such interactions take place spontaneously; they are a "foregone conclusion" that takes place naturally, without forethought. In the case of the child with atypical development, however, the caregiving environment must seek and create situations in which the child can "make you smile."

There is a lot packed into this book's title phrase, "Help him make you smile." It is not as easy to do or as inconsequential as it may seem.

The "help him" refers to the fact that the infant or child who has a developmental disorder affecting the capacity for relatedness may not be able to do this (i.e., make the caregiver smile) on his own. He will not, on his own, behave in such a fashion that the caregiver's smile is assured. He will not be stimulating the pleasure and adoration that normal babies have been programmed to elicit, and the caregiver, to give. This baby's caregiver will need to "help him" to engage in behaviors that are endearing and connecting, at a time when, just because these are not there to begin with, her impulse, instead, may be to withdraw from or reject him, feeling depressed, angry, defeated, despairing, or rejected herself. She will need to stay engaged when there is nothing to engage her. Her engagement, therefore, may be no more at first than *vigilance*, at times heartbreaking, tedious, and discouraging, for any something in her child's repertoire that has the potential, with the help of her response, to genuinely affect her in a happy way.

The behaviors she is after are not necessarily physical or adaptive milestones, like learning to walk, or doing a puzzle, or even learning to talk, although many parents appear to pin their hope for "normalcy" on these kinds of achievements. She will, of course, smile at these, too, in pride or relief. But, for developing and enhancing *intersubjectivity*, she will need to arrange the set, so that, in the context of these physical and adaptive advances, her smile is perceived by the child as a function of something *he* did *to* and *with* her.

The caregiver must try to develop this kind of affective connection with a baby or child who is not, and may never be, like a "normal" baby or child. Will it work? It should, though it depends upon the caregiver's goal, what it is she is hoping for. For to be effective, she must seek, not the whole of a normal contact, but just the beginning of one, a connection, not with the whole of a normal baby, but with a different one, and on his different terms.

"Help him make you smile" then, requires that the caregiver be ready and willing to smile, when the package is not complete, when it is not what she was hoping for and expecting. It implies, and is predicated upon, her acceptance of a child who is different.

It should "work" because, if the child has been able to do something (e.g., make eye contact, reach for her, touch her, initiate a smile) which crosses the interpersonal divide and connects with her, his caregiver will respond, in kind, and genuinely so. She will "connect" back. A bridge will have been formed. That will feel good. The child has therefore made something good happen. Along with other mastery experiences, that will be tucked away in his "becoming a person" file.

It also should work because, by virtue of his actively engaging with her, the child's personhood, in the caregiver's eyes, will have moved up a notch. He will be more there, as a person, with whom she feels she can or might want to connect. It will be easier to be with him; she will be less inclined to withdraw. (In yet another diary, this one about my own feelings at the time of Benjamin's birth, I describe the resistance I felt "to letting loose the love" to a child whom I had been told, by the doctors, might turn out to be "a totally defective organism." This was a very painful experience because I had just given birth, and was biologically and emotionally ready, otherwise, to love my baby.)

The smile, when it comes (i.e., when the caregiver has helped her child do what he needs to do to connect with her, in some way, however small), will be genuine. That smile had not been there before, because the child did not reach out to her. When he does, if ever so slightly, she will smile.

The "smile," of course, is a metaphor for positive regard, for adoration, for the parent feeling content. It is hard to imagine that this would not affect a child, any child, in a more positive, growth-inducing way, than would negative regard, rejection, anxiety, tension, or feelings of despair on the part of his caregiver.

"Help him make you smile" is not a formula for interactions that are to take the place of other interventions that may be necessary for helping the child (e.g., interventions to manage and modify difficult behavior; teach new skills; foster language, etc.). Rather, it simply must be included in the program, and perhaps ideally, integrated with the other interventions, wherever possible. Everything that is done to help the child to perform actions that can be perceived as meaningful and relevant, in coping with novelty, and to experience himself as effective, *especially in an interpersonal context,* but in other realms as well, will contribute to his sense of self. Every time, as well, that he learns a sequence of behaviors which is coherent and effective, which he can repeat, it will become "his," part of his repertoire, part of him, and will contribute to his sense of "personhood." Simultaneously, as his caretaker observes him initiate and execute behavior patterns himself, she will perceive more "personhood" in him. This will likely encourage on her part more encounters with her child that have the potential to forge affective connections between them.

But what if:

a. The baby cannot "read" the facial and bodily cues of the caregiver, so as to discriminate a positive response?
b. The baby does not appear to have an innate propensity to experience certain responses to him as something "positive"?
c. The baby does not appear to care about, see significance for himself in, and feel rewarded (or punished) by the affective responses of the other?

If any or all of these factors prevail, then the dictum "Make mommy smile" appears to beg the question. What is the point, it may be argued, of helping a child "make the caregiver smile," if the child does not even recognize, appreciate, or care about the smile?

There is a great deal we still do not know about the experience of this type of child. Autistic children were once thought to have no attachment needs, and to be incapable of attachments. This has been shown not to be true (Sigman et al. 1986). Similarly, we may find that the autistic child's seeming failure to interpret, and/or lack of interest and responsiveness to, the emotional lives of others may be more apparent than real (e.g., that he may be having emotional reactions that he is not able to communicate) (Sigman et al. 1992.) Or his apparent lack of response may be something that he would change if he could, and he might appreciate efforts on the part of others to help him to do so. I have seen young children as preschoolers who had appeared uninterested in and unresponsive to praise later appear to appreciate and be warmed by positive accepting attitudes towards them. As we have seen, verbal adult autistic individuals often describe an aloneness that they experience and, in what does seem impossible, often express a longing for a connectedness that they have never experienced.

In my clinical work with autistic youngsters and young adults, there almost always seems to be some way in which one can "connect" with the individual, or some means, albeit unconventional, of "making contact." It will be on the child's own terms (i.e., in the atypical way that is the only one available to that child), but often it will result in something that approaches a more familiar form of emotional contact. Depending upon the age of the child and his or her unique characteristics, the connecting may take place, for example, through physical contact (e.g., tickling, rocking, singing, with a quality of primary intersubjectivity), or it may take place through the parent's ability to interpret and therefore respond appropriately to the meaning and purpose of perseverative questioning or an apparently bizarre verbalization. In the latter case, the child has become, by virtue of the parental response, a successful communicator, and the mother's pleasure will be not only in having helped him to do that but in seeing some positive change in his behavior because he was correctly understood. This kind of scenario will need to be repeated again and again for the child to experience and to have the expectation that he can communicate with ("connect with") the other.

Depression about the child and a desperate wish and search for normalcy can interfere with willingness to do things that respect his or her atypical way. Caregivers may be resistant to putting themselves out to connect with the child on his or her terms (see early diary entries). I would argue that we need to respect the child's atypical way, because in so doing, regardless of whether or not the child is able eventually to make a more typical and "human" connection, one has at the very least given this child a message of acceptance for who she is, not a constant demand that she become something that perhaps she cannot be. And she has thus been treated as is deserved by and afforded to any other child.

It may be argued that severely autistic children will not be able to receive the message. They may appear so cut off from an ability to understand others or to be affected by the needs, wishes, and demands of others that only methods which, from the human point of view, may appear aversive and abusive will be effective in managing their extremely maladaptive, self-abusive, or dangerous behaviors. While in special circumstances this may be true, these circumstances must raise questions about the environmental factors that are contributing to such behaviors, and whether these behaviors themselves might have been avoided or decreased had there been, along the way, greater appreciation of the modifications in the environment that this particular individual had required to help him to cope (see, e.g., Gillingham 2000).

Some mention of the "normalization principle" should be made here. Originally conceived as a way of allowing more acceptance of and opportunities for persons with handicaps (Nirje 1969; Wolfensberger 1972), an overzealous and somewhat misguided application of its tenets may have the curious outcome that handicaps become more unacceptable. This is because the goal of normalization has often been interpreted to be that of making the handicap invisible. With the desire to have the person with disabilities "fit in" and be accepted in the community comes the demand that he look and behave as normal (and age appropriate) as possible. And with this comes a corresponding lack of interest in, curiosity about, or acceptance of that which, while it may not be "normal," is normal for that particular person.

"Normalization" then, often translates into efforts to modify the individual, not the environment. It creates anxiety about the ways in which the child is different, efforts to conceal or change him, and an emphasis on training the child to be different versus enjoying the child as he is. Programs attempting to educate mothers regarding how to raise children with developmental handicaps may therefore be geared towards helping them get their children to the next "normal" developmental milestone, or training in the "normal response" when the child does not seem to have it in his or her spontaneous repertoire. In such programs, the atypical child's peculiar, or different, way of doing things is a signal to the parent, family, or educator to get to work to try to change it.

One might ask, Isn't that precisely what was being done in "the trick"? The answer, I believe, is both Yes and No. Teaching Benjamin the trick was motivated, it is true, by a wish for him to perform a particular act that was appropriate to his chronological (rather than developmental) age, and one that was entirely absent in his repertoire. At the time, it arose out of my depression in interacting with him. Fortunately, however, it was taught by expanding upon a behavior that *was* within his repertoire. Moreover, if the success of the attempt were judged on the basis of whether or not the act was executed with the same intentions and goals as it would have had in the hands of the normal sixteen-month-old (i.e., to feed mommy), then it would have to be considered a failure. Benjamin learned in that situation only what he was able and ready to learn at that time—namely, that raising his hand to my mouth brought about a very positive feeling in our interaction. He learned that he could do something to get a response. It later became a communication, "Come play with me." Rather than show that one can "train" the atypical child to be more "normal" (in this case, to "feed mommy"), it demonstrates how hollow would be the victory if one did not allow for the different meaning that the learned behavior might have for the atypical child.

As discussed in the preceding chapter, the danger with a misguided "normalization" approach is that it affords little time for or investment in observing the child's behavior in order to gain an understanding of what it means for the child, and what it might tell about this child's particular needs and ways of communicating them. This may lead one to overlook the functional significance of what is different (i.e., the child's messages in his or her own "language") which, if understood and acknowledged, may form a springboard for more spontaneous and comfortable new growth and development. Moreover, by virtue of understanding, acknowledging, and responding to the child's message, however garbled the "language" in which it is framed, the caretaker has created a situation in which the child has made a connection with her. In contrast, had his unusual gesture and spontaneous way of doing things been perceived merely as something that must be changed, the child would miss out on the usual experiences in infancy of being accepted and enjoyed by his parents for who he is—the experience, again, of making the parent smile.

A misguided "normalization" approach to parenting the child with developmental handicaps, then, runs the risk of these potential negative outcomes:

1. The child cannot feel good about what he or she "really" is;
2. The parent cannot feel good about herself—for example, if the child does not respond well to her efforts to train and educate (i.e., does not become "more normal");
3. One might miss finding a more congenial and possibly more effective mode of changing behavior, one that is based upon an understanding of the behavior's function in the child's life;
4. One's efforts may precipitate even more disturbed or maladaptive behavior, as the child feels forced to perform in ways which are not natural and spontaneous for him or her;
5. One may miss out on any spontaneous developmental progress that may emerge, in either the child or the parent–child interaction, in an atmosphere of greater interest and acceptance; and
6. One may miss opportunities to help the child forge a connection with oneself.

I am not arguing that the atypical child will "flower" on his or her own without appropriate stimulation and expectations. Rather, I am suggesting that, in our efforts to help the child maximize his or her potential and adaptation to society, we set goals for the child and find ways to help the child reach them that are based on an interest in, respect for, and attempt to understand his or her "atypical" world, his or her limitations, and the meaning and function of the child's atypical ways of doing things.

As we have seen, persons with autistic spectrum disorders are thought by many theorists not to have a "theory of mind." In that formulation, however, "mind" appears to refer to "our" minds, in particular. We see in the autistic person a failure to know and to take into account our perspectives. We, however, no more have a theory of the autistic person's mind than they have of ours. We are as ill-equipped to read or take into account the way autistic people think and perceive the world as they may be to read and take into account ours. We do not have their equipment anymore than they have ours.

We can appreciate the enormity of their task and the incredible pain and frustration they must feel in trying to understand us, when we recognize how impossibly difficult it has been for us to understand the autistic individual, how mysterious and out of our reach has been his inner world. Showing humility before and respect for his differences might give the child that edge of self-esteem that may allow him to cope with the implications of his handicap as he matures. This is not to deny the pain that such an individual may yet have to endure because of his or her differences. However, sensitivity on our part to the child's world, when he is young, will likely lead to efforts to change the environment, rather than the child, in an effort to minimize his frustrations and confusion. This, in turn, should allow for experiences of mastery and competence, and thereby foster self-acceptance and the strength to deal with challenges as he matures.

For teaching children with developmental disabilities, Goodman (1992) proposes that one stay where the child is "at," gently expanding his capacities in a horizontal direction and allowing the vertical or progressive movement to emerge as an epiphenomenon of this gentle and respectful stretching. Observing and trying to help Benjamin over thirty years ago, my philosophy was consonant with Goodman's, although I constantly questioned at first what would be best. I have also found, through the years and in clinical work, that there are times when one must, instead, teach and train. Often this is because of some need or demand on the part of oneself or others that the child make "progress" towards greater independence (e.g., become toilet-trained for school). It is very important to assess whether the goals are realistic, whether one needs to lower or modify them to allow the child to experience some success, and whether energies might better be spent working in an area where the child shows some spontaneous inclination for movement. I never had much luck, for example, teaching Benjamin to eat harder solid foods (or to eat one bite at a time). As it turns out, he really cannot manage such foods—he did not then and still does not have the normal pattern of mastication and swallowing.

Benjamin has emerged as a child and young adult with an extraordinary amount of self-confidence and self-esteem. Whether this can be attributed to our caretaking methods or whether he would have been the same or better with others, I will never know. Whether it was at the expense of learning certain skills or competencies, I do not know. But this I do know. The beginning and end of the approach we followed, both its means and its ends, was to accept and enjoy Benjamin. This either fostered or, at the least, did not interfere with the development of his self-confidence and self-esteem. Happy as he is with himself, he continues to "progress," to take on new challenges, and to learn and grow.

Rereading my notes in preparing this book, I find myself laughing and enjoying again Benjamin's special way of "being," all his unusual and "off" efforts to develop and to interact with the world, to copy it, and cope with it, with only his inadequate equipment at his disposal for doing so. Somewhere in those first months and years, we (his family) were able to let go of anxiety about his differences and, instead, respect them, laugh at them, and work with them. Somewhere, it seems, we seemed to have given up worrying about where it would all end up and instead just stayed involved in and marveled at "the moment." And every moment was as dear with Benjamin as with a normal child. Perhaps even more so. His family enthusiastically cheered every tiny new step forward. For the most part, Benjamin himself showed us where to direct him, what he was ready to consider and able to achieve. I do not think any preset program of early intervention would have shown us as well where to take him. You had to be there to "listen" to him, hear the whispers, and see the shadows that pointed the way.

PART THREE

YEARS LATER

~

CHAPTER FIFTY-THREE

Introduction: Same But Different

A persistent theme throughout the diary entries was "same but different." Benjamin's development moved towards intersubjectivity and a concept of self that eventually emerged, something like, but not altogether like, that of a normal child. And all the steps along the way seemed something like, but not altogether like, those taking place in normal development. The observation that development proceeds in similar but also different ways has been mentioned in describing developments related to selfhood and intersubjectivity in children with Down syndrome. With these children, a similar sequence of development was noted, but with differences in the time of appearance, rate of change, and intensity, density, complexity, and maturity of behavior at various stages of development (Cicchetti and Beeghly 1990; Kopp 1990; Berger 1990).

How did the process and the final achievements in Benjamin's development differ from what is "normal"? With respect to process, one may answer that, for certain, it differed in rate—that is, in how long it took to move through the developmental milestones that pave the way towards selfhood and intersubjectivity, how quickly they came, one upon the other. With respect to the final achievements, one might consider answering: lower ceiling. Both these answers, however, beg the question.

With respect to rate, we need to ask, Why did it take longer, what made it go "slower"? What difference in the developmental process accounts for the slower progress? With respect to ceiling, we must take note of the fact that Benjamin did eventually achieve the human capacities of selfhood and intersubjectivity. Therefore, only the quality of the capacities that developed can be at issue, not whether they were achieved at all. Again, we must ask: In what way are they different from the normal, and what accounts for the difference?

Benjamin's story suggests a difference from the start in the strength, speed, and vigor with which he interacted with and made sense of his experience.

There appeared to exist, from the start, a weakness in what we presume to be the innate, constitutionally given ways that the healthy nervous system responds to, processes, and learns from experience. Theories about these early processing mechanisms tend to describe an early, preverbal kind of abstraction from or synthesis of disparate input. In Baldwin's (1894/1968) and Piaget's schemes, for example, these are the processes of assimilation and accommodation; in Werner's (1940/57) theory, it is hierarchical differentiation and coordination of structures; and Gopnick and Meltzoff (1997) speak of hypothesis testing and theory building in their "theory theory" of development. However it is conceptualized, a relative weakness in the processing of experience appears to lead to, or be the result of, a stimulus-bound or "concrete" way of understanding and responding to the world, versus one that is more integrative and abstract (as described by Goldstein 1963).

At the time of Benjamin's birth, Piagetian theory was a widely popular and accepted theory of development. As is clear from the diary, I turned to it, and in particular, to the central concepts of assimilation and accommodation, again and again in trying to understand Benjamin. A decade or so later, neo-Piagetians (e.g., Case 1985; Pascal-Leone 1988) spoke of "M-power," the number of different sources of information that an individual can take into account and integrate, at any one time. The "executive" and/or working memory systems and speed of processing affect ("constrain") the extent and timing of this integration. The slower individual can "keep in mind" and/or integrate information from fewer sources and perspectives.

How do these considerations relate to selfhood and intersubjectivity? As discussed in chapter 46, some theorists have argued that development of a sense of self requires, first of all, the infant's ability to distill out the constant in bodily sensations experienced in myriad passive and active interactions with both inanimate and animate aspects of the external world (see e.g., Baldwin 1894/1968; Escalona 1963; Stern 1985). According to at least some theorists, the ability to recognize similarities and differences—this time between one's own behaviors and that of "the other"—is a prerequisite for intersubjectivity as well, as it would enable one to recognize not only the separateness of "the other" but also the relative identity of oneself with "the other" (e.g., Newson 1978; Hobson 1990b; Gopnick and Meltzoff 1994; Gallese 2005). The relative identity then inspires and forms the groundwork for communication.

The diary entries suggest that Benjamin had significant limitations in his ability to perceive similarities and accommodate novelty, in the speed and vigor of information processing, and in the range and complexity of the material he could integrate at any one time. In keeping with the above models, these limitations, in turn, would likely result in significant delay and difficulty in identifying "self" and in recognizing selfhood in the other. They might also put a distinctive mark on the nature of the intersubjectivity and sense of self that ultimately was achieved; on the steps in the developmental progress towards that end; and on the kinds of support necessary to foster these developments.

There is, however, another way to understand the "same but different" phenomenon in relation to self and intersubjectivity. It evolves from the view that, in normal development, appreciation of the distinction between self and "the world" is innate or a meta-phenomenon of innate processes (see, e.g., Butterworth 1990; Pipp 1990; Hobson 1990b; Baron-Cohen 1988; Gopnick and Meltzoff 1997). Butterworth (1990), for example, following Gibson, develops the thesis that the "optic flow pattern" in sensory perception which takes place when the infant moves provides visual information that informs the infant of his movement relevant to his surroundings and thus forms an early basis for self/non-self differentiation. Appreciation of the commonality of self and other would also be founded upon innate capacities such as an evolution-based understanding of affect expression (Darwin 1872/1965; Trevarthen 1979; Hobson 1990b, 1993b; Ekman 1973), or innate capacities for emotional resonance and imitation (e.g., Stern 1985; Meltzoff 1993). In short, selfhood and intersubjectivity would be considered "hard-wired" or "instinctive" (Trevarthen and Hubley 1978), rather than dependent upon processing interactions with the environment.

If this view is correct, Benjamin, and children like him, would be doubly compromised and/or slowed down in developing selfhood and intersubjectivity—first, because the innate wiring for these human achievements might be absent, distorted, or weak, and second, because there would be compromise as well in their ability to use processing (e.g., perceiving similarities and differences, abstracting from and integrating information) and learning from their experiences to compensate for this deficiency in the course of development.[1]

Several theories of normal development predict stages in a particular order or describe certain developmental phenomena as sequentially emerging from and requiring the scaffolding of other, earlier ones (e.g., that symbolic function requires and emerges from intersubjectivity [as in Hobson 2002]; that representation is an internalization of imitation which must therefore have preceded it [as in Piaget 1952]). However, in the chapters regarding agency, selfhood, and intersubjectivity, there was frequent reference to the ways in which the nature or sequence of developmental phenomena differed from "normal" or typical in Benjamin's early years. Behaviors that appear to reflect innate propensities in typical children had to be "taught" to Benjamin or otherwise learned. There were huge delays in behaviors such as imitation which, in normal children, are the mainstay of early learning. And certain behaviors never appeared at all or seemed to appear "out of sequence."

It may be tempting to view the differences in Benjamin's development as evidence that the developmental theories are wrong. However, an alternative argument is that, in an atypical child, with an atypically organized nervous system, one should not expect to find the same sequence and organization of development as in the normal child (see, e.g., Roeyers, Van Oost, and Bothuyne 1998). To the extent that the different stages do transpire and different capacities emerge, they may do so via different routes than in normal development or through compensatory functions. This view has important implications for interventions. That milestones may be reached through different routes, at different times, and in a different sequence suggests that one should be wary of interventions that propose a uniform developmental curriculum for all children with atypical development, with goals that reflect the timetable and sequence of normal development. Interventions with this curriculum will likely not only be frustrating for child and parent or teacher but also counterproductive. A major lesson to be learned from Benjamin's story appears to be that it is important to respect the differences, and learn from the individual characteristics of each child what the next step should be and how to help him reach it.

In Benjamin's case, the "average expectable environment" that, for the normal child, would provide enough stimulation and experience to move smoothly and effortlessly though the milestones of infancy did not seem to be enough to encourage development progress. Progress seemed so slow in coming that it often appeared that there would be no progress at all, except with constant, specialized stimulation and encouragement from the environment. At the same time, it was difficult to discern what had paved the way for the "quantum leaps" that did, eventually, occur. Perhaps in both normal and atypical development, ongoing stimulation and "nourishment" of existing structures is needed to bring the nervous system to some threshold required for release of a preprogrammed new capacity. In Benjamin's case, perhaps because of the long interval between the leaps, it appeared that there was an even greater need for this "environmental" preparation.

There are a number of factors, then, that might account for the "same but different" quality of various developmental phenomena in atypical children. For one, there may be abnormality in the child's nervous system, compromising the innate foundations of the phenomena found in normal children. There may be abnormality in the child's general learning style, which will affect the extent and nature of the "learning" that can take place to compensate for the absence of or limitations in certain innate capacities. Finally one can expect individual differences as a function of the nature of the child's experience in the world, as these interact in turn with his or her biologically based capacities for learning (Kopp 1990; Berger 1990; Gray 1978). This last underscores the importance of determining the experiences that would most benefit each particular child (see also Berger 1990).

In children like Benjamin, there are general differences from the start that cause a different developmental course towards "same but different" phenomena. In the preceding chapters, I discussed how these differences in Benjamin "played out" with respect to selfhood and intersubjectivity, in particular. In the following pages, I will give you a glimpse of the young man he became and of the "same but different" quality to his selfhood and intersubjectivity that persists to this day.

Note

1. That selfhood and intersubjectivity are innately programmed versus derived through learning from experiences would be evidenced by the relatively normal development of these human characteristics in Down syndrome children who might be otherwise limited in their capacities for abstraction and learning. On the other hand, high-functioning autistic individuals might be able to use cognitive abilities to compensate and circumvent, to some extent, their deficiencies in the interpersonal realms. The final product of course would be "the same but different," not only because the innate underpinnings are impaired but because of limitations as well in abstraction and learning, resulting in a stilted, too-concrete version of social skills.

~

CHAPTER FIFTY-FOUR

Benjamin Today

I would never have predicted the young man Benjamin is today from the infant and toddler described in the diary. That of course would be true were I to try to project what any baby, any normal baby, would be like thirty years later, from its skills and behavior as an infant. In this case, however, I am referring to whether I could imagine Benjamin ever to have any of the capacities of a normal person—the ability to think, plan, remember, talk, communicate, comprehend, initiate, execute, understand, and discuss feelings—when he seemed not to have any of the capacities of a normal infant. With a normal infant, we anticipate a normal adult. With an atypical infant, we simply don't know what to anticipate.

The fact that we cannot anticipate—and probably should not even try—tends to get lost, however, in the diagnosis of disability. There is a tendency to believe that a diagnosis of Down syndrome, autism, PDD, mental retardation, or other such diagnoses automatically lays out a picture of what this child is like now and what he or she will become. But, while the normal infant may grow up to be a normal adult, with what greater specificity than that can we predict the complex and unique individual he will become? The same is true of the retarded or autistic child. He or she may remain retarded or autistic, but this tells us little about the unique and complex older child and adult each infant will eventually become.

Benjamin is quite a character. He is definitely one of a kind, though he shares many features in common with other children with developmental disabilities and/or "pervasive developmental disorders." He does now "think, plan, remember, talk, communicate, comprehend, initiate, execute, understand, and discuss feelings"—but always, with a difference ("same but different"), as examples below will illustrate. He can read, write, ice skate, swim, bike, and ski, play hockey, roller blade—but with a difference. He even now is learning to play the harp. He sings; he takes care of his dog. He has several real passions: Volkswagen Beetles (of which he has an enormous model collection), bats, and vacuum cleaners head the list. He knows everything about these. Until we moved recently, he had his own little "vacuum cleaning business," vacuuming for neighbors. He also had hung out for years at a local Volkswagen repair shop. The high point of a summer evening for Benjamin is "bat-watching," which means sitting on the picnic table at the cottage, counting the bats as they emerge from the attic. Other passions include reptiles, dogs, cars, zebras, frogs, whales, bowling, going fishing, theme parks, and, of course, Gameboy. Also Julie Andrews, *The Sound of Music*, "The Dukes of Hazzard," anything by Walt Disney, *Star Wars*, and about four hundred other videos and DVDs (including, of course, all the Herbie movies), all of which are neatly arranged in his room. He knows, instantly, where any one of them is located.

Benjamin cannot tell time (or rather, can tell it but has no concept of it) or do arithmetic (absolutely no sense of quantity and arithmetic operations). But he can hold his own against any neighborhood kid in Nintendo and Sega video games. He also has a better sense of electronics than any of the rest of us in the family. He is the one we call upon to fix the TV or DVD if something is wrong. He has a very big vocabulary, and a hundred idiomatic expressions, all of which he generally uses correctly—though sometimes not. However, for the most part, he would not be able to give you definitions of the many words he uses, or tell you what his expressions mean. If he did, they would not be correct. His syntax is fairly good, I imagine at about a third- or fourth-grade level. His prosody is off—his voice is somewhat monotonic, although he has learned to add accents for emphasis. When he does this, it sounds "tacked on." He often talks too loud. It is interesting, however, that while the pitch and loudness of his speech is not sufficiently varied, he can sing anything, with *perfect pitch*!

Benjamin runs errands, never forgets what he is supposed to pick up or drop off, and knows how to use the public transit to new places (at least in Toronto, alas not in L.A.). He plans his day, every day, himself, around things that are important to him, or, more likely, things he is currently "obsessed with." He would be very pleased with a day in which he had taken public transit to buy vacuum bags or a new battery for some remote-control toy, or to buy or exchange a video. On his own, until recently, he took care of picking up Ensure (the dietary supplement he needs because he is so incredibly skinny—five feet four inches and only eighty-five pounds) at the drug store (he no longer drinks Ensure). He knows his TV schedule and is enslaved to it. He must watch favorite TV programs such as "Dukes of Hazzard," "Golden Girls," "Cheers," and "Dallas" reruns (Me: "Why do you like 'Dallas'?" Benjamin: "Oh, you know, it's about *relationships* and things like that."); some of the popular sitcoms; various animal shows, hockey games, and standard juvenile fare ("Sesame Street," "Polka Dot Door," "Mr. Rogers," "Power Rangers," etc.). He is a compulsive buyer of videos and DVDs, and often more than one of the same video, if it comes out with a new cover, or some special edition. He uses money he earns at his various small jobs to buy the videos. He takes care of the buying and exchanging of videos by himself (if, for example, there is the slightest imperfection on the cover or in the tape).

Until we moved recently to L.A., Benjamin had been working at five part-time or volunteer jobs—"maintenance associate" at a community center café; stock clerk at a pet store; volunteer work at a day care; volunteer work at a food bank; and, of course, his vacuuming business. He knew his schedule but needed help knowing at what time he had to leave to get to one or another job on time (I set an alarm on his watch). Currently, he vacuums, cleans up, and is a "good will ambassador" at his brother-in-law's film editing firm. He also attends a performing arts program.

As mentioned, Benjamin is extremely thin. Nothing puts weight on him. On the other hand, he does not eat that much, and what he eats is limited by physical factors related to his cleft palate and neurologically based problems in chewing and swallowing. He does not have a normal chewing reflex; he does not have the normal, unconscious motor planning that allows one to chew and swallow, so that he generally fills his entire mouth before trying, often with great difficulty, to swallow. He cannot eat raw vegetables or fruits (apples, carrots). We have been advised to stay away from raisins and nuts because he might aspirate these. He self-selects, with 100 percent accuracy, what he can eat. I never have to worry that he will eat something on which he will choke. On the other hand, I do have to worry that he will stuff too much in his mouth. Stuffing his mouth and stuffing toilets share much in common. In both cases, his behavior appears rather mindless, out of his control—and totally resistant to change.

Benjamin is extremely interested in, troubled by, and compassionate with respect to autism. One of his best friends is a severely autistic nonverbal boy. Benjamin says, "We do not know what is in his world." He correctly diagnoses: "Johnny cannot communicate." He tries in every way, and with more success than most people, to relate to Johnny and to get him to engage with him. He feels frustrated and sad about how difficult it is to know what Johnny is thinking. He very often tries to think of an answer, a solution to the problem or, as he would say, "to solve your answer!" On his own, he came up with this: "Johnny needs to wear one of those hats like in Back to the Future which will pick up his brain waves. Then his mother should have the same kind of hat, and they can connect them, and then the computer in her hat will figure out what the brain waves from his hat mean" (not bad, and probably what we will be doing someday not so far into the future!).

Although Benjamin is sensitive to others' feelings and even acutely aware of them (see, e.g., "Getting It Right" section in "Benjaminisms," the next chapter), he is very egocentric. He tends to do and say what is on his mind, and needs to be reminded to listen or wait for others to have their turn. He can talk spontaneously with rich content about things that are important to him, but he has a lot of trouble answering questions (e.g., in interviews) about topics that are not of special interest to him. In fact, he looks pretty "autistic" at such times. He'll pull at his hair or shred his pants nervously and avoid eye contact and say, "I don't know," to every question.

Benjamin perseverates on topics of Volkswagen Beetles (new and old), vacuum cleaners, bats, and other passions, and everyone who knows him knows how to get onto his wavelength by bringing up one of these topics. When he talks about these things, it is as if he is "in love" with them. He is obsessed with them, talks incessantly about them, and seems to have no idea that others do not share in his love affair. His obsessions help him plan his day and they keep him happy, because he is organized around them. He wakes up each day, knowing what he wants to do, or has to do, as generated by his "passion" of the day.

Benjamin does also get obsessively involved in liking certain women. These are sort of like "crushes" in the romantic sense, but there is no sexual component. He just likes these women with a passion, just as he might a new Volkswagen on the block, and he will arrange his whole day around making sure he can get to them. He will telephone them many times a day. He is, I should add, quite monogamous and loyal with respect to women. He tends to have and pursue only one passion at any one time.

Benjamin can, and often does, also engage in very meaningful, nonperseverative conversations about issues of great importance in his emotional life, and he will simply "blow your mind" with his considerable insight into the feelings of others at these times, and how he tries to cope with serious emotional issues. There are several examples of this in the "Benjaminisms" section.

Benjamin definitely has a "theory of mind" in that he knows how to manipulate you, through anticipating how you would feel and react to certain things; he tries to set you up to give the reaction he wants. But he (often) really does have trouble taking another's perspective, and integrating information from multiple sources (see, e.g., the Sears man story and "Interview" in "Benjaminisms"). He definitely would fail the TOM laboratory tests! Even when he anticipates another's perspective, he may not take it into account (see the letter "to Warren"). And he has no understanding of metaphor. As described earlier, he really cannot act the role of another because he is just too concrete in his thinking. (He *is* Benjamin. Period.) He is quite aware that the other person has thoughts, feelings, and intentions of their own, different from his, which is why, in his way of thinking, he can't "be" that other person (i.e., as an actor).

In the diary, I mentioned at one point that Benjamin appeared to have a sense of his limitations, and to be frustrated by it. If so, it did not last for long! As he matured, and to this day, at the age of thirty-four, Benjamin does not appear to perceive himself as having disabilities or as being different from others with re-spect to his cognitive abilities. He might be aware that he cannot do something that someone else can (e.g., rock climbing, math) or that someone cannot do something that he can do (e.g., play a harp), but there is no value judgment placed on competencies or weaknesses. He literally never compares himself to others; he does not want to be what others are nor do what others can do. He therefore is completely without competitiveness. Benjamin is not aware of cog-nitive disability in himself or others. His concept of disability extends only to ob-servable physical or sensory disabilities (e.g., in a wheelchair, can't walk, can't see, can't hear), or, in the case of his autistic friend, can't talk.

Benjamin certainly is able to recognize himself (i.e., in mirrors, photographs, etc.), but he never looks at himself in the mirror for the purpose of checking on his appearance or to admire himself. He never looks in the mirror when he gets new clothing to see how he looks in it. In fact—he never looks in the mirror! He has no concept of or interest in dressing fashionably, looking "cool." He does not have any investment in his own appearance, although, interestingly, he is very aware of how I look—he'll often comment on my outfit, tell me I look pretty, and so forth. He may be pleased when someone tells him he looks nice, but he has no idea of what he would have to do to look nice and no personal investment in that. Hence, it would never occur to him to note that there was toothpaste all over his shirt, that his collar was stuck in his sweater, that any-one could see by his clothes what he had for breakfast. Recently, for the first time, he noticed and seemed disconcerted by the scar from his cleft lip repair. He also became concerned about an eye tag—he wanted it removed. He had also been upset by the first appearance of body hair. All of these things were of concern to him, not because he wanted to look "nice" but because they just seemed like things that did not belong on him and did not belong "to him." They were not the way *he* was supposed to look.

Benjamin appears to have virtually no concerns about himself. He wants things in the world (a new DVD, a new Gameboy cassette) but not to be more competent or knowledgeable than he is. That does not mean that he is not very interested in learning new things, and is often willing to learn a new skill. It is just that is he is not unhappy about the level of his skills, and he does not pur-sue learning with the goal of being like or catching up with others. However, al-though he has no concerns about himself, Benjamin is not happy at all if some-one is not happy with him. He does not like it at all when someone expresses disapproval about something he has done. This happens very rarely, but it is devastating to him when it does. Since he never intentionally does anything bad, he is extremely upset at himself if he has done something wrong and caused others to be unhappy with him. This only comes about as a result of one or an-other of his compulsions—primarily, stuffing the toilet with paper, resulting in a flood. He will now lie, to cover his tracks, when he knows he has done something wrong. Recently, he went so far as to do a whole laundry of the bath mats, towels, and the like that got soiled, as a way of hiding his "crime" and avoiding my wrath.

So Benjamin clearly is aware of himself (has a sense of himself) and of others. However, although he definitely would be upset if someone disapproved of something he has done, he does not do things out of concern about or with an eye towards what others will think. In general, in going about his business, he does not seem to be thinking about people thinking about him. (With the exceptions mentioned above, he does not judge himself either—he is not embarrassed, for example, by failure or making a mistake.) He does, however, like to please others—that is, *not* to change the way they think about *him*. It is true that he may, now, try to impress someone, by telling them about something that he has done (e.g., took a ride on a blimp) or that he has (e.g., a new Gameboy game), but this seems to be done primarily as a means of initiating contact with them, getting their attention, or joining in and having something to say (e.g., when he is a guest at a "grown-ups" dinner party) when others are engaged in conversation that is beyond him. He already has a very good concept of himself, in any case, and a concept of himself as good. Though he seems entirely content with who he is (except the compulsions), he is not vain, not "conceited." He recognizes the "bad guys" in movies and stories and knows that he is not like them. He harbors ill will to no one, and does not appear to expect it from others. And indeed, he has always been viewed as a good person and treated that way. On the other hand, part of what makes people see him as a good person, and treat him so well, in the first place, may be his "selflessness"(!)—that is, his lack of competitiveness, envy, vanity, and self-aggrandizement.

Benjamin does not think of himself as handicapped. He never compares himself to others and finds himself coming up short. He is not self-conscious about himself. He appreciates that others can do amazing things (sometimes says to me, "Don't you wish you could do that?") and enjoys watching them but doesn't seem to feel in any way inferior or envious. He understands handicap in terms of physical disability, or not being able to talk or communicate. He seems to have no understanding or recognition of cognitive disability, in himself or others. He knows that I can read better than he can, and write, tell time, and so forth, but I think he just assumes I am older, and adult, whereas he thinks of himself as still young, and closer to a child. As an adult, I would be expected to know more. He might "hang out" with normal young people his age who adapt to his level of understanding, and he would never feel that he is in any way different from them. He has many, many friends—amongst normal people of all ages; just about everyone who meets him likes him, loves him, gets a tremendous kick out of the things he says and how he says them. He also has many friends with cognitive and/or physical disabilities. He makes no distinction between normal and disabled. They are all people, his friends.

Benjamin will engage in the same motor stereotypy that became his trademark when he was about three years old. This is hand clapping, usually accompanied by weird vocalizations, and even, if he is standing, some darting and rocking. The stimulus for this is *excitement associated with the passive witnessing of movement*. Thus, hand clapping only happens when Benjamin is watching a video, TV (which is very often), or a movie or when he is a passive spectator of anything involving rapid movement (watching a roller coaster or a hockey game or watching the waves at the beach). It seems to be some kind of overflow phenomenon that is involuntary. On the other hand, he almost seeks out these experiences. It seems quite pleasurable to him to be watching and clapping; though the combined sounds of the clapping and weird vocalizations drive the family crazy, and they are always yelling up to him to "cool it." (He can control it for a few minutes and then it starts up again.)

Clapping is only precipitated by the visual phenomena I've described, though occasionally it might also occur if Benjamin is thinking about these phenomena. It never happens when *he* is in motion (e.g., in a car) or doing something else or talking. It can be prevented by putting something over his hands, such as mittens or gloves. In the house, we tend more simply to just ask him to put on a pair of socks (i.e., on his hands). He'd rather not because, as stated, clapping is pleasurable. Moreover, when he doesn't have the outlet, he may engage in some other stereotyped act, such as biting his thumb (through the sock) and/or rocking.

Benjamin also still has a compulsive habit of stuffing the toilets or sinks with shredded toilet paper. As mentioned earlier, it tends to happen at times of increased excitement (good or bad), anticipation (even positive anticipation, as, e.g., Christmas morning), anxiety, or boredom. He's gotten into a fair amount of trouble because of the plumbing bills that are the result of his compulsions. (He refers to them as his *"repulsions"*!—not without any intent to change the meaning of the word; this is just the way he hears it.) Once, when "yelled at" for one such episode he told me: "I can't help it, it's my brain, my brain is not right, my brain is making me do these things I don't want to do them, I need help; it's my brain that's not good; it doesn't work right."

I mention this because when engaged in his stereotypies or rituals, Benjamin looks quite "autistic" or PDD. His very social nature, his interest in interacting would seem to belie this, yet his pragmatics share as well something of the PDD quality. His thinking is concrete. As described earlier, he is not always clear when one is making a joke or teasing him by presenting as true, and as here-and-now, something that is obviously fantasy. Recall the Christmas story: every Christmas, we "threaten" (playfully) to call Santa Claus if he is not good and pretend to get Santa on the phone to talk to him. He knows we are kidding—sort of; part of him also believes us, gets worried, and pleads with us not to do it (at the same time as he is laughing).

Not a day goes by that Benjamin's special way of looking at things and his special turn of a phrase does not bring on a smile and make my day. He also seems able to speak straight from the heart about serious matters, and his opinions are often very "right on." The "Benjaminisms" are a sample of the many offerings that endear him to me and everyone else who meets him.

How do you sum up or diagnose a Benjamin? I don't think you can. Perhaps the only summary statement that captures most of him would be to say: He's happy. He's almost always happy. He is optimistic. On the other hand, he actively initiates a great deal, on his own, to ensure that he is happy. He self-regulates his happiness, each day, by planning out this or that outing, or contact with a loved person, or phone call, that he knows will make him happy. He makes sure there is always something good coming up to look forward to—for example, a bowling tournament or a trip to a theme park. He begins planning his next birthday party the day after the one he just had! At this point, I would have to say that Benjamin helps himself to smile—every day—at the same time as he has never stopped being able to make me, and everyone else that he meets, smile. The difference is, I don't have to *help* him to do that anymore. He's a pro.

I am not as happy, because I often worry how he will ever handle the losses, when they come, of the people that he loves so much. One of the ways Benjamin keeps himself happy is by never letting go of anything or anybody. Once Benjamin has made contact with someone, once he has established a relationship with them—teachers, workers, friends—he never forgets them. He calls, writes, arranges coffee dates. His birthday parties get bigger each year, because he has invited every teacher from the past and every old and new person he has met and touched or been touched by. If he does lose someone close to him (e.g., they move away), he mourns the loss but also finds a way to keep in touch. Benjamin also throws away nothing. He remembers, "visits," and occasionally uses every toy he's ever had. He has an unbelievable memory, and with this too, he holds on to everything. He has not forgotten anything that he has experienced in the past thirty years. I certainly have. He reminds me.

I, of course, could not endure not having Benjamin. I simply could not endure it. My smile is attached to him.

~

CHAPTER FIFTY-FIVE

Benjaminisms

In the diary, the reader met Benjamin during his first four years of life, as his sense of self and capacity for intersubjectivity were first emerging and slowly developing, in their "same but different" way. Through the following selection of quotes, the reader can now meet Benjamin as an adult and see the vicissitudes of that "same but different" quality over the decades that followed. The quotes are very loosely organized into several categories. Most refer back to characteristics of Benjamin that have been mentioned throughout this book. The reader will recognize problems with imagination, imitation, abstract thinking, pretending, theory of mind, and integration of information. Many of the quotes could fit well into more than one category, however, or somehow defy classification—I was often at a loss as to how to describe the essence of Benjamin's unique turn of a phrase, his special outlook and way of expressing himself. It is perhaps best not to pay too much attention to the headings, and just enjoy the quotes.

The reader may be surprised at how good Benjamin's language is, after the slow and very arduous beginning documented in the diary. He really did very well verbally, after all. But also take note of his age in each of these vignettes. His continuing naïveté and literalness over the years is striking. But so, too, are the flashes of empathy and comprehension. The quotations, in fact, present a complicated picture with respect to Benjamin's understanding of and interactions with others. They illustrate how difficult it may be to pin down exactly what may be wrong about or missing in the capacity for intersubjectivity in individuals with certain developmental disorders. They should bring home how complex these individuals may be and warn against hasty diagnoses and simplified notions about the nature of their differences or difficulties in social interaction. A quote that sparkles with insight and empathy may follow one that clearly reflects a deficit in taking another's perspective. Problems in "theory of mind" abound but in no way interfere with a very strong desire to communicate and the capacity to do so.

There is a great deal of charm in many of these gems. They should make you smile.

Literal

Twelve Years Old
We had a cat named Moonshine. One night, the moon was very bright, and I pointed out to Benjamin how much it was shining. I said, "It's like sunshine, except this would be moonshine." He looked at me in disbelief and said:

B: Moommm! Are you *crazy*? Does a *moon* have fur?

Seventeen Years Old
We are watching a Santa Claus parade. Asked if he wanted to wear a costume and march in the parade next year, he replies, again in disbelief:

B: Are you *kidding*, walk all the way to *the North Pole*??!!

Eighteen Years Old
Kids in his class told him that his parents were Santa Claus. Benjamin said (and again with disbelief!):

B: Are you *crazy*! My parents don't have that much money!! [i.e., to buy presents for everyone]

Doing sheets of homework—additions and subtractions with pictures of little apples. He has to add or subtract apples and write the solution under the pictures. He has been doing sheet after sheet of these for weeks. One night, after doing the compulsory two sheets of apples, there was a third sheet to do. This time, the teacher had drawn little pears. Benjamin is upset:

B: It's *too hard*!

Me: Why, you can do this, it's the same thing as the apples.

B: O o o, *no! NOT* with *PEARS!*

Twenty-Four Years Old
His teacher is very pregnant, in her ninth month. He had learned in school about reproduction—that is, the egg and the sperm.

B: Boy, that egg is getting pretty big now! How is it going to get out!?

Benjamin takes a shop course in "auto mechanics" at school.

Me: What do you do in the auto shop?

B explains (or tries to) the details of changing a tire: "You take this thing and you unscrew the bolts, then you put them over there, and then you put the tire on that thing, . . ."

Me: Oh! So you learned how to change a tire!

B: No.

Me: It sounds like that's what you did. That's how you change a tire!

B: No! We did NOT change the tire.

(I ask him to describe it again; again I surmise he had learned to change a tire; again he rejects this.)

Me: Well, what did you do then?

B: We did *not* change the tire. We put the same one back.

Twenty-Six Years Old

Reads label of medicated mouthwash he needs to take: "Gargle with one tablespoon four times daily." Absolutely *refuses* to do it.

Me: Why?

B: I don't *want* to gargle *with a tablespoon. I don't know how!!!*

Upon his refusing to try Pepto-Bismol:

Me: C'mon Benjamin, it won't kill you.

B: I know it won't kill me . . . but is it good for my stomach?

Twenty-Seven Years Old

Benjamin is working at a workshop. They are trying to find jobs for the clients "in the community." Benjamin is adamant that he does not want to work in the community.

Me: Why don't you want to work in the community?

B: I just don't. I want to stay at the workshop.

Me: Do you know what it means "to work in the community"?

B: Yes. It means you don't work in the workshop. You work outside the workshop.

Me: Right.

B: But what if it rains?

Twenty-Eight Years Old

Benjamin was very excited about a trip to Legoland. He was having trouble waiting. His sister suggested that he relax by meditating, closing his eyes, taking a deep breath. Benjamin did as told.

Anny (in soft tones): Now, picture a beautiful blue ocean.

Benjamin (eyes still closed): But I can't *see!!*

Taking the "Other's" Perspective (or Not!): Playing a Role

Nineteen Years Old

Letter to Uncle Warren

(Warren has just sent him a very expensive model VW Beetle.)

Dear Warren

I like this gift from you. I hope you won't be sad I have one already. I hope we see you soon. I love it. Love B

Twenty-Four Years Old
The Test
I notice a bump and scratch on his forehead. I ask him how he got it:

B: I don't know, will it go away??

Me: Yes, but how did you get it?

B: I don't know.

Me: Did it happen in school?

B: No.

Me: On the way there? On the way home? In the playground?

B: No, I don't know, I don't remember [to all my questions].

Me: That's impossible, Benjamin, you can't have gotten such a big scratch and bump on your head and not know where and how it happened.

B (getting very frustrated and exasperated by the questions): I DON'T KNOW, I don't remember.

(I am becoming exasperated myself, and concerned. Is he concealing something? Does he think he did something wrong and is afraid to tell? Maybe some wrongdoing to him was involved. I therefore press on, and insist that he not hide the truth from me. I even threaten: no videos until he tells me what happened.)

B: Why do you want to know?

Me: I'm your mother. Mothers worry about their children, look after them. If you got hurt, I need to know how. It could be important. Maybe I can help make sure it doesn't happen again.

B: I don't know! I DON'T REMEMBER!!!

(Then, finally, getting quite frustrated by my repeated questions, to which it appears he may, in fact, NOT know the answer, he answers my question, What happened?? one more time):

B: I DON'T *KNOW* ! *Give me a hint!!!*

(In this example, Benjamin clearly [mis]interpreted my asking questions of him as my giving him a test, the answers to which I knew, rather than as an earnest effort on my part to find out from him something I did not know.)

Twenty-Seven Years Old
The Sears Man
Me: The Sears man [department store delivery] is coming today. If someone comes to the door, make sure it is the Sears man before you let him in. How will you find out whether he is the Sears man?

B: I'll ask him.

Me: What will you say?

B: Are you the Sears man?

Me: That would not be the best way to find out who he is. Can you figure out why?

B: No. . . . You said, only let in the man from Sears.

Me: But you are giving him a hint when you ask that way. What if he was a burglar, and you asked him, Are you the Sears man. What would he say?

B: He would say no, because he's not the Sears man.

Me: What if he wanted to come in, so that he could rob the house. If you asked him, are you the Sears man, what would he say?

B: He would say no, because he is not the Sears man.

Me: But then, how would he get in?

B: I wouldn't let him in, because he's not the Sears man.

Me: What if he *said* he was the Sears man, and he wasn't—what if he tried to trick you that way?

B: Then I wouldn't let him in.

Me: But how would you *know* if he was tricking you, how would you know if he was really the Sears man, or if he wasn't?

B: I would ask him. . . . [thinks a bit] Also, I would look to see if his truck was there, or if it said Sears on his pocket.

Me: That would be a good idea!! But what if he parked his car someplace else? How would you know who he was?

(I explain to him the idea that someone might not tell the truth in order to trick him, so that they could get in. I told him it would be better to say, "Who is it?" or "Who are you?" He didn't really see the difference between those questions and the question, "Are you the Sears man" [!] though he probably could learn that he should say, "Who is it?")

Me: OK, let's try it out. Knock Knock. Hi, good morning, can I come in?

B: No.

Me: Why not?

B: Because you are not the Sears man.

Me: How do you know?

B: I don't know. Can we stop this? I won't let anyone in. I promise.

(Obviously, equally a problem here was my way of explaining things to him—though, in part, I was just having fun doing it. Clearly, he needed some very concrete rules, what to say, what to do, and so forth, without my explanations.)

Twenty-Eight Years Old
Job Interview

I introduce the idea of practicing for an interview that Benjamin is scheduled to have regarding volunteer work in a day care.

Me: Let's practice for the interview. I'll be Monica [the interviewer, who has already met him once] and you be Benjamin.

B: But I AM Benjamin.

Me: I know. I'll *pretend* I'm Monica and [teasing] you *pretend* you're Benjamin.

B: But *I* AM Benjamin [not comfortable with the game, getting cranky about it; knows I'm joking with him, but not really sure].

Me: Hi Benjamin, nice to see you again. I understand you want to do volunteer work in the day care?

B: *Ma, NO! You're* not Monica. I don't want to do this.

Me (continuing): Can you tell me a little bit about your experience? Have you ever worked with young children before?

B: [Part laughing at my role-playing, part very uncomfortable, avoiding eye contact, poking his fingers in his eyes, pulling at his hair, etc.]

Me: [I imitate his behavior and say,] Boy, *that* sure looks good in an interview!

B (laughing at me): All right, all right.

Me: So, I understand you want to do volunteer work. Have you worked with young children before?

B: Yes.

Me: Where?

B: Scadding Court [day camp].

Me (now being mom): That's right, Benjamin, but you also worked other places. [He doesn't remember. I remind him of two other day camp jobs he's had—Knox Church and St. Steven's.]

Me: OK, let's practice it again. Hi Benjamin, nice to see you again, how are you today?

B: *I worked in three places: Scadding Court, Knox Church, St.Steven's.*

Me (laughing): No! No !—you have to *wait* for the question, first.

B (laughing): All right, all right.

(We continue with the role play.)

Me: What do you think you would like to do with the children?

B: [answers, correctly] Clean up the toys, lay out the toys, play games with them. That's what I did at the day camp. And they said I was wonderful at it.

(Better, after a bit more practice, but he is still having trouble with eye contact and comfort. So we continue.)

Me: OK. Now, how about *you* be Monica, and *I'll* be Benjamin. [This REALLY throws him.]

B: NO!!! *I'm* Benjamin. Please can we stop this?

Me: Come on, Benjamin, this is fun. Also, this is the way people really learn how to do interviews. It's the way of teaching things. Just try it.

B: All right, all right.

Me: OK, you pretend you're Monica, I'll pretend I'm you.

B: Do you have any experience working with young children?

Me (playing Benjamin): Yes.

(Benjamin doesn't say anything.)

Me: Aren't you going to ask me where I had my experience?

B: No, I don't *have* to. . . . I already know. (!!!!!)

NOT Getting the Point

Twenty-Seven Years Old

Benjamin wants to use money he has just earned to buy a video. I tell him to put it in the bank, save it, don't spend it on yet another video. He is insistent. I explain to him why it is not a good idea to spend it on a relatively unimportant video; wait till a more important video (one that he is waiting for) comes out or wait till he gets some gift money. In the meantime, save his money.

B: All right, all right. You're right. I won't spend my money. But will *you* buy it for me?

Me: NO! I don't want to spend *my* money, either, on that video.

B: You don't have to. *I'll* buy it [i.e., I should give him the money and then he'd go to the store to buy it].

Me: But Benjamin, that will still be my money. I'd still be paying for it.

B: That's OK. I'll pay you back.

Thirty-Three Years Old

The Special Olympics is an international organization sponsoring sports training, competitions, and "Olympics" events for people with developmental disabilities. The athletes all have some degree of cognitive or cognitive/physical handicap. Benjamin has participated in swimming, skiing, floor hockey, soccer, and/or bowling "Special Olympics" for many years. Watching a ski-jumping competition in the (regular) 2004 Olympics on TV, he was impressed with the athletes' expertise:

B: Boy, he's good!! He could even be in the *Special* Olympics!

(This pertains, too, to Benjamin's lack of awareness of his and others' handicaps.)

GETTING the Point
(and APPRECIATING the Other's Perspective)

Benjamin has had knowledge of or experienced several separations and divorces amongst relatives and close friends. These are always very upsetting to him. He simply does not believe separation is ever right, and he is quite articulate about it.

Twenty-Three Years Old

Upon learning of the separation of people he was very close to:

B: It's not right. After fifteen years of marriage, he's separating from Y. Could you believe it, after fifteen years of marriage! It's a mistake, they shouldn't do it! Y will never find another man like L. They should talk about it. I'm going to talk to Y. I'll tell her not to do it. Women are different. They know about these things. Y and A (daughter) are happy on the outside, but inside they are sad.

Benjamin then actually calls Y, on his own initiative. I overheard the conversation:

B: In the future, you will get back together. Don't worry, in the future, you will get back. [Repeats this many times.] It's not right, after fifteen years of marriage. You and L are happy on the outside, but inside you are sad. Don't worry, in the future . . .

The following is one of many conversations during a period of instability when his stepfather was moving back and forth a lot, between the United States and Canada:

B: I wish M was living with us again, under the same roof. I don't like it this way, it's not a family. It's like L and Y, not divorced but separated. Is he coming back? When is he coming back? It was better when he was here. He wants to come back. L doesn't want to go back to Y, but M does want to come back and we should let him. It's too long. He should come back and sleep upstairs in the same bed as you. He should come back and stay, under the same roof, and not go away again. He should not come and then go and then come and then go. *It's too confusing. He should either make up his mind to stay, or not come back at all* [emphasis added].

Me: Which is better, to not come back and forth, or not to come at all?

B: To STAY. He has to make up his mind. Like he comes and then he goes. He lives in Pennsylvania, and then in Toronto. He doesn't want to go to California [where B wants to live because his sisters live there], he never does, he just wants to go to Pennsylvania, and then to Toronto. He has to make up his mind! *He can't do two things at once!!* Make up your mind! What do you want!? [referring to M]

Me: Well, he is trying to and he says he is making up his mind to come back.

B: Well, he loves you. He just doesn't know how to show it.

Benjamin then (spontaneously) offered a plan:

B: You could start off with living under the same roof, but he could stay in the basement [apartment] and then you would begin to see that it could work, and he could then move to upstairs. Get used to each other again, and then see if it can work. You can talk about things, not talk loud and argue, just talk about things. We should all sit down and talk about this . . . you, me, and M. We should talk about this and see. You want me to be happy, right?

Me: Yes, but I need to be happy, too.

B: Well, you'd be happy if I was happy, right?

Me: Yes.

B: SO! We'd *both* be happy!!

Girl (call her Nancy) at school that he likes very much, as a friend, told him she "doesn't want me to talk about being a girlfriend ever again . . . she says she just wants to be my friend, not my girlfriend."

Me: Do you know the difference?

B: Not really.

Me: Girlfriends and boyfriends are in love, and they kiss a lot and want to get married. Nancy doesn't want to do that.

B: I don't want to get married. But I do like Nancy. Friends are better because friends are for life, and girlfriends and boyfriends fight and then they get separated, like Anny and [her former boyfriend], and then they are not friends anymore. I don't want that.

Me: Were you disappointed when she told you that?

B: Well, sort of, but that's life.

Twenty-Six Years Old

Regarding the suicide of a girl in the neighborhood whom he had known:

B: It's *so terrible*!

Me: She must have been really upset about something.

B: She should have gone for therapy. You should never give up hope. She must have been mistreated.

Thirty Years Old

Upon learning that the devoted mother of a very autistic boy has realized that she must now find placement for him. Benjamin already had recognized this—the last time he saw him, quite distressed, Benjamin said, "J is bored. He needs to be in a program all the time." Still, upon learning of the mother's decision, Benjamin was visibly shaken. I assumed this was because it set off anxieties about himself.

Me: Are you upset about J having to move from his home?

B: A little, but it's the right thing. But I am thinking about M [J's mother]. I am thinking about what she must be going through.

Use of Expressions (Not Always Right!)

Twenty-One Years Old

Upon the sudden death of a neighbor, the first death of someone he knew well, Benjamin was quite shook up, and obviously worried about the prospect that this could happen to a family member. By way of reassuring him, I told him (truthfully) that Louis (in contrast to Benjamin's other family members) was a heavy smoker.

B: Well . . . I guess he learned his lesson!

Twenty-Five Years Old

Upon buying yet another model Volkswagen, this one quite overpriced, and being told by me that it was a "rip-off," Benjamin proudly proclaims as he shows off his prize to a visitor:

B: Look at *this* one! It's a RIP-OFF!!

That Special, Very Touching Viewpoint

Twenty-Seven Years Old

To reassure me on the death of a very dear friend of mine:

B: Life goes on; you've got to go on with life. You have to go on seeing and doing things. That way, when you die, at least you have your memories.

Benjamin was to go on a fishing trip the next day, to catch bass. Upon being told that the best bait for catching bass is frogs (which he really likes), Benjamin felt very uncertain whether he would engage in the sport. He thought about it all night. Woke the next morning and announced:

B: *No! NO* frogs. *Worms*, it would definitely be better to use *worms*. Worms don't have families.

That Special Way of Putting Two and Two Together

Twenty-Two Years Old

The Dive

Discussion after he was observed getting ready to do a sitting dive into shallow water:

Me: You should *never never never do that!!!* Do you know what could happen to you if you dive into shallow water?

B: You could bump your head.

Me: No. Not just bump your head; you would hurt your head *very very badly!*

B: Get a concussion?

Me: Or worse. Do you know what a concussion is? It means your head gets broken or your brains get all smashed up.

B: *But I had a flu shot.* (!)

Me: [I explain the irrelevancy of the flu shot, and again stress the horrible damage to your head and the possibility of death if you dove into shallow water.]

B: But, *look on the bright side*, you still have your *heart. That* will keep you healthy. You need your heart to live. Your brain is just for thinking.

Thirty Years Old

Upon learning that a friend had named her baby Benjamin, Benjamin is perplexed and disturbed.

B. He can't be named Benjamin, that's my name.

Me: But there are many people in this world with the name of Benjamin, not just you.

B: Like who?

Me: Well, there's Benjamin Franklin [who he knows a lot about].

B: Yeah, but HE's *dead*!

Thirty-Four Years Old
Jury Duty

His friend Mark, a boy with severe spastic quadriplegia, was recently called to report for jury duty. Although it was unlikely that he would be asked to serve, Mark was quite excited and proud about being called to do his civic duty. Benjamin was quite happy for him too. On the day in question, he told me that Mark would not be at the performing arts program the next day because he had to go to jury duty. He added, "But I don't think he's guilty—I don't think he did it."

Logic

Twenty-Two Years Old

This occurred at the time of the Waco disaster. Looking at the newspaper, he sees a picture of the fire, and reads the headline about a cult leader, but without comprehension.

B: What's a cult leader? What happened?

Me: Some man in Texas thought he was God, and told everybody he was God and they had to do what he said; then he told them to set the house on fire and all die, and they listened to him and they did it.

B: That's *terrible*, that's *crazy*. He must be *crazy*.

Me: He IS crazy.

B (thoughtfully): We-elll, if he's *crazy*, he can't be *God*!

Twenty-Seven Years Old

Benjamin is enamored of a VW Beetle newly arrived at the VW garage for repairs. He is asking us questions (perseveratively) about it.

B: Would you believe it, it's a 1973. How old is it?

Me: Well, what do you think? You were born in 1970 and how old are you?

B: Twenty-seven.

Me: Right. So, this Beetle was born three years after you, in 1973. So about how old would it be?

B: I don't know. Seventy? Three? Nineteen? . . . I don't know.

Me: [I repeat the analogy to his year of birth.]

B (with an air of conviction): Thirty-seven*!!*
Me: How did you get that?
B (with conviction): Well, seventy-three, counting clockwise, is thirty-seven!

Thirty Years Old
B has a "crush" on a colleague of mine who is several years older than he is. When he turned thirty, she teased him that she was the same age as he was—because their *birthdates* were just one day apart.

B: Can you believe it, Maria is the same age as me!!
Me: Do you really think she is? Don't you think she might be a little bit older?
B: Nope. She told me. She's thirty, too.
Me. Ladies sometimes don't like to tell their age. Maybe she is a little older, what do you think?
B: Yeah, I guess she is. Maybe she's older than me. But she *told* me she was thirty.
Me: Well, if she's older than you, how can she also be the same age as you?
B (thinking): Hmm. . . . Height?

Use of Expressions

Twenty-Two Years Old
Discussion regarding a close friend's romantic relationship with a married man:
B: That's not right. If his mother [means wife] knew what he was up to, she'd be very upset. She should be with Jim [a former boyfriend whom B liked]. Jim is single. He should be the stand-by. She should marry Jim, *for my sake.* [emphasis added]

Twenty-Nine Years Old
I can't find a box of soup. I've looked everywhere and suspect Benjamin might have been up to his old tricks—throwing things in the toilet. He denies knowledge of the soup.
Me: Bernard [his worker] thinks you have information you are not telling.
B: Nope, I do *not* know where it is. Have I ever lied to you? Hmmm? If I knew where it was, *you'd be the first to know.*

In a discussion recently about whether "Dallas" was on TV that night, I argued that it was, he argued that it wasn't, as follows:
B: *First of all,* "Dallas" is not on. Second of all, *I rest my case!!*

That Special Turn of Phrase

Twenty-Two Years Old

Regarding taking sailing lessons, on Lake Ontario:

B: You mean I go on the lake, the *big* lake?!! The one with the *horizon? No thank you!!*

Favorite Expressions for the Past Ten Years or So

"Look on the bright side," then gives an alternative view to whatever is concerning the person.

"Might as well!"—Whenever asked to do just about anything

"Why bother!"

"I get the drift."

"The fact is . . ."

"On your behalf . . ."

"May I have the honor?" (Often introducing something quite incongruous, as, for example, "May I have the honor of taking the dead fish out of the fish tank?")

Sophisticated sentence structure and syntax. For example, "The fact that I do [such and such] doesn't mean [such and such]."

Miscellaneous

Twenty-Seven Years Old

Benjamin's turtle (of twelve years) died. We "buried" it in the lake. Benjamin was concerned about what would happen to the body. I tried to explain about its decomposition, in terms of it returning to be just part of the earth and sand. But he wasn't satisfied with the explanation. It was the first time he thought about what happens to something or someone after they die, and he seemed very uncomfortable about the topic.

B: *You* really don't know enough about it. Look it up on the Internet.

Me: I don't know how I would look it up.

B: Look it up under "dies": D-I-E-S!

Twenty-Eight Years Old

In the past, when Benjamin would have trouble getting up for school or work, and claim to not feel well, I would ask: Are you really sick or are you just trying to play hooky? (But I never actually explained what "hooky" meant.) Recently, he came upon the "Jerry Springer Show" (show where people air their laundry and scream and beat up on each other before a live audience; it comes on right before B's favorite show, "Dallas," so he often sees the last few minutes of it).

The guests this particular night are a pair of outrageously dressed and made up male transvestite prostitutes, in black corsets, garters, low-cut tops, and so forth. B doesn't know anything about this sort of thing, but he is definitely taken aback by their appearance and behavior. He tells me, with disbelief:

B: They're really MEN! It's GROSS!

Then, apparently having heard them referred to as "hookers," he says:

B: Mommy, I *promise*—I'll NEVER play hooky!!

And My Favorite

Step-dad: You know Benjamin, I really love you.

B: I know. . . . Who wouldn't!

~

Appendix

The following is a letter to Dr. Hilda Knobloch, who had agreed to assess Benjamin. It accompanied a developmental questionnaire she had sent to me to fill out, prior to her examination of Benjamin.

September 1971

Dear Dr. Knobloch:

I found this form very difficult to fill out (and upsetting). I am not at all certain about many of the dates. Also, at times, I feel I underestimate Benjamin's level, at other times, that I quite seriously overestimate it. I think perhaps that some of my confusion is based on my feeling that it is not only a question of what Benjamin can or cannot do that is at issue, but the quality, the particular style of the way he does even what he can do. There really is no place in the form for getting at that—as I described to you on the phone, he often has a vague, drunken, sleepy, weak, quality. He seems to have less vigor, spontaneity, initiative and interest in exploration than one expects to see in a baby. He's less "lively" in many senses of the word. I see him as relatively underdeveloped in these spheres, not as totally lacking these qualities. He is, that is, often enough excited, vigorous (for him), interested and happy, more so than I tend to expect of him. Finally, I sometimes feel that he does less and acts less, because he has some feedback as to his inability to do more, but that the motivation is not necessarily lacking. He seems timid in his use of his body and often gives up when he doesn't seem to have the strength to complete something he tries.

I have had much concern about the quality and style of his relating. Here, too, he *does* relate to people but it is in a less mature way than his age, and he often tends not to respond. He sometimes seems not to want to bother, as if he is interested elsewhere (though you can always get him to come around, if you play with him). I see as perhaps most lacking *the push to imitate and be like another person*. He enjoys anything shown to him, loves to be entertained, but does not tend to take something he is shown into his own repertoire.

He's not just like a younger baby. He's different. He learns differently. Mainly, he doesn't "express out"—he doesn't communicate his needs *to* someone. He doesn't actively express, proclaim, to you his being. He *reacts* to love, loves to be loved, but doesn't "love out," doesn't imitate, initiate. If he raises his hands to be picked up, which he just did yesterday, tentatively, for the first time, it has the quality of being just the beginning of his response to my lifting him, rather than an expression of his wishes.

Whatever he is, I accept him now and love him. I'd like you to meet him.

Bibliography

Adrien, I. L., M. Perrot, L. Hameury, B. Garreau, C. Barthelemy, and D. Sauvage. "Autism and Family Home Movies: Preliminary Findings." *Journal of Autism and Developmental Disorders* 21 (1991): 1, 43–50.

Alvarez, A. A. *Live Company: Psychoanalytic Psychotherapy with Autistic, Borderline, Deprived and Abused Children.* London: Routledge, 1992.

American Psychiatric Association. *Diagnostic and Statistical Manual of Mental Disorders.* 3rd ed. Washington, D.C.: APA, 1980.

———. *Diagnostic and Statistical Manual of Mental Disorders.* 3rd ed. Washington, D.C.: APA, 1987.

———. *Diagnostic and Statistical Manual of Mental Disorders.* 4th ed. Washington, D.C.: APA, 1994.

———. *Diagnostic and Statistical Manual of Mental Disorders.* 4th training ed. Washington, D.C.: APA, 2000.

Anisfeld, M. "Review: Neonatal Imitation." *Developmental Review* 11 (1991): 60–97.

———. "No Compelling Evidence to Dispute Piaget's Timetable of the Development of Representation and Imitation in Infancy." In *Perspectives on Imitation: From Neuroscience to Social Science, Volume 2: Imitation, Human Development and Culture*, edited by S. Hurley and N. Chater, 107–113. Cambridge, Mass.: MIT Press, 2005.

Anisfeld, M., G. Turkewitz, and S. A. Rose et al. "No Compelling Evidence That Newborns Imitate Oral Gestures." *Infancy* 2, no. 1 (2001): 11–12.

Attwood, T., U. Frith, and B. Hermelin. "Understanding and Use of Interpersonal Gestures by Autistic and Down Syndrome Children." *Journal of Autism and Developmental Disorders* 18, no. 2 (1988): 241–258.

Baldwin, J. M. *The Development of the Child and of the Race.* New York: Augustus M. Kelly, 1894, 1968.

———. *Social and Ethical Interpretation in Mental Development.* New York: Macmillan, 1902.

Baranek, G. T. "Autism During Infancy: A Retrospective Video Analysis of Sensory-Motor and Social Behaviors at 9–12 Months of Age." *Journal of Autism and Developmental Disorders* 29, no. 3 (1999): 213–224.

Baron-Cohen, S. "Social and Pragmatic Deficits in Autism: Cognitive or Affective?" *Journal of Autism and Developmental Disorders* 18, no. 3 (1988): 370–402.

——. *Mind-Blindness: An Essay on Autism and Theory of Mind.* Cambridge, Mass.: MIT Press, 1995.

Baron-Cohen, S., A. M. Leslie, and U. Frith. "Does the Autistic Child Have a 'Theory of Mind?'" *Cognition* (1985): 31–46.

Baron-Cohen, S., H. Tager-Flusberg, and D. J. Cohen, eds. *Understanding Other Minds.* New York: Oxford Medical Publications, 1993.

Baron-Cohen, S., and S. Wheelwright. "The Friendship Questionnaire: An Investigation of Adults with Asperger Syndrome or High-Functioning Autism, and Normal Sex Differences." *Journal of Autism and Developmental Disorders* 33, no. 5 (2003): 509–518.

——. "Empathy Quotient: An Investigation of Adults with Asperger Syndrome or High-Functioning Autism and Normal Sex Differences." *Journal of Autism and Developmental Disorders* 34, no. 2 (2004): 163–176.

Barry, T., L. G. Klinger, J. H. Lee, N. Palardy, T. Gilmore, and S. D. Bodin. "Examining the Effectiveness of an Outpatient Clinic-Based Social Skills Group for High Functioning Children with Autism." *Journal of Autism and Developmental Disorders* 33, no. 6 (2003): 685–702.

Bates, E. *Language and Context: The Acquisition of Pragmatics.* New York: Academic Press, 1971.

——. "Language About Me and You: Pronominal References and the Emerging Concept of Self." In *Self in Transition, Infancy to Childhood,* edited by D. Cicchetti and M. Beeghly, 165–182. Chicago: University of Chicago Press, 1989.

Bates, E., L. Benigni, I. Bretherton, L. Camaioni, and V. Volterra. "Cognition and Communication from 9 to 13 Months: Correlational Findings." In *The Emergence of Symbols, Cognition, and Communication in Infancy,* edited by E. Bates, 69–140. New York: Academic Press, 1979.

Bauman, M. L., and T. L. Kemper. "Neuroanatomic Observations of the Brain in Autism." In *Neurobiology of Autism,* edited by M. L. Bauman and T. L. Kemper, 119–145. Baltimore: Johns Hopkins University Press, 1994.

Bauminger, N., and C. Kasari. "Brief Report: Theory of Mind in High-Functioning Children with Autism." *Journal of Autism and Developmental Disorders* 29, no. 1 (1999): 83–86.

Bauminger, N., C. Shulman, and G. Agam. "Peer Interaction and Loneliness in High Functioning Children with Autism." *Journal of Autism and Developmental Disorders* 33, no. 5 (2003): 489–508.

Beebe, B., and F. F. Lachmann. "Contributions of Mother–Infant Mutual Influence to the Origins of Self and Object Representation." *Psychoanalytic Psychology* 5, no. 4 (1992): 305–337.

Beebe, B., J. Jaffe, S. Feldstein, K. Mays, and D. Alson. "Interpersonal Timing: The Application of an Adult Dialogue Model to Mother–Infant Vocal and Kinesic Interactions." In *Social Perception in Infants,* edited by T. Field and N. Fox, 207–246. Norwood, N.J.: Ablex, 1985.

Beeger, S., C. Rueffe, M. M. Terwagt, L. Stockman. "Theory of Mind-Based Action in Children from the Autistic Spectrum." *Journal of Autism and Development Disorders* 33, no. 5 (2003): 479–487.

Beeghly, M., B. Weiss-Perry, and D. Cicchetti. "Beyond Sensori-Motor Functioning: Early Communicative and Play Development of Children with Down Syndrome." In *Children with Down Syndrome—A Developmental Perspective*, edited by D. Cicchetti and M. Beeghly, 329–368. New York: Cambridge University Press, 1990.

Beglinger, L. J., and T. H. Smith. "A Review of Sub-Typing in Autism and Proposed Dimensional Classification Model." *Journal of Autism and Developmental Disorders* 31, no. 4 (2001): 411–422.

Belsky, J., and R. Isabella. "Maternal, Infant, and Social Contextual Determinants of Attachment Security." In *Clinical Implications of Attachment*, edited by J. Belsky and T. Nezworsky, 41–94. Hillsdale, N.J.: Lawrence Erlbaum, 1988.

Bemporad, J. R., J. J. Ratey, and G. O'Driscoll. "Autism and Emotion: An Ethological Theory." *American Journal of Orthopsychiatry* 57, no. 4 (1987): 477–484.

Berger, J. "Interactions Between Parents and Their Infants with Down Syndrome." In *Children with Down Syndrome—A Developmental Perspective*, edited by D. Cicchetti and M. Beeghly, 101–146. New York: Cambridge University Press, 1990.

Bergman, A. *Ours, Yours, Mine: Mutuality and the Emergence of the Separate Self*. Northvale, N.J.: Jason Aronson, 1998.

Bettleheim, B. *Love Is Not Enough: The Treatment of Emotionally Disturbed Children*. New York: Free Press, 1950.

———. *The Empty Fortress: Infantile Autism and the Birth of the Self*. New York: Free Press, 1967.

Biklen, C. U. "Autism and Praxis." *Harvard Educational Review* 60 (1990): 291–314.

———. *Communication Unbound: How Facilitated Communication Is Challenging Traditional Views of Autism and Ability/Disability*. New York: Teachers College Press, 1993.

Blacher, J., and C. E. Meyers. "A Review of Attachment Formation and Disorder of Handicapped Children." *American Journal of Mental Deficiency* 87, no. 4 (1981): 359–371.

Bloom, L. *One Word at a Time*. The Hague: Mouton, 1973.

Bowlby, J., *Attachment*, vol. 1 of *Attachment and Loss*. New York: Basic Books, 1969.

Bowler, D. M., and J. A. Briskman. "Photographic Cues Do Not Always Facilitate Performance on False Belief Tasks in Children with Autism." *Journal of Autism and Developmental Disorders* 30, no. 4 (2000): 295–304.

Boysen, S. T., K. M. Bryant, and T. A. Shreger. "Shadows and Mirrors: Alternative Avenues to the Development of Self-Recognition in Chimpanzees." In *Self-Awareness in Animals and Humans: Developmental Perspectives*, edited by S. T. Parker, R. W. Mitchell, and M. I. Bocchia, 227–239. New York: Cambridge University Press, 1994.

Bromwich, R. N. "Focus on Maternal Behavior in Infant Interventions." *American Journal of Orthopsychiatry* 46 (1976): 439–446.

Bruner, J., and C. Feldman. "Theories of Mind and the Problem of Autism." In *Understanding Other Minds*, edited by S. Baron-Cohen, H. Tager-Flusberg, and D. J. Cohen, 267–291. New York: Oxford Medical Publications, 1993.

Bruner, J. S. "Organization of Early Skilled Action." In *The Integration of a Child into a Social World*, edited by N. P. M. Richards. Cambridge: Cambridge University Press, 1974.

———. "From Communication to Language—A Psychological Perspective." *Cognition* (1975): 255–287.

Bruner, J. S., and V. Sherwood. "Thought, Language and Interactions in Infancy." In *Frontiers of Infant Psychiatry*, edited by J. D. Call, E. Galenson, and R. L. Tyson, 38–55. New York: Basic Books, 1983.

Buffington, D. M., P. I. Krantz, L. McClannahan, and C. I. Poulson. "Procedures for Teaching Appropriate Gestural Communication Skills in Children with Autism." *Journal of Autism and Developmental Disorders* 23, no. 4 (1998): 538–546.

Buitelaar, J. K., and M. van der Wees. "Are Deficits in the Decoding of Affective Cues and in Mentalizing Abilities Independent." *Journal of Autism and Developmental Disorders* 27, no. 5 (1997): 539–556.

Buss, D., M. G. Haselton, T. K. Shackelford, A. L. Bleske, and J. C. Wakefield. "Adaptations, Exaptations and Spandrels." *American Psychologist* 53 (1998): 533–548.

Butterworth, G. "Self-Perception in Infancy." In *Self in Transition, Infancy to Childhood*, edited by D. Cicchetti and M. Beeghly, 119–138. Chicago: University of Chicago Press, 1989.

Calder, A. J., J. Keane, F. Manes, N. Antoun, and A. W. Young. "Impaired Recognition and Experience of Disgust Following Brain Injury." *Nature Neuroscience* 3 (2000): 1077–1078.

Camaioni, L., P. Pennuchin, F. Muratori, and A. Milone. "Brief Report: A Longitudinal Examination of the Communicative Gestures Deficit in Young Children with Autism." *Journal of Autism and Developmental Disorders* 27, no. 6 (1997) 715–727.

Capps, L., M. Sigman, and P. Mundy. "Attachment Security in Children with Autism." *Development and Psychopathology* 6 (1994): 249–261.

Capps, L., M. Sigman, and N. Yirmiya. "Self-Competence and Emotional Understanding in High Functioning Children with Autism." *Development and Psychopathology* 7 (1995): 137–149.

Carpenter, M., B. F. Pennington, and S. J. Rogers. "Understanding of Others' Intentions in Children with Autism." *Journal of Autism and Developmental Disorders* 31, no. 6 (2003): 569–600.

Carrey, N. J., H. J. Butter, M. S. Persinger, and R. J. Bialik. "Physiological and Cognitive Correlates of Child Abuse." *Journal of the American Academy of Child Adolescent Psychiatry* 34, no. 8 (1995): 1067–1075.

Carter, A. L. "From Sensori-Motor Vocalizations to Words: A Case Study of the Evolution of Attention Directing Communication in the Second Year." In *Action, Gesture and Symbol: the Emergence of Language*, edited by A. Locke, 311–349. London: Academic Press, 1978.

Case, R. *Intellectual Development: Birth to Childhood*. New York: Academic Press, 1985.

———. "The Mind and Its Modules: Towards a Multi-Level View of the Development of Human Intelligence." In *The Mind's Staircase*, edited by R. Case, 343–399. Hillsdale, N.J.: Lawrence Erlbaum, 1992.

———. "Introduction: Reconceptualizing the Nature of Children's Conceptual Structures and Their Development in Middle Childhood." In *The Role of Central Conceptual Structures in the Development of Children's Thought*, edited by R. Case and Y. Okamoto, 1–26, 246. *Monographs of the Society for Research in Child Development* 61:1–2 (1996a).

———. "Summary and Conclusions." In *The Role of Central Conceptual Structures in the Development of Children's Thought*, edited by R. Case and Y. Okamoto, 189–214, 246. *Monographs of the Society for Research in Child Development* 61:1–2 (1996b).

Charlop-Christy, M. H., and L. K. Haymes. "Using Objects of Obsession as Token Reinforcers for Children with Autism." *Journal of Autism and Developmental Disorders* 28, no. 3 (1998): 189–198.

Charlop-Christy, M. H., P. F. Kurtz, and F. Casey. "Using Aberrant Behaviors as Reinforcers for Autistic Children." *Journal of Applied Behavior Analysis* 23 (1990): 163–181.

Charman, T., and S. Baron-Cohen. "Another Look at Imitation." *Development and Pathology* 6, no. 3 (1994): 403–414.

Charman, T., J. Swettenham, S. Baron-Cohen, A. Cox, G. Baird, and A. Drew. "Infants with Autism: An Investigation of Empathy, Pretend Play, Joint Attention, and Imitation." *Developmental Psychology* 33 (1997): 781–789.

Chess, S., and M. Hassibi, "Behavior Deviations in Mentally Retarded children." *Journal of American Academy of Child Psychiatry* 2 (April 9, 1970): 282–297.

Chin, H. Y., and V. Bernard-Opitz. "Teaching Conversational Skills to Children with Autism: Effect on the Development of a Theory of Mind." *Journal of Autism and Developmental Disorders* 30, no. 6 (2000): 569–584.

Chugani, H. T., R. A. Muller, and D. C. Chugani. "Functional Brain Reorganization in Children." *Brain and Development* 18 (1996): 347–356.

Church, J., ed. *Three Babies: Biographies of Cognitive Development*. New York: Vintage Books, 1968.

Cicchetti, D. "How Research on Child Maltreatment Has Informed the Study of Child Development: Perspectives in Developmental Psychopathology." In *Child Maltreatment: Theory and Research on the Causes and Consequences of Child Abuse and Neglect*, edited by D. Cicchetti and V. Carlson, 377–431. Cambridge: Cambridge University Press, 1989.

Cicchetti, D., and M. Beeghly. "Symbol Development in Maltreated Youngsters—An Organizational Perspective." In *Atypical Symbolic Development*, edited by D. Cicchetti and M. Beeghly. San Francisco: Jossey–Bass, 1987.

Cicchetti, D., and M. Beeghly, eds. *Children with Down Syndrome—A Developmental Perspective*. New York: Cambridge University Press, 1990.

Cicchetti D., M. Beeghly, V. Carlson, and S. Toth. "The Emergence of the Self in Atypical Populations." In *Self in Transition, Infancy to Childhood*, edited by D. Cicchetti and M. Beeghly, 309–344. Chicago: University of Chicago Press, 1989.

Cicchetti, D., and K. Schneider-Rosen. "Theoretical and Empirical Considerations on the Investigation of the Relationship Between Affect and Cognition in Atypical Infants." In *Emotions, Cognition and Behavior*, edited by C. E. Izard, J. Kagan, and R. Zajone, 366–406. New York: Cambridge University Press, 1984.

Cicchetti, D., and L. A. Sroufe. "The Relationship Between Affective and Cognitive Development in Downs Syndrome Infants." *Child Development* 47 (1976): 920–929.

———. "An Organizational View of Affect: Illustrations from the Study of Down's Syndrome Infants." In *The Development of Affect*, edited by M. Lewis and L. A. Rosenbaum. New York: Plenum Press, 1978.

Clark, G. N., and R. Seifer. "Facilitating Mother–Infant Communication: A Therapeutic Model for High Risk and Developmentally Delayed Infants." *Infant Mental Health Journal* 14 (1983): 67–82.

Clark, R. A. "The Transition from Action to Gesture." In *Action, Gesture and Symbol: The Emergence of Language*, edited by A. Lock, 231–57. London: Academic Press, 1978a.

Cohen, D. J. "The Pathology of the Self in Primary Childhood Autism and Gilles de la Tourette Syndrome." *Psychiatric Clinics of North America* 3 (1980): 383–402.

Constance, D., and K. A. Bard. "The Comparative and Developmental Study of Self-Recognition and Imitation: The Importance of Social Factors." In *Self-Awareness in Animals and Humans: Developmental Perspectives*, edited by S. T. Parker, R. W. Mitchell, and M. I. Bocchia, 207–226. New York: Cambridge University Press, 1994.

Cooley, C. H. *Human Nature and the Social Order*. New York: Scribner's, 1992.

Coppola, M. A. *Through a Mother's Eyes: A Review of Autism*. Rochester, N.Y.: Coppola, 1983.

Courchesne, E., G. A. Press, and R. Yeung. "Parietal Lobe Abnormalities Detected with MRI in Patients with Infantile Autism." *American Journal of Roentgenology* 160 (1993): 387–393.

Courchesne, E., J. Townsend, and N. A. Akshoomoff et al. "New Finding in Autism: Impairment in Shifting Attention." In *Atypical Cognitive Deficits in Developmental Disorders: Implications for Brain Function*, edited by S. H. Broman and J. Grafman, 101–137. Hillsdale, N.J.: Erlbaum, 1994.

Cowan, P. A. *Piaget: With Feeling—Cognitive, Social and Emotional Dimensions*. New York: Holt, Rinehart and Winston, 1978.

Crocker, A. C. "Exceptionality: Developmental and Behavioral." *Pediatrics* 19, no. 4 (1998): 300–305.

Curcio, F. "Sensori-Motor Functioning and Communication in Mute Autistic Children." *Journal of Autism and Childhood Schizophrenia* 8, no. 3 (1978): 281–292.

Dalyrymple, N. "Environmental Supports to Develop Flexibility and Independence." In *Teaching Children with Autism: Strategies to Enhance Socialization and Communication*, edited by K. A. Quill, 243–264. Albany, N.Y.: Delmar, 1995.

Darwin, C. *The Expression of Emotions in Man and Animals*. London: John Murray, 1872.

Dawson G., D. Hill, A. Spencer, L. Galpert, and L. Watson. "Affective Exchanges Between Young Autistic Children and Their Mothers." *Journal of Abnormal Child Psychology* 18 (1990): 335–345.

deBildt, A., S. Systema, C. Ketalaars, D. Kraijer, E. Mulder, F. Volkmar, and R. Minderaa. "Interrelationship Between Autism Diagnostic Observation Schedule-Generic (ADOS-G), Autism Diagnostic Interview-Revised (ADI-R), and the Diagnostic and Statistical Manual of Mental Disorders (DSM-IV-R) Classification in Children and Adolescents with Mental Retardation." *Journal of Autism and Developmental Disorders* 34, no. 2 (2004): 129–138.

deBildt, A., S. Systema, C. Ketalaars, D. Kraijer, F. Volkmar, and R. Minderaa. "Measuring Pervasive Developmental Disorder in Mentally Retarded Children and Adolescents." *Journal of Autism and Developmental Disorders* 33, no. 6 (2003): 595–606.

Decety, J., and T. Chaminade. "The Neurophysiology of Imitation and Intersubjectivity." In *Perspectives on Imitation: From Neuroscience to Social Science, Volume 1: Imitation, Mechanisms of Imitation and Imitation in Animals*, 119–140. Cambridge, Mass.: MIT Press, 2005.

de Hirsch, K., J. Jansky, and W. Langford. *Predicting Reading Failure: A Preliminary Study of Reading, Writing and Spelling Disabilities in Preschool Children.* New York: Harper and Row, 1966.

DeMyer, M. K., G. D. Alpern, S. Barton, W. E. DeMyer, D. Churchill, J. N. Hingten, C. Q. Bryson, W. Pontius, and C. Kimberlin. "Imitation in Autistic, Early Schizophrenic and Non-Psychotic Normal Children." *Journal of Autism and Childhood Schizophrenia* 2 (1972): 264–287.

Dimberg, U., M. Thunberg, and K. Elmehend. "Unconscious Facial Reactions to Emotional Facial Expressions." *Psychological Science* 11 (2000): 86–89.

Eagle, R. S. "Accessing and Assessing Intelligence in Individuals with Low Functioning Autism." *Journal on Developmental Disabilities* 9, no. 2 (2002): 45–53.

Eagle, R. S., and E. Struening. "Estimates of Intelligence in Severely Quadriplegic Children as a Function of Severity of Physical Handicap, Test Procedures, SEC, Home Environment, and Educational Experience." *Society of Behavioral Science* 19, no. 2 (1987): 61.

Edwards, D. "Social Relations and Early Language." In *Action, Gesture and Symbol: The Emergence of Language,* edited by A. Lock, 449–470. London: Academic Press, 1978.

Eibl-Eibesfeldt, I. "Human Ethological Concepts and Implications for the Science of Man." *Behavioral and Brain Sciences* (1979): 1–57.

Ekman, P. "Cross-Cultural Studies of Facial Expression." In *Darwin and Facial Expressions—A Century of Research in Review,* edited by P. Ekman, 169–222. New York: Academic Press, 1993.

Emde, R. N. "Moving Ahead: Integrating Influences of Affective Processes for Development and for Psychoanalysis." *International Journal of Psychoanalysis* 80, no. 2 (1999): 317–339.

———. "The Prerepresentational Self and Its Affective Core. *The Psychoanalytic Study of the Child* 38 (1983): 165–193.

Emde, R. N., and C. Brown. "Adaptation to the Birth of a Down's Syndrome Infant: Grieving and Maternal Attachment." *Journal of the American Academy of Child Psychiatry* 17 (1978): 299–323.

Emde, R. N., and H. K. Buchsbaum. "'Didn't You Hear My Mommy?' Autonomy with Connectedness in Moral Self Emergence." In *Self in Transition, Infancy to Childhood,* edited by D. Cicchetti and M. Beeghly, 35–60. Chicago: University of Chicago Press, 1990.

Emde, R. N., E. L. Katz, and J. K. Thorpe. "Emotional Expression in Infancy: II Early Deviations in Down's Syndrome. In *The Development of Affect,* edited by M. Lewis and A. Rosenblum. New York: Plenum Press, 1978.

Escalona, S. "Patterns of Infantile Experience and the Developmental Process." *Psychoanalytic Study of the Child* 18 (1963): 197–244.

Fadiga, L., L. Craighero, G. Buccino, and G. Rissolatti. "Speech Listening Specifically Modulates the Excitability of Tongue Muscles: A TMS Study." *European Journal of Neuroscience.* Cited in Iacoboni, M., "Understanding Others: Imitation, Language, and Empathy," in *Perspectives on Imitation: From Neuroscience to Social Science, Volume 1: Imitation, Mechanisms of Imitation and Imitation in Animals,* edited by S. Hurley and N. Chater, 77–100. Cambridge, Mass.: MIT Press, 2005.

Fein, D., B. Penningon, P. Markovitz, M. Braverman, and I. Waterhouse. "Towards a Neuropsychological Model of Infantile Autism: Are the Social Defects Primary?" *Journal of the American Academy of Childhood Psychiatry* 25, no. 2 (1986): 198–212.

Feldman, H., S. Goldin-Meadow, and L. Gleitman. "Beyond Herodotus: The Creation of Language by Linguistically Deprived Deaf Children." In *Action, Gesture and Symbol: The Emergence of Language*, edited by A. Lock, 351–414. London: Academic Press, 1978.

Ferrier, L. "Word, Context and Imitation." In *Action, Gesture and Symbol: The Emergence of Language*, edited by A. Lock, 471–484. London: Academic Press, 1978.

Field, T. "Interaction and Attachment in Normal and Atypical Infants." *Journal of Consulting and Clinical Psychology* 55, no. 6 (1987): 833–859.

Fogel, A. "Research Approaches to Relationship Development." In *Action and Thought: From Sensorimotor Schemes to Symbolic Operations*, edited by G. E. Forman. New York: Academic Press, 1982.

Fonagy, P., and M. Target. "Predictions of Outcome in Child Psychoanalysis: Retrospective Study of 763 Cases at the Anna Freud Centre." *Journal of the American Psychiatric Association* 44, no. 1 (1996): 27–77.

Fonagy, P., S. Redfern, and T. Charman. "The Relationship Between Belief-Desire Reasoning and a Projective Measure of Attachment Security (SAT)." *British Journal of Developmental Psychology* (December 1995): 1–25.

Fraiberg, S. "Blind Infants and Their Mothers: An Examination of the Sign System." In *The Effect of the Infant on Its Caregiver*, edited by M. Lewis and L. A. Rosenblum, 215–232. New York: John Wiley and Sons, 1974.

———. "Congenital Sensory and Motor Deficits and Ego Formation." *Annual of Psychoanalysis* no. 3 (1977a): 169–194.

———. *Insights from the Blind*. New York: International, 1977b.

Freeman, B. J. "Guidelines for Evaluating Interventions Programs for Children with Autism." *Journal of Autism and Developmental Disorders* 27, no. 36 (1997): 653–676.

Frith, U. *Autism: Explaining the Enigma*. Oxford: Blackwell, 1989.

Frith, U., and A. Happe. "Beyond 'Theory of Mind.'" *Cognition* 50 (1994): 115–132.

Gallese, V. "From Grasping to Language: Mirror Neurons and the Origins of Social Communication." In *Towards a Science of Consciousness*, edited by S. Hameroff, A. Kasniak, and D. Chalmers, 165–232. Cambridge, Mass.: MIT Press, 2000a.

———. "The Inner Sense of Action: Agency and Motor Representation." *Journal of Consciousness Studies* 7, no. 10 (2000b): 23–40.

———. "'The Shared Manifold' Hypothesis—From Mirror Neurons to Empathy." *Journal of Consciousness Studies* 8, no. 5–7 (2002): 33–50.

———. "The Manifold Nature of Interpersonal Relations: The Quest for a Common Mechanism." *Philosophical Transactions of the Royal Society of London* (2003): 517–528.

———. "'Being Like Me': Self-Other Identity, Mirror Neurons, and Empathy." In *Perspectives on Imitation: From Neuroscience to Social Science, Volume 1: Imitation, Mechanisms of Imitation and Imitation in Animals*, edited by S. Hurley and N. Chater, 101–118 Cambridge, Mass.: MIT Press, 2005.

Gallup, G. G. Jr. "Chimpanzees: Self Recognition." *Science* 167 (1970): 341–343.

———. "Self-Recognition in Primates: A Comparative Approach to the Bidirectional Properties of Consciousness." *American Psychologist* 32 (1977): 329–338.

———. "Toward a Comparative Psychology of Self-awareness: Species Limitations and Cognitive Consequences." In *The Self: An Interdisciplinary Approach*, edited by G. R. Goethals and J. Strauss, 121–135. New York: Springer Verlag, 1991.

Gara, L., and C. Goldfarb. "The Autistic Child: What Can You Do?" *The Canadian Journal of Diagnosis* (February 1999): 147–155.

Gavida-Payne, S., and Z. Stoneman. "Family Predictors of Maternal and Paternal Involvement in Programs for Young Children with Disabilities." *Child Development* 68 (1997): 701–717.

Gergerly, G. "From Self-Recognition to Theory of Mind." In *Self-Awareness in Animals and Humans: Developmental Perspectives*, edited by S. T. Parker, R. W. Mitchell, and M. I. Bocchia, 51–60. New York: Cambridge University Press, 1994.

Giannini, A. J., D. Tamulonis, M. C. Giannini, R. H. Loisell, and G. Spirtos. "Defective Response to Social Cues in Moebius' Syndrome." *Journal of Nervous and Mental Disease* 172 (1984): 174–175.

Gibson, J. J. *The Ecological Approach to Visual Perception.* Boston: Houghton-Mifflin, 1979.

Gillberg, C. "Subgroups in Autism: Are There Behavioural Phenotypes Typical of Underlying Medical Conditions?" *Journal of Intellectual Disability Research* 36 (1992): 201–214.

Gillberg, C., and G. Ehlers. "High Functioning People with Autism and Asberger Syndrome: A Literature Review." In *Asperger Syndrome or High-Functioning Autism?*, edited by E. Schopler, G. B. Mesibov, and L. J. Kunce, 79–106. New York: Plenum Press, 1998.

Gillberg, C., and S. Steffenburg. "Autistic Behavior in Moebius Syndrome." *Acta Paediatr Scand* 78, no. 2 (1989): 314–316.

Gillingham, G. *Autism: Handle with Care! Understanding and Managing the Behavior of Children and Adults with Autism.* Edmonton: Tacit Publishing, 1995.

———. *A New Understanding! Solving the Mystery of Autism, Asperger's and PDD-NOS.* Edmonton: Tacit Publishing, 2000.

Goldberg, S. "Social Competence in Infancy: A Model of Parent–Infant Interactions." *Merrill Palmer Quarterly* 23 (1977): 164–77.

Goldfarb, C. "Pediatric Flash: Pitfalls in the Diagnosis of Pervasive Developmental Disorders." *Contemporary Pediatrics* (December 1998): 11–12.

Goldman, A. I. "Imitation, Mind-Reading, and Simulation." In *Perspectives on Imitation: From Neuroscience to Social Science, Volume 2: Imitation, Human Development and Culture*, edited by S. Hurley and N. Chater, 78–94. Cambridge, Mass.: MIT Press, 2005.

Goldstein, K. "Abnormal Conditions in Infancy." *Journal of Nervous and Mental Disease* 128 (1959): 538–557.

———. *The Organism: A Holistic Approach to Biology Derived from Pathological Data in Man.* Boston: Beacon Press, 1963.

Gomez, J. C. "Mutual Awareness in Primate Communication: A Gricean Approach." In *Self-Awareness in Animals and Humans: Developmental Perspectives*, edited by S. T. Parker, R. W. Mitchell, and M. I. Bocchia, 61–80. New York: Cambridge University Press, 1994.

Gomez, J. C., E. Sarria, and J. Tamarit. "The Comparative Study of Early Communication and Theories of Mind: Ontogeny, Phylogeny, and Pathology." In *Understanding Other Minds*, edited by S. Baron-Cohen et al., 397–426. New York: Oxford Medical Publications, 1993.

Goodman, J. F. *When Slow Is Fast Enough*. New York: Guilford Press, 1992.

Goodman, R. "Infantile Autism: A Syndrome of Multiple Primary Deficit." *Journal of Autism and Developmental Disorders* 19 (1989): 409–424.

Gopnick, A., and A. N. Meltzoff. "Minds, Bodies and Persons: Young Children's Understanding of the Self as Reflected in Imitation and Theory of Mind Research." In *Self-Awareness in Animals and Humans: Developmental Perspectives*, edited by S. T. Parker, R. W. Mitchell, and M. I. Bocchia, 166–186. New York: Cambridge University Press, 1994.

——. *Words, Thoughts, and Theory*. Cambridge, Mass.: MIT Press, 1997.

Gordon, B. "Commentary: Neural Systems Perspective for Behavioral Treatment for Autism." *Journal of Autism and Developmental Disorders* 30, no. 5 (2000): 503–508.

Gore, J. C. "Abnormal Ventral Temporal Cortical Activity During Face Discrimination Among Individuals with Autism and Asperger Syndrome." *Archives of General Psychiatry* 57 (2000): 331–340.

Grandin, T. "The Learning Style of People with Autism: An Autobiography." In *Teaching Children with Autism: Strategies to Enhance Communication and Socialization*. Albany, N.Y.: Delmar, 1995a.

——. "Thinking in Pictures and Other Reports from My Life with Autism." New York: Doubleday, 1995b.

Gravida-Payne, S., and Z. Stoneman. "Family Predictors of Maternal and Paternal Involvement in Programs for Young Children with Disabilities." *Child Development* 68, no. 4 (1997): 701–717.

Gray, C. A. "Social Stories and Comic Strip Conversations with Students with Asperger Syndrome and High-Functioning Autism." In *Learning and Cognition in Autism*, edited by E. Schopler and G. B. Mesibov, 167–198. New York: Plenum Press, 1998.

Gray, H. "Learning to Take an Object from the Mother." In *Action, Gesture and Symbol: The Emergence of Language*, edited by A. Lock, 159–182. London: Academic Press, 1978.

Greenfield, J. *A Child Called Noah*. New York: Rinehart and Winston, 1972.

Greenfield, P. M. "Structural Parallels Between Language and Action in Development." In *Action, Gesture and Symbol: The Emergence of Language*, edited by A. Lock, 415–445. London: Academic Press, 1978.

Greenspan, S. I. *Infancy and Early Childhood: The Practice of Clinical Assessment and Intervention with Emotional and Developmental Challenges*. Madison, Conn..: International Universities Press, 1992a.

——. "Reconsidering the Diagnosis and Treatment of Very Young Children with Autistic Spectrum or Pervasive Developmental Disorder." *Zero to Three* 13, no. 2 (October–November 1992b): 1–9.

——. "Current Issues in Lifespan Development: Part I. Research Support for the Comprehensive Developmental Approach to Autistic Spectrum Disorders and Other Developmental and Learning Disorders: The Developmental, Individual Difference." *Los Angeles Psychologist* (May/June 2004): 9–13.

Greenspan, S., B. Kalmanson, R. Shahmoon-Shanok, S. Weider, G. Williamson, and M. Canzalone. "Assessing and Treating Infants and Young Children with Severe Difficulties in Relating and Communicating." *Zero to Three* (1997): 19–29.

Greenspan, S. I., and Weider, S. *The Child with Special Needs: Encouraging Intellectual and Emotional Growth.* Reading, Mass.: Addison and Wesley, 1998.

Gresham, F. M., and D. L. Macmillan. "Early Intervention Project: Can Its Claims Be Substantiated and Its Effects Replicated?" *Journal of Autism and Developmental Disorders* 28, no. 1 (1998): 5–13.

Grossman, J. B., A. Carter, and F. R. Volkmar. "Social Behavior in Autism." *Annals of the New York Academy of Sciences*, 807 (January 15, 1997): 440–454.

Guillaume, P. *Imitation in Children.* Chicago: University of Chicago Press, 1971.

Hadwin, J., S. Baron-Cohen, P. Howlin, and K. Hill. "Does Teaching Theory of Mind Have an Effect on the Ability to Develop Conversation in Children with Autism?" *Journal of Autism and Developmental Disorders* 27, no. 5 (October 1997): 519–538.

Happe, F. *Autism: An Introduction to Psychological Theory.* Cambridge, Mass.: Harvard University Press, 1995a.

———. "The Role of Age and Verbal Ability in the TOM Task Performance of Subjects with Autism." *Child Development* 66 (1995b): 843–855.

———. "The Brain Regions Critical in Allowing Us to Understand Another Person's Thoughts." *British Psychological Society's Centenary Conference.* Glasgow, U.K.: 2001.

Happe, F., and U. Frith. "The Neuropsychology of Autism." *Brain* 119 (1996): 1377–1400.

Harris, P. "Grasping Action." In *Perspectives on Imitation: From Neuroscience to Social Science, Volume 2: Imitation, Human Development and Culture*, edited by S. Hurley and N. Chater, 173–177. Cambridge, Mass.: MIT Press, 2005.

Hart, D., and S. Fegley. "Social Imitation and the Emergence of a Mental Model of Self." In *Self-Awareness in Animals and Humans: Developmental Perspectives*, edited by S. Parker et al., 149–165. New York: Cambridge University Press, 1994.

Hartman, H. *Ego Psychology and the Problem of Adaptation.* New York: International Universities Press, 1939/58.

Hatfield, E., L. Richard, and R. L. Rapson. *Love and Sex: Cross-Cultural Perspectives.* Boston: Allyn and Bacon, 1996.

Hawke, W. A. "Psychiatric Aspects of Mental Retardation." In *Psychological Problems of the Child and His Family*, edited by P. Steinhauer and Q. Rae-Grant, 265–283. Toronto: Gage Publishing, 1977.

Heflin, L. J., and R. L. Simpson. "Interventions for Children and Youth with Autism: Prudent Choices in a World of Exaggerated Claims and Empty Promises. Part 1: Intervention and Treatment Option Review." *Focus on Autism and Other Developmental Disabilities* 13, no. 4 (Winter 1998): 194–211.

Hermann, D. *Helen Keller, A Life.* New York: Alfred A. Knopf, 1998.

Heyes, C. "Imitation by Association." In *Perspectives on Imitation: From Neuroscience to Social Science, Volume 1: Imitation, Mechanisms of Imitation and Imitation in Animals*, edited by S. Hurley and N. Chater, 159–176. Cambridge, Mass.: MIT Press, 2005.

Hobson, R. P. "Beyond Cognition: A Theory of Autism." In *Autism: New Perspectives on Diagnosis, Nature and Treatment*, edited by G. Dawson, 22–48. New York: Guilford, 1989.

———. "On the Origins of Self and the Case of Autism." *Development and Psychopathology* 2 (1990a): 163–181.

———. "On Psychoanalytic Approaches to Autism." *American Journal of Orthopsychiatry* 60 (1990b): 324–336.

———. *Autism and the Development of Mind.* Hillsdale, N.J.: Erlbaum, 1993a.

———. "Through Feeling and Sight to Self and Symbol." In *The Perceived Self: Ecological and Interpersonal Sources of Self Knowledge,* edited by U. Neisser, 254–279. Cambridge: Cambridge University Press, 1993b.

———. "Understanding Persons: The Role of Affect." In *Understanding Other Minds,* edited by S. Baron-Cohen, H. Tager-Flusberg, and D. J. Cohen, 104–227. New York: Oxford Medical Publications, 1993c.

———. *Cradle of Thought: Exploring the Origins of Thinking,* London: Macmillan, 2002.

Hobson, R. P., A. Lee, and R. Brown. "Autism and Congenital Blindness." *Journal of Autism and Developmental Disorders* 29, no. 1 (1999): 45–56.

Hobson, R. P., J. Ouston, and A. Lee. "What Is in a Face? The Case of Autism." *British Journal of Psychology* 79 (1988): 601–623.

Hofer, M. A. "Relationships as Regulators: A Psychobiologic Perspective on Bereavement." *Psychosomatic Medicine* 1, no. 46 (1984): 183–197.

Horne, G., and S. Horne. "Brianna's Story." *Moebius Syndrome Newsletter,* 1999. www.ciaccess.com/moebius/feb99/story.htm (February 1999).

Howe, D. "Disabled Children, Parent-Child Interaction and Attachment." *Child and Family Social Work* 11, no. 2 (2006): 95–106.

Hunt, J. M. *Intelligence and Experience.* New York: Ronald Press, 1961.

Hurley, S., and N. Chater, eds. *Perspectives on Imitation: From Neuroscience to Social Science, Volume 1: Imitation, Mechanisms of Imitation and Imitation in Animals.* Cambridge, Mass.: MIT Press, 2005a.

———. *Perspectives on Imitation: From Neuroscience to Social Science, Volume 2: Imitation, Human Development and Culture.* Cambridge, Mass.: MIT Press, 2005b.

Hwang, B., and C. Hughes. "The Effects of Social Interactive Training on Early Social Communicative Skills of Children with Autism." *Journal of Autism and Developmental Disorders* 30, no. 4 (2000): 331–344.

Iacaboni, M. "Understanding Others: Imitation, Language, and Empathy." In *Perspectives on Imitation: From Neuroscience to Social Science, Volume 1: Imitation, Mechanisms of Imitation and Imitation in Animals,* edited by S. Hurley and N. Chater, 77–100. Cambridge, Mass.: MIT Press, 2005.

Ingram, D. "Sensori-Motor Intelligence and Language Development." In *Action, Gesture and Symbol: The Emergence of Language,* edited by A. Lock, 261–282. London: Academic Press, 1978.

Inhelder, B. *The Diagnosis of Reasoning in the Mentally Retarded.* New York: Chandler Publishing Company, 1968.

James, W. *The Principles of Psychology, vol 1.* New York: Dover, 1890.

Jones, S. "Why Don't Apes Ape More." In *Perspectives on Imitation: From Neuroscience to Social Science, Volume 1: Imitation, Mechanisms of Imitation and Imitation in Animals,* edited by S. Hurley and N. Chater, 291–301. Cambridge, Mass.: MIT Press, 2005.

Kadmanson, B. "Diagnosis and Treatment of Infants and Young Children with Pervasive Developmental Disorders." *Zero to Three* 13, no. 2. (October–November 1992): 21–26.

Kagan, J. *The Nature of the Child.* New York: Basic Books, 1984.

Kanner, L. "Autistic Disturbance in Affective Contact." *Nervous Child* 2 (1943): 217–250.

———. "Irrelevant and Metaphorical Language in Early Childhood Autism." *American Journal of Psychiatry* 3 (1946): 242–246.

———. "The Concept of Wholes and Parts in Early Infantile Autism." *American Journal of Psychiatry* 108 (1951): 23–26.

———. "Follow-up Study of Eleven Autistic Children Originally Reported in 1943." *Journal of Autism and Child Schizophrenia* 1 (1971): 119–145.

Kasari, C., M. Sigman, and P. Baumgartner. "Pride and Mastery in Children with Autism." *Journal of Child Psychology and Psychiatry* 34 (1993): 353–362.

Kasari, C., M. Sigman, P. Mundy, and N. Yirmiya. "Affective Sharing in the Context of Joint Attention: Interactions of Normal, Autistic, and Mentally Retarded Children." *Journal of Autism and Developmental Disorders* 20, no. 1 (1990): 87–100.

Kasting, A. "Parent Involvement: Changing Perspectives from 1965–1990." *Canadian Children* 15, no. 2 (1990): 1–11.

Klin, A. "Understanding Early Infantile Autism. An Application of G. H. Mead's Theory of the Emergence of Mind." *L.S.E. Quarterly*, no. 73 (1989): 336–356.

Klin, A., S. S. Sparrow, A. deBildt, D. Cicchetti, D. J. Cohen, and F. R. Volkmar. "A Normed Study of Face Recognition in Autism and Related Disorders." *Journal of Autism and Developmental Disorders* 29, no. 6 (1999): 499–508.

Koegel, L. K. "Interventions to Facilitate Communication in Autism." *Journal of Autism and Developmental Disorders* 30, no. 5 (2000): 383–392.

Koegel, L. K., and Koegel, R. L. "Motivating Communication in Children with Autism." In *Learning and Cognition in Autism*, edited by E. Schopler and G. Mesibov, 73–87. New York: Plenum Press, 1985.

Koegel, R. L., and L. K. Koegel, eds. *Teaching Children with Autism: Strategies for Initiating Positive Interactions and Improving Learning Opportunities*. Baltimore: Brookes, 1995.

Koegel, R. L., M. C. O'Dell, and L. K. Koegel. "A Natural Language Teaching Paradigm for Non-verbal Autistic Children." *Journal of Autism and Developmental Disorders* 17 (1987): 187–200.

Kohut, H. *The Restoration of the Self*. New York: International Universities Press, 1977.

Kopp, C. B. "The Growth of Self-Monitoring Among Young Children with Down Syndrome." In *Children with Down Syndrome: A Developmental Perspective*, edited by D. Cicchetti and M. Beeghley, 231–251. New York: Cambridge University Press, 1990.

Krantz, P. J., and L. R. McClannahan. "Teaching Children with Autism to Initiate with Peers: Effects of a Script-Fading Procedure." *Journal of Applied Behavior Analysis* 26 (1993), 121–132.

Larkin, A. S., and S. Garry. "Brief Report: Progress Reported in Three Children with Autism Using Daily Life Therapy." *Journal of Autism and Developmental Disorders* 25, no. 4 (1998): 339–342.

Laushley, K. M., and L. J. Heflin. "Enhancing Social Skills of Kindergarten Children with Autism Through the Training of Multiple Peers as Tutors." *Journal of Autism and Developmental Disorders* 30 (2000): 183–194.

LeVine, R. A. "Enculturation: A Bio-social Perspective on the Development of the Self." In *Children with Down Syndrome—A Developmental Perspective*, edited by D. Cicchetti and M. Beeghly, 99–118. New York: Cambridge University Press, 1990.

Lewin, R., ed. *Child Alive*. New York: Anchor Books, 1975.

Lewis, M., and J. Brooks-Gunn. *Social Cognition and the Acquisition of Self.* New York: Plenum, 1978.

Lewy, A. L., and G. Dawon. "Social Stimulation and Joint Attention in Young Autistic Children." *Journal of Abnormal Child Psychology* 20, no. 6 (1992): 535–566.

Libby, S., S. Powell, D. Messer, and R. Jordan. "Imitation of Pretend Play Acts by Children with Autism and Down Syndrome." *Journal of Autism and Developmental Disorders* 27, no. 4 (1997): 365–384.

Lock, A., ed. *Action, Gesture and Symbol: The Emergence of Language,* London: Academic Press, 1978a.

———. "The Emergence of Language: On Being Picked Up." In *Action, Gesture and Symbol: The Emergence of Language,* edited by A. Lock, 3–20. London: Academic Press, 1978b.

Lord, C. "The Complexity of Social Behavior in Autism." In *Understanding Other Minds,* edited by S. Baron-Cohen, H. Tager-Flusberg, and D. J. Cohen, 292–316. New York: Oxford Medical Publications, 1993.

———. "Follow-up of Two Year Olds Referred for Possible Autism." *Journal of Child Psychology and Psychiatry* 36 (1995): 1365–1382.

———. "Commentary: Achievements and Future Directions for Intervention Research in Communication and Autistic Spectrum Disorders." *Journal of Autism and Developmental Disorders* 30, no. 4 (2000): 393–398.

Lord, C., S. Risi, L. Lambrecht, E. Cook, B. L. Leventhal, P. DiLavore, A. Pickles, and M. Rutter. "The Autism Diagnostic Observation Schedule-Generic: A Standard Measure of Social and Communication Deficits Associated with the Spectrum of Autism." *Journal of Autism and Developmental Disorders* 30, no. 3 (2000): 205–224.

Lovaas, O. J. *The Autistic Child: Language Development through Behavior Modification.* New York: Irvington Publication, 1977.

———. "Behavioral Treatment and Normal Educational and Intellectual Functioning in Young Autistic Children." *Journal of Consulting and Clinical Psychology* 55 (1987): 3–9.

———. *Teaching Individuals with Developmental Delays: Basic Intervention Techniques.* Austin, Tex.: Pro-Ed, 2003.

Loveland, K. A. "Autism, Affordances and the Self." In *The Perceived Self: Ecological and Interpersonal Sources of Self Knowledge,* edited by U. Neisser, 237–253. Cambridge: Cambridge University Press, 1993.

Loveland, K. A., B. Tunali-Kotoski, D. A. Pearson, K. A. Brelsford, J. Ortegon, and R. Chen. "Imitation and Expression of Facial Affect in Autism." *Development and Psychopathology* 6, no. 3 (1994): 433–444.

Mahler, M. S. *On Human Symbiosis and the Vicissitudes of Individuation.* Madison, Conn.: International Universities Press, 1968.

Mahler, M. S., and P. Elkisch. "Some Observations of the Ego in the Case of Infantile Psychosis." In *Psa Study of the Child,* vol. 8, 252–261. New York: International Universities Press, 1953.

Mahler, M. S., F. Pine, and A. Bergman. *The Psychological Birth of the Human Infant.* New York: Basic Books, 1975.

Marfo, K. "Interaction Between Mothers and Their Mentally Retarded Children: Integration of Research Findings." *Journal of Applied Developmental Psychology* 5 (1984): 45–69.

———. "Correlates of Maternal Directiveness with Children Who Are Developmentally Delayed." *American Journal of Orthopsychiatry* 22, no. 2 (1992): 219–233.

Maurice, C. *Let Me Hear Your Voice: A Family's Triumph Over Autism.* New York: Fawcett Columbine, 1993.

Maurice, C., G. Green, and S. C. Luce. *Behavioral Intervention for Young Children with Autism: A Manual for Parents and Professionals.* Austin, Tex.: Pro-Ed, 1996.

McGee, G. G., R. S. Feldman, and M. J. Morrier. "Benchmarks of Social Treatment for Children with Autism." *Journal of Autism and Developmental Disorders* 27 (1997): 353–363.

McGee, G. G., P. J. Krantz, D. Mason, and L. E. McClannahan. "A Modified Incidental Teaching Procedure for Autistic Youth: Acquisition and Generalization of Receptive Object Labels." *Journal of Applied Behavioral Analysis* 16 (1983): 329–338.

McIntosh, H. "Research Unearths New Treatments for Autism." *APA Monitor* 30, no. 8 (1999): 4.

Mead, G. H. "The Genesis of Self and Social Control." *International Journal of Ethics* 35, no. 3 (1935): 251–277.

Meaney, M. J., D. H. Aitken, M. Bhatnager, S. R. Bodnoff, J. B. Mitchell, and A. Sarrieau. "Neonatal Handling and the Development of Adrenocortical Response to Stress." In *Advances in Touch*, edited by N. Gunzenhauser, T. B. Brazelton, and T. Fields, 11–20. Skillman, N.J.: Johnson and Johnson, 1990.

Meltzoff, A. N. "Foundations for Developing a Concept of Self: The Role of Imitation in Relating Self to Other, and the Value of Social Mirroring, Social Modeling and Self-Practice in Infancy." In *Children with Down Syndrome—A Developmental Perspective*, edited by D. Cicchetti and M. Beeghly, 139–164. New York: Cambridge University Press, 1990.

———. "The Role of Imitation in Understanding Persons and Developing a Theory of Mind." In *Understanding Other Minds*, edited by S. Baron-Cohen, H. Tager-Flusberg, and D. J. Cohen, 335–366. New York: Oxford Medical Publications, 1993.

———. "Imitation and Other Minds: The 'Like Me' Hypothesis." In *Perspectives on Imitation: From Neuroscience to Social Science, Volume 2: Imitation, Human Development and Culture*, edited by S. Hurley and N. Chater, 55–78. Cambridge, Mass.: MIT Press, 2005.

Meltzoff, A. N., and M. K. Moore. "Imitation of Facial and Manual Gestures by Human Neonates." *Science* 198 (1977): 75–78.

———. "Newborn Infants Imitate Adult Facial Gestures." *Child Development* 54 (1983): 702–709.

———. "Imitation in Newborn Infants: Exploring the Range of Gestures Imitated and the Underlying Mechanisms." *Developmental Psychology* 25 (1989): 954–1062.

Mesibov, G. B. "Implications of the Normalization Principle for Psychotic Children." *Journal of Autism and Developmental Disorders* 6, no. 9 (1976): 360–365.

———, ed. *Journal of Autism and Developmental Disabilities: Special issue: Preschool Issues in Autism* 27, no. 6 (1997).

Mitchell, P. *Introduction to Theory of Mind: Children, Autism and Apes.* New York: St. Martin's Press, 1997.

Mitchell, P., and S. Isaacs. "Understanding of Verbal Representations in Children with Autism: the Case of Referential Opacity. *British Journal of Developmental Psychology* 12 (1994): 431–453.

Mitrani, T., and J. Mitrani, eds. *Encounters with Autistic States: A Memorial Tribute to Frances Tustin.* Northdale, N.J.: Jason Aronson, 1997.

Moore, C. "Theories of Mind in Infancy." *British Journal of Developmental Psychology* 14 (1996): 9–40.

Morgan, S. "Autism and Piaget's Theory: Are the Two Compatible?" *Journal of Autism and Developmental Disorders* 16, no. 4 (1986): 441–458.

Moses, L. J. "Foreword." In *Self-Awareness in Animals and Humans: Developmental Perspectives,* edited by S. T. Parker, R. W. Mitchell, and M. I. Boccia, x–xvii. New York: Cambridge University Press, 1994.

Muir, E. "Watching, Waiting and Wondering: Applying Psychoanalytic Principles to Mother–Infant Intervention." *Infant Mental Health Journal* 13, no. 4 (1992): 319–328.

Mundy, P., and M. Crowson. "Joint Attention and Early Social Communication: Implications for Research on Intervention with Autism." *Journal of Autism and Developmental Disorders* 27, no. 6 (1997): 653–676.

Mundy, P., and M. Sigman. "The Theoretical Implications of Joint Attention Deficits in Autism." *Development and Psychopathology* 1 (1989a): 173–183.

———. "Second Thoughts on the Nature of Autism." *Development and Psychopathology* 1 (1989b): 213–217.

Mundy, P., M. Sigman, and C. Kasari. "A Longitudinal Study of Joint Attention and Language Development in Autistic Children." *Journal of Autism and Developmental Disorders* 20 (1990): 115–128.

———. "The Theory of Mind and Joint Attention Deficits in Autism." In *Understanding Other Minds,* edited by S. Baron-Cohen, H. Tager-Flusberg, and D. J. Cohen, 181–203. New York: Oxford Medical Publications, 1993.

Murray, D. G. *This Is Stevie's Story.* Nashville, Tenn.: Abingdon Press, 1967.

Murray, L., A. Fiori-Crowley, R. Hooper, and P. J. Cooper. "The Impact of Post-Natal Depression and Associated Adversity on Early Mother–Infant Interactions and Later Infant Outcome." *Child Development* 67 (1996): 2512–2526.

National Research Council, Committee on Educational Interventions for Children with Autism. *Educating Children with Autism,* edited by C. Lord and J. McGee. Washington, D.C.: National Academy Press, 2001.

Neisser, U. "The Self Perceived." In *The Perceived Self: Ecological and Interpersonal Sources of Self Knowledge,* edited by U. Neisser, 3–24. Cambridge: Cambridge University Press, 1993.

Nelson, K., *Narratives from the Crib.* Cambridge, Mass.: Harvard University Press, 1992.

Newson, J. "Dialogue and Development." In *Action, Gesture and Symbol: The Emergence of Language,* edited by A. Lock, 31–34. London: Academic Press, 1978.

Nirje, B. "The Normalization Principle and Its Human Management Implications." In *Changing Patterns in Residential Services for the Mentally Retarded,* edited by R. Kugel and W. Wolfensberger, 42–65. Washington, D.C.: President's Committee on Mental Retardation, 1969.

Njardvik, U., J. L. Matson, and K. E. Cherry. "A Comparison of Social Skills in Adults with Autistic Disorder, Pervasive Developmental Disorder Not Otherwise Specified, and Mental Retardation." *Journal of Autism and Developmental Disorders* 29, no. 4 (1999): 287–296.

Oke, N. J., and L. Schreibman. "Training Social Initiations to a High Functioning Autistic Child: Assessment of Collateral Behavior Changes and Generalizations in a Case Study." *Journal of Autism and Developmental Disorders* 20, no. 4 (1990): 479–497.

O'Leary, D. D., B. L. Schlagger, and R. Tuttle. "Specification of Neocortical Areas and Thalamocortical Connections." *Annual Review of Neurosciences* 17 (1994): 419–439.

Osterling, I., and G. Dawson. "Early Recognition of Children with Autism: A Study of First Birthday Home Videotapes." *Journal of Autism and Developmental Disorders* 24 (1994): 247–258.

Oxford English Dictionary, 2nd ed. Oxford: Oxford University Press, 1989.

Ozonoff, S. "Executive Function in Autism." In *Learning and Cognition in Autism,* edited by E. Schopler and G. B. Mesibov, 199–217. New York: Plenum Press, 1995.

Ozonoff, S., and R. E. McEvoy. "A Longitudinal Study of Executive Function and Theory of Mind Development in Autism." *Development and Psychopathology* 6, no. 3 (1994): 415–432.

Ozonoff, S., and J. N. Miller. "Teaching Theory of Mind: A New Approach to Social Skill Training for Individuals with Autism." *Journal of Autism and Developmental Disorders* 25 (1995): 415–433.

Park, C. C. *The Siege: The First Eight Years of an Autistic Child, with Epilogue 15 Years Later.* Boston: Little, Brown and Company, 1982.

———. *Exiting Nirvana : A Daughter's Life with Autism.* Boston: Little, Brown and Company, 2001.

Parker, S. T., and C. Milbrash. "Contributions of Imitation and Role-Playing Games to the Construction of Self in Primates." In *Self-Awareness in Animals and Humans: Developmental Perspectives,* edited by S. T. Parker, R. W. Mitchell, and M. I. Bocchia, 101–126. New York: Cambridge University Press, 1994.

Parker, S. T., R. W. Mitchell, and M. I. Boccia, eds. *Self-Awareness in Animals and Humans: Developmental Perspectives.* New York: Cambridge University Press, 1994.

Pascal-Leone, J. "Organismic Processes for Neo-Piagetian Theories: A Dialectical Causal Account of Cognitive Development." In *The Neo-Piagetian Theories of Cognitive Development: Towards an Integration,* edited by A. Demetrious, 25–65. Amsterdam: North-Holland (Elsevier), 1988.

Phillips, W., J. C. Gomez, S. Baron-Cohen, V. Laa, and A. Riviere. "Treating People as Objects, Agents or 'Subjects': How Young Children with and without Autism Make Requests." *Journal of Child Psychology and Psychiatry* 36, no. 4 (1995): 1383–1398.

Piaget, J. *The Origins of Intelligence in Children.* New York: International Universities Press, 1952.

———. *Play, Dreams and Imitation.* New York: W.W. Norton, 1962.

Pine, F. *Developmental Theory and Clinical Process.* New Haven, Conn.: Yale University Press, 1987.

———. *Drive, Ego, Object and Self: A Synthesis for Clinical Work.* New York: Basic Books, 1990.

Pipp, S. "Sensorimotor and Representational Internal Working Models of Self, Other and Relationship: Mechanisms of Connection and Separation." In *Children with Down Syndrome—A Developmental Perspective,* edited by D. Cicchetti and M. Beeghly, 243–264. New York: Cambridge University Press, 1990.

Plooij, F. X. "Some Basic Traits of Language in Wild Chimpanzees." In *Action, Gesture and Symbol: The Emergence of Language*, edited by A. Lock, 113–131. London: Academic Press, 1978.

Pomeroy, John C. "Subtyping Pervasive Developmental Disorder: Issues of Validity and Implications for Child Psychiatric Diagnosis." In *Asberger Syndrome or High Functioning Autism?* edited by E. Schopler, G. B. Mesibov, and L. J. Kunce, 29–60. New York: Plenum Press, 1998.

Povinelli, D. "Monkeys, Apes, Mirrors, and Minds: The Evolution of Self-Awareness in Primates." *Human Evolution* 2 (1996): 493–507.

Povinelli, D. J. "Monkeys, Apes, Mirrors and Minds: The Evolution of Self-Awareness in Primates. *Human Evolution* 2, no. 6 (1987): 493–509.

Prizant, B. "Brief Report: Communication, Language and Social-Emotional Development. Issues for Persons with Autism Who Are Non-Speaking or Have Limited Speech." *Journal of Autism and Developmental Disorders* 26, no. 2 (1996): 173–178.

Prizant, B. M., and A. L. Schuler. "Facilitating Communication: Language Approaches." In *Handbook of Autism and Pervasive Developmental Disorders*, edited by D. I. Cohen and A. M. Donnellan, 316–332. New York: Wiley, 1987.

Prizant, B. M., and A. M. Wetherby. "Enhancing Language and Communication in Autism: From Theory to Practice." In *Autism: New Perspectives on Diagnosis, Nature and Treatment*, edited by G. Dawson, 282–309. New York: Guilford Press, 1989.

Richards, M. P. M. "The Biological and the Social." In *Action, Gesture and Symbol: The Emergence of Language*, edited by A. Lock, 21–30. London: Academic Press, 1978.

Rieffe, C., M. M. Terwogt, and L. Stockmann. "Understanding Atypical Emotions Among Children with Autism." *Journal of Autism and Developmental Disorders* 30, no. 3 (2000): 195–204.

Rizolatti, G. "The Mirror Neuron System and Imitation." In *Perspectives on Imitation: From Neuroscience to Social Science, Volume 1: Imitation, Mechanisms of Imitation and Imitation in Animals*, edited by S. Hurly and N. Chater, 55–76. Cambridge, Mass.: MIT Press, 2005a.

Robins, D. L., D. Fein, M. L. Barton, and J. A. Green. "The Modified Checklist for Autism in Toddlers: An Initial Study Investigating the Early Detection of Autism and Pervasive Developmental Disorder." *Journal of Autism and Developmental Disorders* 31, no. 2 (2001): 131–144.

Rochat, P. *Early Social Cognition: Understanding Others in the First Months of Life*. Mahwah, N.J.: Erlbaum, 1999.

Rodier, P. M., J. L. Ingram, B. Tisdale, S. Nelson, and J. Romano. "Embryological Origin for Autism: Developmental Anomalies of the Cranial Nerve Motor Nuclei." *Journal of Comparative Neurology* 370 (1996): 247–261.

Roeyers, H., P. Van Oost, and S. Bothuyne. "Immediate Imitation and Joint Attention in Young Children with Autism." *Development and Psychopathology* 10 (1998): 441–450.

Rogers, S. "Interventions That Facilitate Socialization in Children with Autism." *Journal of Autism and Developmental Disorders* 30, no. 5 (2000): 399–410.

Rogers, S. J., and B. F. Pennington. "A Theoretical Approach to the Deficits in Infantile Autism." *Development and Psychopathology* 3 (1991): 137–162.

Rogers, S. J., S. Ozonoff, and C. Maslin-Cole. "A Comparative Study of Attachment Behavior in Young Children with Autism or Other Psychiatric Disorders." *Journal of the American Academy of Child and Adolescent Psychiatry* 30 (1991): 483–488.

Rosen, L. "Selected Aspects in the Development of the Mother's Understanding of Her Mentally Retarded Child." *American Journal of Mental Deficiency* 59 (1953): 522–528.

Rutter, M. "Autism Research: Lessons from the Past and Prospects for the Future." *Journal of Autism and Developmental Disorders* 35, no. 2 (2005): 241–258.

Rutter, M., and the English and Romanian Adoptees (ERA) study team. "Developmental Catch-up, and Deficit, Following Adoption After Severe Global Early Privation." *Journal of Child Psychology and Psychiatry* 39, no. 4 (1996): 465–477.

Sander, L. "Infant and Caretaking Environment." In *Explorations in Child Psychiatry*, edited by E. J. Anthony, 129–166. New York: Plenum Press, 1975.

Savage-Rumbaugh, S. *Ape Language—From Conditioned Response to Symbol.* New York: Columbia University Press, 1986.

Savage-Rumbaugh, S., S. G. Shanker, and T. J. Taylor. *Apes, Language and the Human Mind.* New York: Oxford Universities Press, 1998.

Schanberg, S. "Genetic Basis for Touch Effects." In *Touch in Early Development*, edited by T. Field, 67–80. Hillsdale, N.J.: Erlbaum, 1994.

Schneider-Rosen, K., and D. Cicchetti. "The Relationship Between Affect and Cognition in Maltreated Infants. Quality of Attachment and the Development of Visual Self-Recognition." *Child Development* 55 (1984): 648–658.

Schopler, E., G. B. Mesibov, and K. Hearsey. "Structured Teaching in the TEACCH System." In *Learning and Cognition in Autism*, edited by E. Schopler and G. B. Mesibov, 243–268. New York: Plenum Press, 1995.

Schopler, E., G. B. Mesibov, and L. J. Kunce, eds. *Asperger Syndrome and High or Functioning Autism?* New York: Plenum Press, 1998.

Schultz, R. T., I. Gauthier, A. Klin, R. K. Fulbright, A. W. Anderson, F. Volkmar, P. Skudlarski, C. Ladadie, D. J. Cohen, and J. C. Gore. "Abnormal Ventral Temporal Cortical Activity During Face Discrimination Among Individuals with Autism and Asperger Syndrome." *Archives of General Psychiatry* 57, no. 3 (2000): 331–340.

Schur, H. "An Observation and Comments on the Development of Memory." *Psychoanalytic Studies of the Child* 21 (1966): 488–475.

Sellin, B. *Messages from an Autistic Mind: I Don't Want to Be Inside Me Anymore.* New York: Basic Books, 1995.

Seltzer, M. M., M. W. Krauss, M. T. Shattuck, G. Orsmond, A. Swe, and C. Lord. "The Symptoms of Autism Spectrum Disorders in Adolescence and Adulthood." *Journal of Autism and Developmental Disorders* 33, no. 6 (2003): 565–583.

Serra, M., A. E. Jackson, P. L. C. van Geert, and R. B. Minderaa. "Brief Report: Interpretation of Facial Expression, Posture, and Gestures in Children with a Pervasive Developmental Disorder Not Otherwise Specified." *Journal of Autism and Developmental Disorders* 3, no. 28 (1998): 257–264.

Serra, M., L. M. Althaus, L. M. J. deSonneville, A. D. Stant, A. E. Jackson, and R. B. Minderaa. "Face Recognition in Children with a PDD-NOS." *Journal of Autism and Developmental Disorders* 33, no. 3 (2003): 303–318.

Shields, M. M. "The Child as Psychologist: Construing the Social World." In *Action, Gesture and Symbol: The Emergence of Language*, edited by A. Lock, 529–556. London: Academic Press, 1978.

Shotter, J. "The Cultural Context of Communication Studies: Theoretical and Methodological Issues." In *Action, Gesture and Symbol: The Emergence of Language*, edited by A. Lock, 43–78. London: Academic Press, 1978.

Siegler, R. S., and K. Crowley. "The Microgenetic Method: A Direct Means for Studying Cognitive Development." *American Psychologist* 46, no. 6 (1991): 606–620.

Sigman, M. "Infants at Risk of Autism: A Longitudinal Study." UCLA Center for Autism Research and Treatment (CART), proposed study, infor@autism.ucla.edu/infant.php, 2004.

Sigman, M., C. Kasari, and J. Kwon et al. "Responses to the Negative Emotions of Others by Autistic, Mentally Retarded and Normal Children." *Child Development* 63 (1992): 796–807.

Sigman, M., P. Mundy, T. Sherman, and J. Ungerer. "Social Interactions of Autistic, Mentally Retarded and Normal Children and Their Caregivers." *Journal of Child Psychology and Psychiatry* 27, no. 5 (1986): 647–655.

Simon, R. "Extraordinary Memory of Autistic Children: I. Types of Memory Reported by Mothers of Autistic Children as Compared to Memory Forms Reported by Mothers of Normal Toddlers." Unpublished paper, 1969.

Simons, J., and S. Oshi. *The Hidden Child: The Linwood Method for Reaching the Autistic Child*. Brentwood, Md.: Woodbine House, 1985.

Skoyles, J. R. "Neural Plasticity and Exaptation." *American Psychologist* 54, no. 6 (1999): 438–439.

Sloboda, A. "Origins and Development of High Ability." *Ciba Foundation Symposium*, Ciba Foundation, Chesterton, England: John Wiley and Sons, 1993.

———. "Music Performance Expression and the Development of Excellence." In *Musical Perception*, edited by R. Aiello and A. Sloboda, 152–169. New York: Oxford University Press, 1994.

Spiker, D., and M. Ricks. "Visual Self Recognition in Autistic Children: Developmental Relationships." *Child Development* 55 (1984): 214–225.

Sroufe, L. A. "An Organizational Perspective on the Self." In *Children with Down Syndrome—A Developmental Perspective*, edited by D. Cicchetti and M. Beeghly, 281–308. New York: Cambridge University Press, 1990.

Stahmer, A. C. "Teaching Symbolic Play Skills Using Pivotal Response Training." *Journal of Autism and Developmental Disorders* 25, no. 2 (1995): 123–142.

Stechler, G., and S. Kaplan. "The Development of the Self—A Psychoanalytic Perspective." *The Psychoanalytic Study of the Child* 35 (1980): 85–105.

Steele, S., R. M. Joseph, and H. Tager-Flusberg. "Brief Report: Developmental Change in Theory of Mind Abilities in Children with Autism." *Journal of Autism and Developmental Disorders* 33, no. 4 (2003): 461–468.

Stern, D. N. *The Interpersonal World of the Infant: A View from Psychoanalysis and Developmental Psychology*. New York: Basic Books, 1985.

Stone, N. W., and B. H. Chesney "Attachment Behavior in Handicapped Infants." *Mental Retardation* 16 (1978): 8–12.

Stone, W. L., E. E. Coonrod, and O. Y. Ousley. "Brief Report: Screening Tool for Autism in Two-Year Olds (STAT) : Development and Preliminary Data." *Journal of Autism and Developmental Disorders* 30, no. 6 (2000): 599–607.

Stone, W. L., O. Y. Ousley, P. J. Yoder, K. L. Hogan, and S. L. Hepburn. "Nonverbal Communication in Two- and Three-Year Old Children with Autism." *Journal of Autism and Developmental Disorders* 27, no. 6 (1997): 677–696.

Szajnberg, N. M. "Moebius Syndrome: Alternatives in Affective Communication." *Developments in Medical and Child Neurology* 16 (1994): 459–462.

Szatmari, P., G. Bartolucci, R. Bremner, S. Bond, and S. Rich. "A Follow-up Study of High-Functioning Autistic Children." *Journal of Autism and Developmental Disorders* 19, no. 2 (1989): 213–225.

Tager-Flusberg, H. "What Language Reveals About the Understanding of Minds in Children with Autism." In *Understanding Other Minds*, edited by S. Baron-Cohen, H. Tager-Flusberg, and D. J. Cohen, 138–157. New York: Oxford Medical Publications, 1993.

Tizard, B., and C. Hodges. "The Effect of Early Institutionalized Rearing on the Development of 8 Year Old Children." *Journal of Child Psychology and Psychiatry* 19 (1977): 99–118.

Tizard, B., and J. Rees. "The Effect of Early Institutionalized Rearing on the Behavior Problems and Affectional Relationships of 4 Year Old Children." *Journal of Child Psychology and Psychiatry* 16 (1975): 16–73.

Tomasello, M. "On the Interpersonal Origins of Self-Concept." In *The Perceived Self: Ecological and Interpersonal Sources of Self Knowledge*, edited by U. Neisser, 174–164. Cambridge: Cambridge University Press, 1993.

Travis, L. L., and M. Sigman. "Social Deficits and Interpersonal Relationships in Autism, Mental Retardation and Developmental Disabilities." *Research Reviews* 4, no. 2 (1998): 65–72.

Trevarthen, C. "Early Attempts at Speech." In *Child Alive*, edited by R. Lewin, 57–74. New York: Anchor Press/Doubleday, 1975.

———. "Communication and Cooperation in Early Infancy: A Description of Primary Intersubjectivity." In *Before Speech: The Beginning of Interpersonal Communication*, edited by M. M. Bulliwa, 321–347. New York: Cambridge University Press, 1979.

Trevarthen, C., and P. Hubley. "Secondary Intersubjectivity: Confidence, Confiding and Acts of Meaning in the First Year." In *Action, Gesture and Symbol: The Emergence of Language*, edited by A. Lock, 183–229. London: Academic Press, 1978.

Tustin, F. *Autistic States in Children*. London: Routledge and Kegan Paul, 1981.

Twachtman, D. D. "Methods to Enhance Communication in Verbal Children." In *Teaching Children with Autism: Strategies to Enhance Communication and Socialization*, edited by K. A. Quill, 133–162. New York: Delmar, 1995.

Urwin, C. "The Development of Communication Between Blind Infants and Their Parents." In *Action, Gesture and Symbol: The Emergence of Language*, edited by A. Lock, 79–110. London: Academic Press, 1978.

Volkmar, F., and D. J. Cohen. "The Experience of Infantile Autism: A First Person Account by Tony W." *Journal of Autism and Developmental Disorders* 15 (1985): 47–54.

Volkmar, F. R., and A. Klin. "Asberger Syndrome and Non-Verbal Learning Disabilities." In *Asberger Syndrome and High or Functioning Autism?* edited by E. Schopler, G. B. Mesibov, and L. J. Kunce, 107–122. New York: Plenum Press, 1998.

Vygotsky, L. S. *Mind in Society*. Cambridge, Mass.: Harvard University Press, 1978.

———. *Thought and Language*. Rev. ed. Edited by A. Kozulin. Cambridge, Mass.: MIT Press, 1986.

Weider, S. "'Opening the Door': Approaches to Engage Children with Multisystem Developmental Disorders." *Zero to Three* 13, no. 2 (1992): 10–15.

Wellman, H. M. "Early Understanding of Mind: The Normal Case." In *Understanding Other Minds*, edited by S. Baron-Cohen, H. Tager-Flusberg, and D. J. Cohen, 10–39. New York: Oxford Medical Publications, 1993.

Werner, E., G. Dawson, J. Osterling, and N. Dinno. "Brief Report: Recognition of Autism Spectrum Disorder Before One Year of Age: A Retrospective Study Based on Home Videotapes." *Journal of Autism and Developmental Disorders* 30, no. 2 (2000): 157–162.

Werner, H. *Comparative Psychology of Mental Development*. Rev. ed. New York: International University Press, 1940, 1957.

Werner, H., and B. Kaplan. *Symbol Formation*. New York: Wiley, 1963.

Wesner, D., J. Dowling, and F. Johnson. "What Is Maternal–Infant Intervention? The Role of Infant Psychotherapy." *Psychiatry* 45 (1982): 307–315.

Wetherby, A. "Ontogeny of Communicative Functions in Autism." *Journal of Autism and Developmental Disorders* 16, no. 3 (1986): 295–315.

———. "Language Interventions for Autistic Children: A Look at Where We Have Come in the Past 25 Years." *Journal of Speech Language Pathology and Audiology* 13, no. 4 (1989): 15–28.

Wetherby, A., and B. M. Prizant. "Profiling Communication and Symbolic Abilities in Young Children." *Journal of Childhood Communication Disorders* 15 (1993): 23–32.

White, B. L. "Motivation Reconsidered: The Concept of Competence." *Psychological Review* 66 (1959): 297–333.

White, B. L., B. Kaban, and J. Attanucci. *The Origins of Human Competence*. Lexington, Mass.: D.C. Heath, 1979.

Williams, J., A. Whiten, T. Suddendorf, and D. Perrett. "Imitation, Mirror Neurons and Autism." *Neuroscience and Biobehavioral Reviews* 25 (2001): 287–295.

Wimmer, H., and J. Perner. "Beliefs About Beliefs: Representation and Constraining Function of Wrong Beliefs in Young Children's Understanding of Deception." *Cognition* 11 (1983): 103–148.

Wimpory, D. C., R. P. Hobson, J. M. G. Williams, and S. Nash. "Are Infants with Autism Socially Engaged? A Study of Recent Retrospective Parental Reports." *Journal of Autism and Developmental Disorders* 30, no. 6 (2000): 525–536.

Wing, L. "Language, Social and Cognitive Impairments in Autism and Severe Mental Retardation." *Journal of Autism and Developmental Disorders* 1, no. 1 (1981): 31–44.

———. "The Continuum of Autistic Disorders." In *Diagnosis and Assessment in Autism*, edited by E. Schopler and G. M. Mesibov, 91–110. New York: Plenum Press, 1988.

———. "The History of Asperger Syndrome." In *Asperger Syndrome and High or Functioning Autism?* edited by E. Schopler, G. B. Mesibov, and L. J. Kunce, 12–28. New York: Plenum Press, 1998a.

———. "Syndromes of Autism and Atypical Development." In *Handbook of Autism and Pervasive Developmental Disorders*, 2nd ed., edited by D. J. Cohen and F. R.Volkman. New York: John Wiley and Sons, 1998b.

———. "Reflections on Opening a Pandora's Box." *Journal of Autism and Developmental Disorders* 35, no. 2 (2005): 197–204.

Wing, L., and J. Gould. "Severe Impairments of Social Interaction and Associated Abnormalities in Children: Epidemiology and Classification." *Journal of Autism and Developmental Disorders* 9 (1979): 11–29.

Winnicott, D. W. *The Motivational Process and the Facilitating Environment*. New York: International Universities Press, 1965.

Wolf, D. "Understanding Others: A Longitudinal Case Study of the Concept of Independent Agency." In *Action and Thought: From Sensorimotor Schemes to Symbolic Operations*, edited by G. Forman, 297–327. New York: Academic Press, 1982.

Wolfensberger, W. *The Principle of Normalization in Human Services*. Toronto: National Institute on Mental Retardation, 1972.

Wooton, A. J. "Object Transfer, Intersubjectivity and Third Position Repair: Early Developmental Observations of One Child." *Journal of Child Language* 21 (1994): 543–564.

Wright, K. "The Tarzan Syndrome." *Discover* (November 1996): 88–98.

Yirmiya, N., O. Erel, M. Shaked, and D. Solomonica-Levi. "Meta-Analyses Comparing Theory of Mind Abilities of Individuals with Autism, Individuals with Mental Retardation and Normally-Developing Individuals." *Psychological Bulletin* 124 (1998): 283–307.

Yirmiya, N., T. Pilowsky, D. Solomonica-Levy, and C. Shulman. "Brief Report: Gaze Behavior and Theory of Mind in Individuals with Autism, Down Syndrome, and Mental Retardation of Unknown Etiology." *Journal of Autism and Developmental Disorders* 29, no. 4 (1999): 333–342.

Zajone, R. B. "Feeling and Thinking: Preferences Need No Inferences." *American Psychologist* 35 (1980): 151–175.

Zwaigenbaum, L., S. Bryson, P. Szatmari, I. Smith, and W. Roberts. "A Study of Infant Siblings of Children with Autism Spectrum Disorders." Project supported by the National Alliance for Autism Research, Canadian Autism Intervention Research Network. www.caairn-site.com/studies/babysibs_full.html, 2001.

Index

ABA. *See* applied behavioral analysis

abstraction: autism and, 66–67; cognition and, 41, 52–54, 65–67, 106, 115–17, 121–23, 129, 214, 257n1; MR and, 65–67

ADOS. *See* Autistic Diagnostic Observation Schedule

affection: ability to manipulate, 158; behavior showing, 38, 56–57, 83, 90–91, 99, 101–2, 104, 116, 120, 129, 132, 135, 138, 143, 149; gestures of, 49, 70, 80, 88–91, 96, 99–100, 116, 120, 122, 129, 132, 135, 138, 143. *See also* love

affective attunement, 198

affective connectedness, 215, 227, 244

affective relatedness, 199, 203–4

affordance, 31, 58

agentivity, 190

aliment, 53–54, 65–66, 94, 100, 159, 218, 228

anger, 35; gestures of, 122, 141–43, 231–32; understanding of, 122, 140, 231–32

animal, 78, 87; intersubjectivity of, 199

anticipation, 160

anxiety, 140–41, 165

appeal, 94–95, 203

applied behavioral analysis (ABA), 113–14

Arnaud, Jean-Jacques, 196n2

art: making of, 145, 158

AS. *See* Asperger's syndrome

ASD. *See* autistic spectrum disorder

ashram, 25

Asperger's syndrome (AS): autism compared with, 13n2; DSM and, 13n2; MR with, 13n2

assertiveness, 30

assimilation-accommodation: innateness of, 218, 254; lack of input for, 61, 72, 100; MR and, 52–54, 65–66, 107, 146, 228–31; optimal discrepancy for, 231; promoting, 220, 230–31; sensori-motor level characteristic of, 93–94; slowness in, 45; success with, 123, 157

attention: calling to, 34, 44, 46, 49, 55–57, 59, 62–63, 71, 91, 193; lack of, 19–20, 160

attunement, 19–22

Attwood, T., 226

atypical child: cognition in, 161, 220, 223; developmental disability of, 7, 50; emotion-action integration in, 129; facial expressions in, 75–76; integrative capacity in, 213; intersubjectivity of, 2, 12–13, 118,

~

About the Author

Rita S. Eagle received her B.A. from Barnard College, Columbia University, and her Ph.D. in Clinical Psychology from New York University. She has forty-five years of experience in assessment, therapy, teaching, and research, with a focus on cognitive and emotional development in individuals with developmental disabilities, including autistic spectrum disorders, mental retardation, and cerebral palsy. Dr. Eagle has also worked in child welfare matters, with a particular interest in the separation experience of children who have lost or been denied access to their parents. She has worked in private practice, and in clinical, educational, and research venues in New York City, Toronto, and California, including Master's Children Center in New York City (with Drs. Margaret S. Mahler and Fred Pine), the Research Center for Mental Health at New York University, the Rusk Institute for Rehabilitative Medicine at New York University Medical Center, and the Clarke Institute of Psychiatry and Surrey Place Center in Toronto. Currently, she is associated with Harbor Regional Center in Los Angeles, California. Dr. Eagle has published research and clinical papers in the *Journal of Autism and Developmental Disorders*, the *American Journal of Orthopsychiatry*, *Canadian Psychology*, the *Journal of Psychotherapy, Research and Practice*, the *Journal of Divorce*, and the *Journal of Developmental Disabilities*. She has three children, including Benjamin, the inspiration for this book, now thirty-six years old, who has mental retardation and features of an autistic spectrum disorder.